Our Suffering Brethrer

Our Suffering Brethren

FOREIGN CAPTIVITY and NATIONALISM
in the EARLY UNITED STATES

DAVID J. DZUREC III

University of Massachusetts Press
Amherst and Boston

Copyright © 2019 by University of Massachusetts Press
All rights reserved
Printed in the United States of America

ISBN 978-1-62534-407-6 (paper); 406-9 (hardcover)

Designed by Sally Nichols
Set in Minion Pro and Whitney

Cover design by Milenda Nan Ok Lee
Cover art: James B. Dennis, *The Battle of Queenston, Oct. 13, 1813*, engraved by T. Sutherland
Courtesy River Bank Art Museum.

Library of Congress Cataloging-in-Publication Data
Names: Dzurec, David J., III, author.
Title: Our suffering brethren : foreign captivity and nationalism in the early United States / David J. Dzurec III.
Description: Amherst : University of Massachusetts Press, [2019] | Includes bibliographical references and index.
Identifiers: LCCN 2018053113| ISBN 9781625344069 (hardcover) | ISBN 9781625344076 (paper) | ISBN 9781613766545 (ebook) | ISBN 9781613766552 (ebook)
Subjects: LCSH: United States—Foreign relations—1783–1815. | United States—Politics and government—1783–1809. | United States—Politics and government—1809–1817. | Captivity—Political aspects—United States—History. | Americans—Foreign countries—History. | Prisoners of war—United States—History. | Nationalism—United States—History. | Political culture—United States—History.
Classification: LCC E310.7 .D98 2019 | DDC 327.73009/033—dc23 LC record available at https://lccn.loc.gov/2018053113

British Library Cataloguing-in-Publication Data
A catalog record for this book is available from the British Library.

Parts of Chapter 1 were first published as "Prisoners of War and American Self-Image during the American Revolution," *War in History* 20, no. 4 (2013): 430–51 by SAGE Publications Ltd. All rights reserved. Copyright © 2013 by David Dzurec. First published November 7, 2013. Available at http://online.sagepub.com. Parts of Chapter 3 first appeared in "'A Speedy Release to Our Suffering Captive Brethren in Algiers': Captives, Debate, and Public Opinion in the Early American Republic," *The Historian* 71, no. 4 (2009): 735–56. Copyright © 2009 Phi Alpha Theta. Published by John Wiley and Sons. First published December 4, 2009. Sections of Chapter 6 appeared in "Failure at Queenston Heights: The Politics of Citizenship and Federal Power during the War of 1812," *New York History* 94, nos. 3–4 (April 2014): 205–20. Copyright © 2014 by The New York State Historical Association.

For my family

Contents

Preface ix

INTRODUCTION

1

1. "Obligations Arising from the Rights of Humanity"
Prisoners of War and American Self-Image in the Revolution

16

2. "The More We Are Treated Ill Abroad"
The Continental Congress, Public Opinion, and American Captives in Algiers, 1783–1787

39

3. "A Speedy Release to Our Suffering Captive Brethren in Algiers"
The Washington Administration and the Challenge of Public Opinion

61

4. "Millions for Defence, but Not a Cent for Tribute"
Debate and Public Sentiment during the Tripolitan War, 1801–1805

86

5. "We Shall Ever Be Prey of the Jealous and Monopolizing Spirit of the English"
Impressment and Party Ideology in Jefferson's Second Term

109

6. "Floating Hells of Old England"
The Prisoner Debate and Federalist Opposition to the War of 1812

131

7. Mr. Madison's Other War
The Dartmoor Massacre, the End of the Barbary Wars, and American Self-Confidence, 1815–1816

161

CONCLUSION

"To Promote Each Other's Welfare, and Mutual Feelings of Peace and Good Will"
The Insecurity Bookending an Era of Free Security

191

Notes   199

Index   229

Preface

In October 1785, John Jay noted that "the more we are treated ill abroad, the more we shall unite and consolidate at home."[1] Jay's observation was in many ways more insightful than he knew. Throughout the early history of the United States, threats to American security served to shape American politics and fuel an emerging nationalism. The model of American politics that emerged as partisans attempted to claim the mantle of "defender of American liberty" not only defined the earliest days of American politics but also shaped the DNA of our national political culture. While this book specifically explores the period before what Richard Hofstadter has labeled the "era of free security," partisan efforts to claim the mantle of "defender of American liberty and security" continued into the twenty-first century. An understanding of the earliest years of American politics helps us gain a better understanding of the shape of American politics today.

Although the scope of this project has expanded, it began with a far more narrow focus. I was initially drawn to the experience of captivity during the American Revolution. As my researched progressed, however, it became clear to me that the power of captivity narratives went well beyond the 1780s and ultimately helped to shape American culture and politics into the first decades of the nineteenth century. What started as a study of captivity in New England and the Great Lakes region, quickly grew into a study that spanned the Atlantic, touching three continents. Despite obstacles imposed by distance and geography, stories from Europe and North Africa had as much impact on the culture and politics of the Revolutionary and early United States as did stories from the American frontier. The external threats to American liberty remained a key to American politics until 1816, following the end of the War of 1812 and the end of the Barbary threat. It was only then that Americans truly felt secure in the larger world and the era of free security could begin.

Regarding sources and use of sources, this book draws extensively on reports, newspapers, and letters. I have worked to faithfully render words, expressions, and sentences in their original forms or styles and only employed "*sic*" when it is absolutely needed for clarity. Unless otherwise indicated, the italics in quoted sources appear in the original document. Finally, while I have received assistance and feedback in myriad forms and from innumerable sources, ultimately, the mistakes in this book are my own.

With that in mind, I owe a great debt to a great many people who have helped to make this project a reality. Lucy Murphy, Randy Roth, Saul Cornell, and John Brooke all helped shape the early contours of this book. Dominic DeBrincat, Robb Haberman, John Maas, Hugh Randall, Nathan Kozuskanich, Alison Efford, and Brian Kennedy all offered encouragement, support, and friendship along the way. Alan Taylor, Paul Gilje, and Andrew Robertson offered helpful feedback on a variety of occasions. Doug Bradburn, Andrew Fagal, and the members of the Upstate Early American Workshop provided feedback on several chapters and provided a great sense of community. I am also indebted to a number of anonymous reviewers who provided feedback both on the book manuscript and portions of the work that have appeared as journal articles in *War in History, New York History,* and *The Historian.*

At the University of Scranton, I have been fortunate to work with outstanding colleagues, students, and supportive administrators. In the History Department, Will Conover, Mike DeMichele, Roy Domenico, Larry Kennedy, Susan Poulson, and Bob Shaffern have all provided a great deal of encouragement and support. Katy Shively Meier (now at Virginia Commonwealth) and Adam Pratt shared in the process of completing manuscripts. Students Erin Dunleavy, Kristen Yarmey, and Julia Frakes, in sharing their work and providing research assistance, brought a sustaining enthusiasm to the project. Associate Dean Harry Dammer, Dean Brian Conniff, and Provosts Hal Bailey and Joe Dreisbach have been supportive throughout my time at the university. I also owe a debt of gratitude to Bill Burke for his support in both my academic and athletic endeavors. At the University of Massachusetts Press, the entire editorial staff, but especially Brian Halley and Rachael DeShano, have been a great help in working though the publication process.

Finally, I could not have completed any of this without my family. Some of my earliest memories are of my parents balancing their own academic research in food science and nursing with the challenges of raising five children. Their love and support continue to be a model for me as I strive to achieve the same balance. My siblings, Kate, Paul, Dan, and Charlie, have always challenged me to be my better self and shared a lifetime of experiences. My children, David, Emily, and Noah, who are all surprised and thrilled that their dad could actually write a book, have been a continual inspiration. My wife, Brooke, has been a loving and supportive partner throughout this project and our lives together. None of this would have been possible without her.

Our Suffering Brethren

INTRODUCTION

In late 1776, Charles Herbert of Newburyport, Massachusetts, became a captive of the British navy. Herbert, a crewman aboard the American privateer *Dalton*, kept a journal of his experience, which he "concealed, while writing, in his boots, and as each page became full, it was conveyed to a chest with a double bottom, and there secreted until he left prison." Herbert's captivity had begun on Christmas Eve 1775, when the British man-of-war *Raisonnable* tracked down and seized the *Dalton* off the west coast of Spain. Upon capture the British officers ordered Herbert and his fellow crewmen "down into the cable-tier," where the Americans found "nothing but bare cable to lay upon, and that very uneven." Worse still, the captive crew were "almost suffocated with heat" and provided with "nothing but a few rags and a dozen old blankets." In the months that followed the men of the *Dalton* saw little improvement in their condition, experiencing varying degrees of discomfort and facing cold, illness, vermin infestation, and "the itch" while they were held on the prison ships. In those first few months of captivity, Herbert recorded that he and his fellow captives were taken aboard the *Dalton* and the Royal Navy ships *Raisonnable*, *Belleisles*, *Torbay*, and *Buford* before they were finally transferred to Mill Prison in Plymouth, England.[1]

The frequent relocation of the *Dalton*'s crew was the result of a legal dilemma that became one of the central issues in the War of American Independence. From the earliest days of the conflict, American prisoners posed a fundamental problem for British officials. Treating these captives as prisoners of war would be an acknowledgment of U.S. sovereignty and independence. However, handling the captive crewmen as rebellious subjects, as British officials were initially inclined to view them, technicially made these rebels civil prisoners. Such a categorization, if they were brought ashore, would allow the crewmen to claim their rights as Englishmen and the right of release on bail while they awaited trial.[2]

American officials were quick to recognize the dilemma that their captive countrymen presented to the British and sought to use it to their advantage. In the earliest days of the conflict, General George Washington called on General Thomas Gage, commander of British forces in North America, to provide American prisoners with a "more tender treatment" in line with the accepted international practices for prisoners of war.[3] While an act of Parliament would ultimately resolve this dilemma in early 1777, the plight of captive Americans in the preceding months served as a rallying cry to the Patriot cause. Seizing on the issue, American officials worked to highlight British cruelty and encourage popular support for their efforts in the first years of the Revolutionary conflict.[4]

In addition to the practical issues presented by American captives, the conflict with the colonies raised questions about the very nature of British American identity. Herbert's experience again proves instructive. After the Americans had been in captivity nearly a month, the wives of several British crewmen were allowed to view the "American prisoners." In anticipation of seeing an actual American, these women asked, "'What sort of people are they?' 'Are they white?' 'Can they talk?' Upon being pointed to where some of them stood, 'Why!' exclaimed they, 'they look like our people, and they talk English.'"[5] The surprise of these women at discovering the commonality between themselves and the American prisoners highlights an English perception of Americans as "other," a view that predated the American Revolution. Although the number of Englishmen who believed British colonists in North America to be something other than white Anglophones may have been relatively small, the process of defining Americans as something other than fully British began well before the Revolution. As historian Richard Merritt has observed, "Englishmen began to identify the colonial population as 'Americans' persistently after 1763—a decade before Americans themselves did so."[6] The categorization of the colonists as less than English was greatly disturbing to many in British North America, especially as the attitude came at a time of increased nationalism following the British victory in the French and Indian War. It was this definition of Americans as not fully English, as Linda Colley and T. H. Breen note, that served as a critical precondition of the American Revolution.[7]

While Americans had chafed at the notion that they were anything other than Englishmen in the years leading to the Revolution, the outbreak of war in 1775 left participants on all sides conflicted in their loyalties. The uncertainties embodied in the definitions of identity characterized one of the great challenges of the American Revolution. Although wars against a distinct "other" based on nationality or religion had long served to draw the various facets of the British Empire together, the American Revolution lacked any such easy categorizations. Within England itself, reaction to the conflict with the colonies was profoundly mixed. In Parliament and in the press, expressions of support for the war were often countered with declarations of opposition to the conflict. Across the Atlantic, the colonists themselves were split over how to respond to their growing alienation from their parent country. It is estimated that between one-fifth and one-third of Americans chose to remain loyal to England, dismissing their rebellious countrymen as traitors who failed to appreciate the blessings of British Empire. By way of contrast, supporters of the Patriot cause believed loyalists to be complicit in English tyranny, pointing to prisoner accounts of captivity and suffering as a clear example of the corrupt nature of the British government.[8]

Prisoner narratives, like the story of Charles Herbert, were a key component in the larger Patriot effort to define the British as "other." The utility of these narratives was nothing new. During the colonial era, captivity narratives of British Americans suffering at the hands of Native Americans and French forces served to reinforce the colonists' British identity while reminding Americans of the savagery of the French Empire. In the initial phase of the Revolution, printers throughout New England reissued several colonial narratives of "captivity and deliverance" that might offer solace to Americans resisting a new enemy. These older narratives offered a model for a new round of stories of captivity that drew a wide cross-section of Americans into efforts to define the Patriot cause. In many ways, because these narratives were so closely tied to the project of defining the American cause, they were also a key step in democratizing American politics. Highlighting the stories of average Americans' suffering at the hands of a barbarous "other," these new captivity narratives allowed many colonists, who might otherwise have been excluded, to join a national conversation about what it meant to be an American.[9]

In the decades that followed the Revolution, the plight of captive Americans and efforts on their behalf continued to play a role in shaping American politics and identity. The narratives of American prisoners of war gave way to stories of American sailors imprisoned in North Africa and, at the beginning of the nineteenth century, returned to stories of Americans' suffering at the hands of the British. While the experience of captivity was only a part of the larger "unleashing of democratic urges," captives of the British and North Africans became a symbol of the young nation's struggle to establish itself and helped unite the American people to push their government to protect their fellow countrymen abroad.[10] An examination of this struggle and the national discussion of the fate of the captive Americans between 1775 and 1816 offers a key to understanding the insecurity that informed and shaped the development of American identity, nationalism, and political culture in the young United States.

These experiences and accounts of captivity, especially before 1816, fueled a collective insecurity that contributed to a national conversation about what it meant to be an American. In the era before what historian C. Vann Woodward has labeled the "era of free security," public concern about the safety of Americans in the larger Atlantic world played a critical role in defining American political institutions and identity. Partisans often played on this insecurity to advance their visions for the nation and their political cause. During the American Revolution, supporters of the Patriot cause worked assiduously to depict their British adversaries as cruel and savage captors. During the Confederation period, advocates of a stronger national government increasingly pointed to the threat of Barbary captivity as another justification for a stronger national government. Following the ratification of the U.S. Constitution, both Federalists and Republicans worked to turn concerns about American security abroad to their political advantage.[11]

The politics of public opinion played a central role in the evolution of the captivity debate during the eras of the Revolution and Early American Republic. Although never employing the term *public opinion* during the Revolution, leaders of the Patriot cause masterfully employed the ordeal of their captive countrymen to develop public support for their cause. While Congress and American military officials laid the initial foundation for a debate over the treatment of prisoners during the Revolution, outrage over the suffering of their "famished, tortured, murdered fellow citizens" soon took on a life of its own in public discussions, becoming a valuable tool in the cause of Independence.[12] In the years that followed the Revolution, American public opinion continued to evolve, fed by growing avenues of communication, most notably the expanding American press. Almost immediately following the end of the Revolution, news of American sailors sold into slavery in Algiers sparked a national discussion about how best to respond to this new threat to American freedom abroad. In the face of a seemingly unresponsive government, public opinion on the eve of the Constitutional Convention seemed to favor private efforts to free captive Americans.[13]

Following the ratification of the Constitution, many believed that an energized national government might limit the need for the type of popular politics embodied by earlier public efforts to redeem captive Americans. Members of the Washington administration, while recognizing the power of public opinion, hoped to return to a more deferential style of politics. Yet, as they were quick to realize, such a model in the wake of the American Revolution was no longer viable. Faced with this reality, the nascent Federalists were, as historian Todd Estes notes, "often ideologically elitist" and "operationally democratic." In fact, in a number of cases—Alexander Hamilton's efforts to establish public credit, the Jay Treaty debates, and cultivating support for U.S. neutrality during the French Revolution—Federalists made use of public opinion to great effect, if in a limited way.[14]

Challenging the Federalists' limited model of public opinion in late 1791, James Madison declared that "public opinion sets bounds to every government and is the real sovereign in every free one." Madison and many of his fellow newly minted Republicans saw open lines of communication between the government and its citizens as the key to reading, hearing, and shaping public opinion. Madison argued that "whatever facilitates a general intercourse of sentiments, [such] as good roads, domestic commerce, a free press, and particularly a *circulation of newspapers through the entire body of the people* and *Representatives going from and returning among every part of them*" ought to be understood as a political virtue.[15] Yet Madison's definition of public opinion, as both Estes and political scientist Colleen Sheehan state, was not a simple expression of popular sentiment (or outright democracy). Instead,

Madison saw the intercommunication between the government and the people as offering an opportunity (if not a responsibility) for representatives to influence and guide public opinion. In his larger reflection, Madison went as far as to demonstrate how the structural and institutional mechanisms of government were intended to assist in the expression and refinement of public opinion.[16]

For both Federalists and Republicans, then, reining in the "democratic urges" of the Early Republic required a means with which to refine public opinion to a form that best fit their vision for the new nation. The examination of the debates surrounding the plight of American captives in the earliest years of the Republic offers an opportunity to explore how both Federalists and Republicans employed nascent nationalism to exploit the fear of an "other" and thus to control the force of public opinion. Discussion of American captivity often fused nationalism with a distinct and politically partisan element, strengthening and enhancing the viability of that nationalism. Thus, the debates over captivity reveal not only the role of foreign affairs in the development of American national identity but also demonstrate how partisan debate, as each side jockeyed to claim the mantle of American nationalism, was a driving force in the development of this new identity. During those debates, sometimes one side and then another, and sometimes both sides simultaneously, staked out stridently nationalist positions. Somewhat ironically, the partisan debates over captivity during this period, with their nationalist cast, united rather than divided the nation in the era of the Early Republic.[17]

Although the threat of captivity was only one of myriad challenges facing the young nation in the first four decades of its existence, stories of the imprisonment of American citizens by a foreign power attracted a national audience in a way that few other issues did. Reprinted in newspapers throughout the nation, these accounts helped to bring Americans together, even if occasionally along partisan lines, in defense of the liberty of their fellow countrymen. During the Revolution, the plight of Americans held aboard the prison ships in New York's Wallabout Bay or their mistreatment in Canadian prisons provided a powerful symbol for the Patriot cause and a concrete example of the growing corruption and malevolence of the British Empire and justified the need to throw off English rule. In the years that followed Independence, the inability of the new government to quickly end threats to American liberty represented by the Barbary corsairs and the British practice of impressment were a focal point uniting citizens of the United States to demand action and helping to drive the development of factional politics.

The role of international events in shaping American politics and identity in the early years of the United States was necessarily influenced by the experiences of sailors. As a number of recent studies have illustrated, maritime encounters were the lens through which Americans viewed the world beyond North America. Even before the American Revolution, as historian Denver Brunsman demonstrates, the British practice of impressment, which Americans viewed as a threat to the livelihood of North American sailors, sparked a series of anti-impressment riots, which were one of the first signs of tension between North American colonists and British officials.[18] Following the Revolution, sailors continued to serve as a conduit for information from the larger world and helped to form the basis for American knowledge about other countries and peoples. American sailors were the major supplier of newspapers, broadsides, books, and pamphlets from around the globe. In addition to these very public texts, the diaries, letters, and journals of sailors supplemented official news from abroad with personal stories of the "other." Sailors were a critical component of the "Republic of Letters."[19] While collecting, transporting, and distributing information, sailors also forced Americans to think critically about notions of American citizenship. Questions about who could rightfully claim the title *American* and about what rights, responsibilities, and duties accompanied that title were all the more pressing as a growing number of American citizen-sailors found themselves on foreign shores.[20] Serving as the front line of American engagement with the world, as historian Brian Rouleau notes, "sailors were nineteenth-century America's largest class of representatives overseas. . . . Maritime history *is* the history of early U.S. foreign relations."[21] Whether traveling through the Atlantic Ocean, Pacific Ocean, or Mediterranean Sea, American sailors shaped Americans' perceptions about their place in the world.[22]

This story of captivity and partisan nationalism occurs at the intersection of several important trends in the historiography of the American Revolution and Early Republic. The first of these trends is a growing understanding of the significance of foreign affairs within the struggle to establish a stable state system in the years following the Revolution.[23] The second trend includes well-established considerations of American nationalism and public discourse.²⁴ The third is the emerging understanding of the significance of sailors to defining American identity in the earliest years of the Republic.²⁵

On the first trend, scholars have long recognized the importance of foreign affairs and American security in the context of the greater Atlantic world as critical components of the ratification of the U.S. Constitution. In the years between the First and Second World Wars, numerous historians saw American efforts to unite their new nation under a central government as a model to the world, as modern nations sought to develop international bodies, such as the League of Nations, to prevent war through promoting community, collaboration, and economic ties.²⁶ Beginning in the 1950s, these earlier formulations were overshadowed by growing socioeconomic and ideological interpretations of the period. And by the late twentieth century, studies of the liberal tradition in American political thought and of the rise of the "Republican synthesis" acted to push aside earlier concerns over security and foreign affairs and came to dominate much of the debate surrounding the making of the Constitution.²⁷ Despite this imbalance, in recent years a number of historians, including Frederick Marks, Peter Onuf, and David Hendrickson have continued to explore the significance of foreign threats and interstate stability in shaping American policy during the eras of the American Revolution and Early Republic.²⁸ Uncovering what Hendrickson has labeled the "lost world of the American Founding" helps explain why the plight of American captives was so significant to the public in the earliest years of the United States. This concern for the struggles of their fellow citizens held by a foreign power allowed the issue to become one of widespread public discussion and the source of a nationalist impulse that helped drive the development of American political culture.

Building on this recognition of the importance of foreign relations to the early United States, historian Walter Hixson employs a "cultural analysis" of the construction of national identity and foreign policy to highlight the significant connection between the two. He concludes that "foreign policy plays a profoundly significant role in the process of creating, affirming, and disciplining conceptions of a national identity." Hixson argues that this entanglement of foreign policy and national identity is marked by a "pathological violence" and "cultural hegemony" driven by "unacknowledged internal anxieties."²⁹ Indeed, both violence and hegemony were powerful forces in shaping American identity and foreign policy in the early days of the United States, but I argue that between 1776 and 1816, American anxiety was not only acknowledged but actively integrated into the national conversation about American identity and the place of the United States in the world.

In the face of external threats to American liberty and its related growing anxiety, citizens across a wide social and economic spectrum rallied on behalf of their captive countrymen. The proliferation of newspapers and pamphlets during the Revolutionary Era and the Early Republican period was critical in disseminating knowledge of emerging threats to American liberty to a broader public. More important still, the growth of this print culture allowed Americans to express their feelings on the issue to a larger audience than any ever before possible to reach. Through this proliferation, the "conversation of the people" began to challenge the "words of the authoritative few," enabling a new model of civil society to emerge. Political actors came to include a wide cross-section of citizens. In the Early American Republic, debate occurred between and among American citizens, in the press, and in public displays such as parades and civic festivals. Local events became national events as newspapers narrated community activities to a nationwide audience. The public debate was opened wide to expression of political and social dissent.[30]

Stories recounting the experiences of American sailors overseas, both their successes and their failures, helped to define the parameters of national conversations about what it meant to be American. As stories of American captivity in foreign lands made their way to a broader public, Americans increasingly attempted to decipher the meaning of these trials and tribulations for their nascent national identity. In many ways, faced with the challenge of "unbecoming British" and lacking a cohesive sense of what they were to become afterward, Americans found in the captivity of their fellow countrymen abroad, particularly sailors, the polar opposite of what it was to be an American. Although a sense of insecurity is not an ending point for national identity, it did serve a critical role in drawing the American people together in a hostile world.[31] These stories of captivity ignited a national conversation that would help define the contours of a new American nationalism.

Thus a conversation begun during the Revolution with Americans consuming stories of British-held prisoners of war rolled forward into the Confederation period, the attacks by Barbary corsairs laying bare the inherent weakness of the Articles of Confederation. The debate lingered even as Federalists and Republicans struggled to shape the future of the United States following the ratification of the Constitution. These discussions, rather than tearing down the young United States, helped to unite Americans around a common cause and aided the development of an "imagined community" in the face of varied and ongoing threats to American security. Following the end of the War of 1812 and the final American settlement with the Barbary States of North Africa in late 1815 and early 1816, the vulnerability that had marked the first conversations of what it meant to be American was replaced by a sense of security both at home and in the larger Atlantic world. That shift in national confidence marked the beginning of the "era of free security."[32]

In tracing the plight of captive Americans between 1776 and 1816, this book brings together these historiographic trends—the significance of early American foreign relations, the development of American nationalism, and the role of sailors in the development of both histories—to demonstrate how the captivity of sailors abroad manifested as a sense of insecurity at home. That belief or perception was a critical force in defining an American public sphere and shaping American politics in the late eighteenth and early nineteenth centuries. While the end of the War of 1812 and of the conflict with the Barbary States marked the beginning of "free security," it did not bring an end to the politics of fear in the United States. In many ways, as I attempt to demonstrate here, the deployment of fear as a political tool to shape American public opinion in the period before "free security" became an integral and lasting part of American nationalism and political culture. Tellingly, while this book explicitly explores the period between Independence and the termination of the Barbary Wars, recent works such as Kariann Akemi Yokota's *Unbecoming British,* Sam Haynes's *The Unfinished Revolution,* and Rachel Hope Cleves's *The Reign of Terror in America* demonstrate how uncertainty, insecurity, and even outright fear remained a part of American politics throughout the nineteenth century.[33] More striking still are the parallels between American political behavior at either end of the era of free security. So deeply embedded was this insecurity that with the outbreak of the Cold War in the second half of the twentieth century, American politics during this post–World War II era came to bear a striking resemblance to the politics of the first half of the nineteenth century. Just as Federalists and Republicans vied to demonstrate their ability to protect Americans abroad more than a century before, in the face of a global communist threat both Democrats and Republicans sought to outdo one another by demonstrating their power to contain and even roll back communism overseas and in neighboring countries.[34]

Beginning with the American Revolution, the first chapter explores the how the suffering of American prisoners in British hands helped inform and define the cause of Independence. In the midst of the difficult transition from British colony to independent nation and faced with the task of creating a new national identity, supporters of the Patriot cause seized on narratives of British cruelty toward prisoners as a means to unite Americans in defense of their fellow countrymen and paint their former colonial masters as a "cruel and barbarous" enemy. Echoing captivity narratives of the colonial generations, stories of British "savagery" replaced French and Indian atrocities as the greatest threat to American liberty and helped to unite many Americans in the cause of Independence.[35]

Chapters 2 and 3 explore how the capture of American sailors by Algerian corsairs in the context of the federal inability to redeem their captive countrymen led private citizens to act when the government could not. As had been the case during the American Revolution, stories of captive Americans immediately attracted national attention. When Algerian corsairs seized the American merchant ships *Maria* and *Dauphin* in 1785, news of the capture sent shockwaves throughout the young nation. The powerlessness of the government to redeem the captive crewmen revealed the limits of federal authority under the Articles of Confederation, convincing many Americans of the need to take matters into their own hands and laying the foundation for an increasingly participatory political culture in the new nation. The ongoing failure of Congress to secure the release of the twenty-one sailors led groups of American citizens to undertake private efforts on behalf of their fellow countrymen. Although these endeavors were ultimately put on hold as news of the Constitutional Convention offered hope that the American crewmen might be redeemed through official channels, these initial enterprises demonstrated a decidedly democratic understanding of the place of American citizens in foreign affairs.[36]

Despite expectations that the Washington administration might provide greater security to the citizens of the new nation and bring a quick resolution to the Algerian crisis, the seizure of nearly a hundred American sailors in 1793, in addition to those already in captivity, revived the democratic impulse of the Revolution and renewed private efforts to free the American sailors in North Africa. Many officials within the federal government sought to limit the voices of the American people in formal debate, but following the 1793 attacks, many members of the American public were unwilling to be shut out and silenced. In the face of the continued failure of the Washington administration to provide for American security abroad, concerned citizens revived movements, begun before the ratification of the Constitution, to secure the release of the prisoners held in Algiers. Despite the objections of the president and many of his supporters, citizens throughout the United States responded to the crisis in Algiers in petitions, letters, and newspapers and through the theater, expressing their frustration with their government's inaction and impotence. From members of Congress to the captive sailors in Algiers, a wide range of Americans made their voices heard in the debate over Algiers. The force of this reaction would ultimately force the federal officials who had opposed any public input to recognize the power of a motivated citizenry and respond to their demands.

Chapters 4 through 6 explore the efforts of the Federalists and Republicans, following the election of 1800, to employ a nationalist vision aimed at harnessing the response of a wider American public to foreign threats to American liberty. Examining the contours of this radically altered political landscape through the lens of captivity offers a new way of understanding the evolving relationship between the minority Federalists, the majority Republicans, and the American people. Chapter 4 explores how Jefferson's efforts to square Republican ideology with a military response to the Tripolitan threat resulted in a protracted conflict and a widespread public debate over the administration's handling of the war. Fulfilling a long-standing desire to employ a military response to the Barbary threat, Jefferson's initial efforts to protect Americans abroad met with mixed results. Following news of a Tripolitan declaration of war against the United States, Jefferson carefully balanced a limited military response with his desire to remain within the bounds of his constitutional authority. Despite Jefferson's optimism that this limited military force would bring a quick end to the Tripolitan threat, the half-measure ultimately failed. The result was a military engagement that lasted far longer than almost any American had foreseen, opening the door for a vitriolic public debate about the administration's handling of the conflict with Tripoli. Although the final settlement of the conflict was celebrated as an American victory, with both Republicans and Federalists attempting to claim some of the credit, had the administration moved more assertively from the start, a costly war and a deeply partisan national debate might have been avoided all together.

Paralleling the previous one, chapter 5 explores how the Jefferson administration's efforts to bring an end to the practice of impressment not only failed to stop the British practice but served as fodder for a wave of partisan attacks in the national press. In the face of the continuing threat of impressment, the celebration of a victory in Tripoli was quickly overshadowed by American vulnerability at the hands of the European powers. Even as Americans celebrated the exploits of their "gallant tars," they were unsure of how to proceed against the most powerful navy in the world. Although the celebration of the victory in Tripoli had been marked by a surge in national pride and might have allowed the American public to shift its attention away from international affairs, the ongoing attacks on American sailors, highlighted by the engagement between the American *Chesapeake* and the British *Leopard*, reminded Americans of U.S. vulnerability on the global stage. Once again attempting to adhere to Republican ideology and possibly a bit chastened by the high cost of the conflict with Tripoli, the Jefferson administration enacted a politically divisive and economically debilitating embargo. The failure of the embargo to successfully bring an end to impressment once again drew the ire of the Federalist minority, bringing Americans into a national debate over administration policy.[37]

With the failure of American efforts to secure freedom of the seas through nonintercourse, the United States finally resorted to a military solution in 1812. Chapter 6, focusing on the debate over the treatment of prisoners of war, examines a moment of transition for the Federalists and Republicans, with each party seeming to adopt the other's traditional views on government. Throughout the conflict, Federalists cast their opposition to the war and administration as a defense of the Republic from the threat of tyranny. Republicans countered that they were simply employing federal power to defend the nation in the face of Federalist treason.

Chapter 7 examines how the Madison administration's use of decisive force to terminate the Barbary threat in 1815 played a critical role in establishing the perception of American victory in the War of 1812 and ushering in the era of free security. Although General Andrew Jackson's victory at the Battle of New Orleans in early January 1815 is often cited as the critical moment in creating American self-confidence in the wake of the War of 1812, a closer examination of the year 1815 immediately following the conclusion of the conflict reveals a more complicated story. The surge in national self-confidence that followed Jackson's victory was soon undercut by the shooting deaths of American prisoners of war held at England's Dartmoor Prison in April 1815. In the days that followed the Dartmoor Massacre, the celebration of Jackson's victory at New Orleans faded from the American press and was replaced by news of a fresh episode of British cruelty toward helpless Americans. The national attention paid to the "horrid massacre" of the Americans at Dartmoor also recast Jackson's victory at the Battle of New Orleans. Much as the *Chesapeake-Leopard* affair diminished celebrations of victory in Tripoli nearly a decade before, the Dartmoor shootings tarnished the glory of New Orleans. The April carnage once again forced Americans to confront their weakness and vulnerability abroad. Rather than celebrating a glorious victory in a "second war of American independence," Americans were forced into a national discussion of the tragic incident at Dartmoor.[38]

The momentary distraction represented by Dartmoor was ultimately overshadowed by news of a final settlement with the Barbary States. During the conflict with England, Algerian ships had renewed their attacks on American shipping. At the conclusion of the War of 1812, the Madison administration sent what was at the time the largest American fleet ever assembled to the Mediterranean to bring a final end to the Barbary threat. Within a matter of weeks, as reports of this fleet's success began to appear in the American press, coverage of the incident at Dartmoor was pushed aside by news of this diplomatic success. The victory of the American fleet, which finally quashed the Barbary menace, provided the American people with an important coda to their "victory" in the war with England. Bringing a real end to the threat of North African piracy enabled the people of the United States to claim not only that they had defeated their colonial masters a second time but also that by defeating the Barbary threat, they had succeeded where all the nations of Europe had failed. By September 1815, the *Niles' Weekly Register* reported that the American people had begun "to assume, more and more, a NATIONAL CHARACTER."[39] In the wake of this overwhelming victory, as Americans celebrated the success of their nation on the international stage, they could now afford—ironically—to turn their attention away from that stage.

Americans spent the first half-century following Independence well aware of their vulnerability in the larger Atlantic world. The continued failure of the federal government to secure the liberty of its captive citizens overseas repeatedly drew the nation into public discussions of how to better secure the legacy of the American Revolution. An examination of the collective debates surrounding the treatment of captive Americans that emerged during the era of the Revolution and the Early Republic provides insight into the development of the young nation's political culture and nationalism. The threat of foreign captivity in the decades following Independence simultaneously served to bring the American people together in defense of their fellow countrymen while dividing them along partisan lines. Both the successful and failed attempts at the redemption of American hostages in the Early Republic played a critical role in defining the shape of American politics.[40] In the end, the efforts of both Federalists and Republicans to claim the mantle as defender of American liberty abroad, while playing on American fears that grew out of this insecurity, helped to create a language of American nationalism that would define the United States in the decades and centuries to follow.

CHAPTER 1

"Obligations Arising from the Rights of Humanity"

Prisoners of War and American Self-Image in the Revolution

On the last day of the year 1775, the Reverend Nathan Fiske stood before his congregation in Brookfield, Massachusetts, and delivered *An Historical Discourse Concerning the Settlement of Brookfield and Its Distresses during the Indian Wars.* Fiske's sermon traced the "transactions or sufferings" of the town's early settlers. Brookfield was well acquainted with the ravages of war. Almost immediately after its founding, the town became the front line in the conflict that the colonists called King Philip's War. Located along the western edge of seventeenth-century English settlement in North America, the eighty residents of Brookfield faced the constant threat of attack. In August 1675, a Nipmuc raid resulted in the near total destruction of the town. During Queen Anne's War a little more than a decade later, the residents of Brookfield again endured the harsh reality of war with nearly twenty inhabitants of the town killed and a handful of others taken captive. Fiske contrasted the hardships faced by the early settlers of Brookfield with their striking resilience, noting that despite these challenges, the town had continued to grow with "amazing rapidity." By the middle of the eighteenth century, the people of Brookfield no longer feared that they might find their "dwellings in ashes" or their families "carried captive through a perilous, dreadful wilderness."[1]

By 1775, however, Fiske believed that the "dangers and distresses, the cruelties and sufferings" of their forefathers had been "renewed in part in our day." Fiske drew a direct line between the experience of the people of Brookfield in the late seventeenth century and that of the American people in the late eighteenth century:

> When our fore-fathers took sanctuary in these then inhospitable shores, it was to secure to themselves and their progeny "peace, liberty and safety." When they purchased lands of the natives, they thought them their own: and when they cultivated them for their children whom they hoped to leave free and happy, they little thought their posterity would be disturbed in their possessions by *Britons*, more than themselves were by savage Indians. And at the conclusion of the last war, which seemed to put an end to our fears of any molestation from the Savages for time to come, who could have thought that the same nation that then assisted us in conquering them, would ever have laid such a plan . . . who could have thought that *Britons* would practice what the uncultivated tribes of Indians have refused to do: and that they themselves would distress and destroy our most populous towns on the sea coast, when the Savages could not be prevailed on by flatteries or gifts to molest our back settlements?

Now engaged in a battle with England, the people of Massachusetts once again faced the horrors of war. Fiske hoped that the example of the previous generations might provide some solace to Americans defending themselves against an unresponsive and increasingly repressive government. Just as the first settlers of Brookfield had endured the threat of Native American attack, so too, he believed, could Americans now survive the assault of the "savage" Britons.[2]

Fiske's meditation on the "increase and improvements" at Brookfield was part of a larger effort to define the Patriot cause in opposition to the British "other" and to unite the colonies against a common threat to American liberty. Fiske's sermon was just one in a cacophony of voices competing for attention during the American Revolution.[3] Despite the discordant turmoil that marked public discussion in the early days of the Revolution, Fiske's denunciation of British cruelty joined a growing body of literature that attempted to redefine Americans' relationship with England. Paralleling Fiske's message in both argument and historical focus was the reissue of John Williams's *The Redeemed Captive* and Mary Rowlandson's *The Sovereignty and Goodness of God*, each originally published almost a century before the American Revolution. Between 1770 and 1776, both narratives were reprinted nine times. Publishers throughout New England advertised their new editions, promising descriptions of "a most barbarous and cruel treatment" and a narrative of "captivity and deliverance." Both themes resonated with Americans who saw their own plight reflected in the accounts of Indian captivity. Just as Williams and Rowlandson were ultimately redeemed following their trial at the hands of a "barbarous and cruel" captor, Americans hoped that they too would ultimately achieve Independence following their own time of trial.[4]

While consideration of historical violence provided a starting point for Americans as they tried to make sense of the conflict with England, it was stories of the sufferings of their fellow countrymen that soon became one of the central pillars of the Patriot cause. From the prisons came tales of horrid conditions and an endless string of cruelty practiced by British guards. News from the frontier brought a constant stream of new brutality and savagery conducted by the British and their Indian allies. As accounts of British violence appeared in newspapers, broadsides, and stand-alone volumes, the colonial captivity narratives were subsumed into a new body of literature detailing American suffering at the hands of the British. While the Patriot cause was made up of disparate factions ranging from shoemakers and sailors to New England and Virginian elites, stories of British cruelty and American suffering helped define the Patriot cause in a way that could be understood at all levels of society.[5] The experience of every prisoner was unique, but taken together, these stories of captivity and suffering defined and explained the values and rights that all Americans were fighting for. Descriptions of British cruelties and savagery inflicted on American prisoners represented the direct opposite of the personal rights and individual liberty that Independence promised all Americans. The plight of American prisoners during the Revolution became a shorthand for the struggle of the entire nation as it tried to secure its independence from the savage Britons.

Defense of the American prisoners during the Revolution began at the highest level. As early as August 1775, George Washington decried the treatment of American prisoners in a letter to Thomas Gage, commander of British forces in North America. In his communication Washington noted that American soldiers were being detained in "a common Gaol appropriate for Felons." Washington requested that Gage adhere to the "Obligations arising from the Rights of Humanity" and offer those who had been captured "a more tender treatment." He went on to warn that if prison conditions did not improve, he would be forced to respond in kind, and, despite his own aversion to such actions, British soldiers held by American forces "would feel its effects." Gage was quick to respond, claiming no wrongdoing on the part of British jailers and decrying the hardships British soldiers had endured in American prison camps, "laboring . . . to gain their daily subsistence, or reduced to the wretched alternative, to perish by famine or take arms against their King and country."[6]

Washington and members of Congress recognized the value of this debate in defining their cause. In September 1775, Continental Congress ordered that the exchange between the two generals be published in newspapers throughout the colonies. The members of Congress understood that their ultimate success was dependent on the support of the American people, and they believed the best way to achieve such support was to make clear the righteousness of the American cause in the face of a vicious, brutal enemy. When the Continental Congress established its own rules for the treatment of prisoners seized by American forces in May 1776, it made sure that these guidelines were distributed to newspaper editors throughout the country and published without delay. The congressional rules gave responsibility for the care of captives to the states in which they had been captured, but it required that detainees "be treated as prisoners of war, but with humanity, and be allowed the same rations as the troops in the service of the United Colonies."[7]

From the very first, Congress attempted to claim the virtue of moral superiority for Americans in the conflict. Although the practice of claiming the cause of right was a long-standing practice in European warfare, the American Revolutionaries pushed the limits of this strategy to a level that was "all together unusual in eighteenth-century wars."[8] One of the key components of these efforts was the consistent and near-constant use of the press. Nearly every resolution passed by Congress denouncing British actions, as well as Washington's carefully crafted letters calling for the more-humane treatment of captives, found their way into a sympathetic press. Revolutionary elites understood that efforts in support of the American cause needed to be fought not only on the battlefield but in the print medium as well. The ordeal faced by American prisoners held by the British military gave Congress plenty of ammunition to continue its fight for the moral supremacy throughout the war and served to aid in drawing supporters to the Patriot cause.

British officials, despite their long experience with combat operations in North America, found themselves uncertain about how to handle American captives, given the complex circumstances surrounding the American uprising. On the one hand, American combatants who took up arms against the

King were technically traitors and subject to execution. Indeed, a fair number of British officials favored such action. Among them was Captain Frederick Mackenzie of the Royal Welch Fusiliers, who declared that "rebels taken in arms forfeit their lives by the laws of all Countries." Failure to enforce these laws, Mackenzie argued, "encourages them to continue their opposition," for without punishment of death, "captivity has nothing dreadful in it." On the other hand, British officials were slow to send these "rebels" to the gallows. Fearful of public reaction to the execution of American prisoners yet overwhelmed by the sheer number of them, colonial authorities resorted to using makeshift prisons throughout North America. The results for American prisoners were mixed. Although spared execution, captive Americans faced prison conditions far more harsh than those endured by traditional prisoners of war.[9]

Traditionally, the British held prisoners of war for relatively limited periods of captivity. Their standard practice was to negotiate an exchange of prisoners in short order, thus minimizing the costs of providing for captives and replenishing their own ranks with the return of British soldiers. While in British hands, traditional prisoners of war were provided with a two-thirds ration along with basic medical care, shelter, and clothing. But treating American prisoners in this fashion would have been a de facto recognition of the American cause and rebel authority. Thus, although the British military had a great deal of experience in treating captive enemy combatants, there were no clear guidelines on how to address the complex challenge of detaining rebellious Americans. This problem resulted in an ad hoc approach to dealing with American detainees.[10]

The greatest departure from traditional prisoner practice was in the treatment of officers. Despite Washington's protest, Gage limited the rights traditionally offered captured officers, denying them prisons apart from their enlisted men and refusing them parole. His policy made clear that he would not recognize commissions granted by the Continental Congress or George Washington. Such treatment of American officers, however, lent credence to American charges of incivility leveled against British prison officials. Gage eventually abandoned the practice of limiting these rights but continued a delicate political dance, seeking to avoid official recognition of the American cause while dealing with the reality of an ever-growing prison population. But a muddled policy left thousands of American captives in deplorable conditions without adequate food and supplies, in makeshift prisons, and with a status situated somewhere between traitor and prisoner of war.[11]

The outset of the war suggested to the British almost nothing about the difficulties that they would face in dealing with American prisoners. British forces held the earliest captive Americans in Boston, and their numbers never grew beyond a few dozen. When the British evacuated Boston in March 1776, these few prisoners were granted their freedom. The American incursions into Canada, however, signaled the beginning of the need for a more-serious prisoner policy. In relatively short order, both Halifax and Quebec emerged as long-term sites for the incarceration of captive Americans. In both Canadian cities, the lack of British planning quickly became apparent. Without any formal military housing public jails, warehouses, abandoned buildings, and a variety of other structures were repurposed to hold American prisoners. As the war stretched into several years and the theatre of war extended farther into U.S. territory, British military authorities established makeshift prison facilities in the occupied cities of Philadelphia, Charleston, Savannah, and New York.[12]

Across the Atlantic, in the earliest years of the war, the uncertain status of American prisoners relegated privateers and members of the Continental and state navies captured by the British navy to prison ships in various British ports. Captured in the summer of 1776, the crewmen of the American privateer *Yankee* were among the first Americans to experience life aboard a British prison ship. The twenty-five man crew found themselves anchored in the Thames and confined to the very vessel they had previously sailed. As their confinement continued through the summer, conditions aboard the *Yankee* quickly deteriorated. Before long sympathetic Londoners began to decry the "putrid steams" that emerged from the ship and the suffering of the "miserable wretches" trapped on board.[13]

In a letter addressed to the lord mayor of London, "Humanitas" called on the "head of this great city (justly famed for its great humanity even to its enemies)" to work to alleviate the "truly shocking" and "barbarous" conditions faced by the twenty-five American prisoners. Regardless of the detainees' perceived wrongdoing in acting as privateers, Humanitas argued, the prisoners were "entitled to common humanity" and should not be detained under conditions that bore striking resemblance to "the memorable black hole at Calcutta." This treatment of the crew of the *Yankee* was made all the more egregious by the fact that "English prisoners, taken by the Americans, have been treated with the most remarkable tenderness and generosity." The growing concern over the fate of the American prisoners led Parliament to act in early 1777.[14]

The passage of North's Act in March 1777 temporarily solved the prisoner dilemma in England. The act still denied American prisoners in England the status of prisoners of war, while simultaneously depriving them of the rights of traditional civil prisoners. Consequently, the act allowed British officials to detain the "rebels" on English soil indefinitely without trial or bail. Many of the sailors who had previously been held aboard the prison ships soon found themselves in England's Forton and Mill prisons.[15]

Conditions in the English prisons were far better than any in North American facilities. In large part because they were established prisons rather than makeshift structures in British-held North America, prisoners in Forton and Mill received treatment more reasonable than that endured by their counterparts on the other side of the North Atlantic. The sailors at Forton and Mill were given proper medical care, opportunity to exercise in fresh air and sunshine, and daily access to washing troughs, soap, and water. Despite these precautions, smallpox remained a very real threat, and the isolation and helplessness of prison life could take a toll on prisoners' mental health. American prisoners incarcerated at Forton and Mill also received a smaller quantity of rations than did their European counterparts in British prisons. French and Spanish prisoners of war received ten and one-half pounds of bread per week; the Americans, only seven. The rationale behind this difference lay in the refusal to officially designate Americans as prisoners of war. When the Americans complained about their rations, their British captors bluntly informed them that as rebels, they would be issued only seven pounds of bread per week and that only officially recognized prisoners of war were to receive ten pounds.[16]

The relatively healthier conditions in English prisons led to a much-lower death rate than that found in their North American counterparts. Although American officials issued a steady stream of criticism and demands for investigations into conditions at Forton and Mill, those prisons provided little grist for the American propaganda mill.[17] Prison conditions in New York City stood in stark contrast to those in Britain and evolved in a nearly opposite fashion. The increasing prison population in North America ultimately led British officials to turn to prison ships to relieve the overcrowding. In New York as in Halifax and Quebec, the British first employed public jails to house captives, but as those sites filled, they began to employ whatever buildings could be found. Before long the sugar houses along New York's waterfront became the primary sites for the detention of prisoners. These buildings, designed to store rum, sugar, and molasses, tended to be poorly maintained year round, oppressively hot in the summer, and terribly drafty in the winter, the latter condition exacerbated by the lack of fuel for heating. Within a matter of months, even the sugar houses were inadequate in number to hold New York's growing prisoner population. Soon churches, buildings at King's College, and even New York's City Hall were pressed into service as prisons.[18]

As the prison population in New York expanded and it became increasingly clear that the makeshift prisons onshore were inadequate, British military authorities in New York turned to prison ships as an expedient means to deal with the ever-growing prison population. By October 1776, the first of the prison ships to be employed in the thirteen colonies appeared in Brooklyn's Wallabout Bay. Located across from the southern tip of Manhattan, the bay provided an ideal location for anchoring these floating detention centers. The proximity of the harbor allowed for easy transport of prisoners from the city, while the harbor provided anchorage away from other shipping traffic. From a security standpoint, the harbor offered a water barrier that, in conjunction with the surrounding mud flats and its location in the heart of British-controlled New York, made prisoner escape extremely difficult. For the prisoners unfortunate enough to find themselves trapped aboard these vessels, the suffering was nearly interminable.[19] While the twenty-five-man crew of the *Yankee* suffered the "inhumanity" of their "stinking apartment" in London, captives in New York found conditions far worse. Prison ships in New York often held in excess of two hundred men with meager rations and little, if any medical care. Under such conditions, the mortality rate aboard these prison ships was near 40 percent.[20]

Within weeks of the first prisoners' transfer to Wallabout Bay, denunciations of the treatment of prisoners aboard prison ships began to appear in the American press. The first of these was the reprint of Humanitas's letter to the lord mayor of London. Newspapers in Connecticut, Massachusetts, Pennsylvania, and New Hampshire published for all to read the London comparison of British brutality and American "tenderness and generosity" toward prisoners of war.[21] The suffering of the American prisoners in Wallabout Bay in the winter of 1776–1777 underscored Humanitas's earlier description of the horrors experienced aboard the prison ship *Yankee*. Reports of the wretched conditions in New York were quickly disseminated through the Patriot press. By January 1777, accounts out of New York described how captains and lieutenants, "many of whom had formerly lived in affluence," were confined between decks "with Indians, Mulattoes, and Negro slaves" and denied even the most basic rations, often going "twelve or sixteen hours without a drop of fresh water." And "as to their provisions, the allowance is very small and the quality unwholesome." Most shocking, according to one account, was that the "prison ship had neither Doctor nor medicine chest" to provide for the care of prisoners. The experience of Americans confined to the prison ships in both England and New York confirmed Americans' worst fears or suspicions about British brutality and inhumanity.[22]

Those prisoners who remained onshore found conditions little better than those of their fellow captives on board the prison ships. Although Americans detained onshore managed to avoid some of the wretched conditions of the floating hulks, they were more likely to experience abuse at the hands of their guards. Prisoners who were fortunate enough to receive "any trifle of food or drink" often experienced "the but [sic] end of a musket" when their good fortune was observed by British soldiers.[23] In reporting these conditions, one prisoner stated that "the New England people can have no idea of such barbarous policy." Had the "Gentleman of Honor and Distinction," who was held in New York, known what awaited him in detention, he wrote, he might have wished to "fall by the sword of the Hessians" instead of suffering in detention under such barbaric conditions. Worse still, the prisoner reported, his fellow captives were dying at a rate of twenty or thirty a day "and thrown out upon the highway and open fields, with this impious and horrid expression, 'D—n the rebel, he's not worth a grave.'"[24]

Such accounts fueled American speculation about the reason for this brutal behavior from the British. In a letter reprinted in newspapers throughout New England and eventually making its way to Europe, "Misercors" argued that British cruelty was a calculated policy designed to punish American prisoners for their service in the rebellion. In his essay, Misercors declared that the moldy bread, the bilge-water-soaked pork, and the lack of drinking water were all forms of retaliation on the part of the British. "By these means and in this way," he argued, "above fifteen hundred brave Americans who had nobly gone forth in the defense of their injured, oppressed country . . . died in New York." These deaths were made all the more atrocious given that many of those Americans who suffered in British prison "were very amiable, promising youths, of good families, the flower of our land." Such treatment of American citizens suggested that British cruelty knew no bounds. Misercors declaimed: "Where in history can we find an instance of more horrid treatment of prisoners? Even the famous instance of Calcutta is not to be compared with this." Such treatment, which, Misercors believed, was "the effect of cool reflection and a preconcerted system," ought to raise "the indignation of every friend to right, to mercy and to mankind." Thus, he argued, Americans ought not allow "our famished, tortured, murdered fellow citizens to cry for vengeance in vain."[25]

Misercors was not alone in his denunciation of British actions. During his address to New York's Convention of Representatives in January 1777, Governor George Clinton condemned British policy that left American captives to "starve and languish, and die in prisons."[26] In that same month, the Continental Congress appointed a seven-man committee to investigate the ever increasing accounts of British cruelty. In the ensuing months, the "committee appointed to enquire into the conduct of the enemy" found ample evidence of British brutality, reporting back to Congress in April 1777 "that in every place where the enemy has been, there are heavy complaints of oppression, injury, and insult suffered by the inhabitants." The committee's findings confirmed accounts of the sufferings experienced by American prisoners, who "were, in general, treated with the greatest barbarity," which stood in marked contrast to the "humane treatment" offered those "taken by the United States." On the whole, the neglect and abuse endured by American captives "was never known to happen in any similar case in a Christian country."[27]

Although Congress ordered that the "committee who brought in the report, publish the same with affidavits," there was no need for the committee itself to take any action. Within a few days, the report was serialized in the *Pennsylvania Evening Post* and subsequently reprinted in newspapers around the country. John Adams forwarded one of these copies of the *Evening Post* to his wife, Abigail, noting that the report would "give you, some Idea, of the Humanity of the present Race of Brittons." The lesson of this report and the countless other reports of British cruelty, Adams argued, could not be studied enough. "It would convince every American," he wrote, "that a Nation, so great a Part of which is thus deeply depraved, can never again be trusted with Power over Us." Furthermore, Adams hoped that British actions would excite American passions in their prosecution of the war, for the "public may be clearly convinced that a War is just, and yet, until their Passions are excited, will carry it languidly on."[28]

As Adams hoped, the Congressional report was merely one instance of a wave of reports chronicling British cruelties. In the months that followed, stories of prisoner abuse appeared in newspapers around the nation. From Boston, the *Independent Chronicle* reported that captive American sailors were being "whipped with a wire cat of nine tails that drew blood every stroke." In Philadelphia, the *Pennsylvania Packet* published accounts of "numerous instances of prisoners of war perishing in all the agonies of hunger, from their severe treatment." Notably, these accounts were not limited to the English-language press. In May 1777, the German newspaper *Wochentliche Philadelphische Staatsbote* reported that a British officer had shot and stabbed American soldier Philip Jones following his capture by British forces in southern New Jersey. Tales of British cruelty, brutality, and viciousness continued to echo throughout the newly independent states, providing a foil for an emerging American character and reminding Americans of the cause for which they were fighting.[29]

Conditions aboard the prison ships proved a near constant source of propaganda for the American cause, and severe weather in the winter of 1778–1779 exacerbated the issue. Following a Christmas Eve blizzard and a wave of extreme cold, the city was brought to a standstill. As supplies of food and fuel dwindled and with temperatures well below freezing, the prisoners found themselves last in line for limited supplies. In the face of such dire conditions, British officials released 136 prisoners from the prison ships in New York, transporting them to New London, Connecticut. Although the release of prisoners might have been viewed as an act of compassion, it only provided more ammunition for Patriot charges of British cruelty. "In this short run [from New York to New London]," several Patriot papers reported, "16 died on board [*sic*]" and "upwards of 60 when they landed were scarcely able to move," and the remainder were "greatly emaciated and infeebled." The plight of these prisoners, these newspapers declared, stood as yet another example of the "inhumanity of the Britons," which had been carried out "from the beginning of this war, & through every stage of it." Horrified by the prisoners' condition and their reports of starvation, the Connecticut General Assembly called for local officials to collect from the former prisoners testimony "stating the particulars of the severe usage and sufferings" from their time in captivity. In a footnote to the legislative act, the Assembly called on the "printers in this State ... to insert the above resolution in their respective papers."[30]

Throughout the war, official reports and hearings on the treatment of prisoners and their subsequent publication continued to be a critical component of the Patriots' efforts to articulate and define their cause. In early 1781, the

Continental Congress launched another round of hearings on prison conditions. The focus of this new battery of hearings was the British prison ship *Jersey*.[31] The investigation into treatment of prisoners aboard the *Jersey* began with the testimony of George Batterman of Rhode Island, who had been taken captive while traveling as a civilian passenger on an American privateer vessel. In his 1781 testimony, Batterman described the punishing conditions—overcrowding, disease, and hunger—endured by those incarcerated on the prison ships. Although on board the *Jersey* for only a brief period, Batterman charged that the British had "taken this method of starving us for the want of water to kill us, or make us enter into their service. They never allow a man that is sick to go to the hospital ship, till they are so weak and low that they often expire before they get out of the ship." Based on Batterman's testimony and other reports of mistreatment, Congress retreated from its earlier stance that American-held prisoners receive humane treatment and decreed that "British prisoners receive the same allowance and treatment, in every respect, as our people, who are prisoners, receive from the enemy." Batterman's testimony, which appeared in newspapers throughout the United States, only added to the growing public concern over the treatment of American prisoners by the British. As it had throughout the war, Congress again made sure that the proceedings from these hearings made their way into the American press.[32]

Although British officials had downplayed accusations of brutality throughout the war, the American investigation of the *Jersey* marked their first concerted effort to refute the charges of abuse. Spearheading the official British response was David Sproat, commissary general for naval prisoners in North America. Sproat was a Philadelphia Tory and an outspoken opponent of Independence and had lost a self-described "pritty [sic] little fortune" as a result of his loyalty to Great Britain. In the face of Patriot hostility, Sproat had fled to New York and eventually managed to earn an appointment in the British bureaucracy. He believed that anyone caught "in the very acts of Rebellion and Murder" had no right to kind treatment. To many supporters of the Patriot cause, the commissary general's dismissal of prisoner complaints was a glaring example of British cruelty and depravity. Sproat's inability or unwillingness to recognize the suffering of the American prisoners was simply an outgrowth of his earlier rejection of the Patriot cause of Independence and represented his identification with the savage British.[33]

Sproat dismissed reports of mistreatment as scurrilous and argued that allegations of abuse were "not founded on matters of fact, but merely calculated to deceive the world into a belief of the necessity of using our people that fall into their hands ill, and inflame the minds of those already crowded by such impressions." In fact, he had personally boarded the prison ships, the British commissary general noted, in an effort to ensure that each prisoner received "the full quantity of good, sound, wholesome provisions." He went on to claim that from the day of his appointment as commissary general, he had worked with British officials to make the prison ships as comfortable as possible for those onboard. He highlighted the acquisition of "two excellent large stoves" to provide heat for the prisoners during the cold winter months. Aboard the hospital ships, he explained, "every sick or wounded person [was] furnished with a cradle, bedding, and surgeons appointed to take care of them." Striking back at his critics, Sproat declared British treatment of prisoners more humane than the American treatment of British prisoners. He noted that British soldiers taken captive by American forces had been "thrown into jail and shackled with heavy irons," that loyalists had fled the country for fear of being "thrown into a dungeon and there treated with every species of insult, outrage, and cruelties," and that prisoners held in Pennsylvania had been fed on bread and water "when meat was plenty." All of this occurred "under the nose of the very people" who had leveled charges of brutality against the British. Most importantly, he had tried repeatedly to establish a prisoner exchange so as to bring an end to the suffering of "the poor prisoners on both sides in distress," but American officials had been unwilling to cooperate. According to Sproat, if anyone bore the blame for the suffering of both English and American prisoners, it was those who supported the cause of American Independence.[34]

Sproat's defense of British prison policies was only one aspect of the British campaign to refute American charges. In response to the congressional hearings, British military authorities launched their own inquiry into the conditions onboard the *Jersey*. Backed by testimony from six *Jersey* prisoners and conducted by four British officers, the investigation found little on the ship that could be considered the fault of the the jailers. Ultimately, they concluded that the prisoners had only their own poor hygiene to blame for the less-than-comfortable conditions on the prison vessel. In support of these findings the officers pointed to the testimony of the six Americans, "being the oldest prisoners in [British] possession," who "collectively and voluntarily" declared that "they firmly believed their situation was made at all times as comfortable as possible, and that they were in no instance oppressed or ill-treated." Beyond the living conditions, the prisoners noted that they regularly received 66 ounces of bread, 43 ounces of beef, 22 ounces of pork, 8 ounces of butter, 1 pint of peas, and 2 pints of oatmeal. The prisoners concluded "their general testimony with an affirmation that they have never been and are not now crowded in the prison ship."[35]

In addition to the testimony of the "oldest" of the *Jersey*'s prisoners, a number of British officers who oversaw the prison ships offered sworn testimony that they had done their best to offer the captives reasonable living conditions. Jeremiah Downer, a "mariner, a native of Boston, in New England," noted that during his time as commander of "his Majesty's prison ship Strombolo, in the harbor of New York . . . the provisions issued to the prisoners confined on board, were of the same goodness and quality as those issued to the seaman belonging to the Stombolo, and the same as that time were issued to the seaman in the Royal Navy." Peter Robertson, "acting Purser of his Majesty's prison ship the *Jersey*," testified that all provisions issued to those on board the prison ships "have always been the same in goodness and quality as were supplied to the crews of his Majesty's said hospital ship and the other King's ships on the North-American station during said period." Finally, Admiral Mariot Arbuthnot, swore an oath that he "uniformly ordered provisions to be issued to the naval prisoners of the same kind, species, goodness and quality as at the same times were furnished to the Royal Navy."[36]

British officials made sure to publicize in the Loyalist press the results of their findings, highlighting the American prisoners' accounts, which corroborated their conclusions. The Loyalist newspapers published the complete proceedings, including Sproat's letter and the testimony of the prisoners and the officers. Despite this public relations effort, the veracity of the British claims about the quality of life on the prison ships was dubious, as the 47 percent death rate suggests. In all likelihood, the prisoners who had denied the existence of unsanitary conditions or cruel treatment aboard British prison ships had been offered freedom in exchange for their testimony. Regardless of the truth of these British claims, the fact that the British military went beyond simply denying the charges of prisoner mistreatment and not only commissioned an investigation but sought out prisoner confirmation of the committee's findings, suggests the impact that the reports of prisoner mistreatment were having on the conduct of the war.

Unconvinced and undeterred by the British efforts, the Patriot press went on publishing any and all accounts alleging and detailing the mistreatment of

American prisoners. Within weeks of the release of the official British inquiry into conditions on the *Jersey*, Patriot papers countered with an account of thirty-three British-held prisoners who had been freed as part of a prisoner exchange. The prisoners, according to one report, were "in a very sickly and emaciated condition, owing to the inhuman treatment they experienced while with the enemy." The prisoners' conditions and their experience aboard the ships were "beyond description, and, if possible, exceed the enemy's former refinements in barbarity." The account published by the Patriot press was a direct refutation of much of the testimony produced in the British hearings. Most pointedly, the prisoners themselves contradicted the sworn testimony of British admiral Mariot Arbuthnot; they "had repeatedly petitioned the Admiral, but their petitions remained unanswered." With no improvement in their living conditions, the prisoners reported that because of a lack of water, they "were obliged to ally their thirst with urine . . . [and] that latterly about seven or eight die in a day." Despite the new British awareness of the power of the stories about prisoner mistreatment, by 1781 there was little they could do to stem the rising tide of the public perception of British cruelty by 1781.[37]

While American officials often integrated individual prisoners' stories into a larger single narrative contrasting British cruelty and American virtue, for many prisoners the utility of their suffering to the American cause was at best secondary. The primary goal of most prisoners was to regain their freedom. That desire manifested itself in a variety of ways. The delayed recognition of Americans as true prisoners of war meant that escape was one of the only, albeit an extremely dangerous, means to freedom available to many captives. In the North American prisons, the likelihood of success in any escape attempt diminished the longer prisoners remained in captivity. Poor nutrition and unsanitary conditions often left prisoners in a weakened state and unable to endure the physical demands of flight. The importance of good health to any escape attempt may help to explain the vast difference between the number of prisoners who successfully escaped in North America compared to those in England, where hundreds of prisoners, primarily officers, escaped each year.[38]

If outright escape was dangerous and unlikely, British officials offered another avenue by which prisoners might end their captivity—enlistment in the British armed forces. British recruitment efforts were by no means subtle. By 1776, recruiters often approached prisoners within days of their confinement and offered assurances that they would protect the identity of any defectors.[39] Although the exact numbers in North America are hard to determine, one historian has calculated that more than 10 percent of the American prisoners in England petitioned for a royal pardon with the promise to enter the king's service at some point and that nearly all of these petitions were accepted.[40] Whatever the North American numbers American officials filed formal protests against the practice in both 1777 and 1781. Despite prison conditions the vast majority of prisoners remained in captivity until they were exchanged or paroled.[41]

Although most prisoners refused to enlist in the British military in exchange for their freedom, their actions do not necessarily symbolize a loyalty to the cause of Independence. Life in the British military was in many ways less appealing than life in British prison. Following a wave of enlistments in the British service at Mill prison in December 1778, a petition asserting loyalty to Congress and denouncing those who joined the British military received less than half of the remaining prisoners' signatures.[42] In most cases, historians have little evidence to provide insight into the motives behind prisoners' decisions and are largely left with official inquiries and press reports. In a few cases, however, American prisoners provided a full accounting of their time in British detention, echoing the captivity narratives of an earlier generation.

The emergence of a Revolutionary War captivity literature was spearheaded by Ethan Allen and John Dodge.[43] Reflecting the earlier narratives of John Williams and Mary Rowlandson, Allen and Dodge presented to the American people stand-alone accounts of their time in captivity. Like their colonial predecessors and reflective of the larger American effort to cast the British as "other," Allen and Dodge crafted narratives that highlighted their own virtue during their captivity while condemning the inhumanity of a savage and powerful enemy. With a ready-made audience created by the continued attention to prison conditions and building on the celebrity of Ethan Allen following his exploits in upstate New York and Canada, publishers reprinted both Allen's and Dodge's narratives several times during the war. (There was even a British edition of Dodge's account.) These memoirs of wartime captivity fit perfectly into the larger American efforts to control the narrative of the conflict with Britain. In both cases, Allen and Dodge served as exemplars of American virtue in the face of British power, tyranny, and cruelty, giving a face to the emerging definition of American liberty. The degree to which these individual accounts conform to the larger narrative of the American struggle suggests possible gaps between the prisoners' actual experiences and their memoirs.

Both Dodge's and Allen's accounts are possibly hybrids that integrate their actual experiences within the framework of traditional captivity narratives and straddle the line between fiction and reality. Walking that line was part of their effort to connect their stories to the cause of Independence, to gain the sympathy of the public, and, of course, to realize a profit from the sale of their work. The variety of motives, however, does not diminish the value of their narratives. In many ways, conforming to the larger narrative of American suffering at British hands suggests just how integral this theme had become to the American cause.[44]

Ethan Allen's ordeal as a prisoner of war began in September 1775. He was one of thirty-eight Americans captured in a failed raid on the British position at Montreal. His earlier success in the war, particularly in the seizure of Fort Ticonderoga and in his attempts to encourage the Caughnawaga people and the Montreal merchants to turn against England, made him a primary target of British frustration and anger as the war dragged on. Allen's captivity spanned the Atlantic; he was eventually transferred him to New York by way of Ireland, North Carolina, and Halifax. Only when he reached British-occupied New York did his captors finally grant him parole, allowing him to split his time between Manhattan and Long Island. Nearly three years passed before Allen regained his freedom following a prisoner exchange in May 1778.[45]

Allen published his *Narrative of Colonel Ethan Allen's Captivity* almost immediately following his release. From the first, it was a success. The narrative went through eight editions in the first two years after its publication, and another nineteen editions in the following half-century. Allen's account contained many characteristics of Williams's and Rowlandson's earlier narratives, substituting British for Indian captors. Just as Williams and Rowlandson sought to highlight their ability to cling to their Christian ideals in the face of Indian captivity, Allen went to great lengths to describe his zeal to maintain his moral superiority as an American in the face of British cruelty. Allen missed no opportunity to highlight an instance of British barbarity. From the first moments in British hands, he and several members of his force were "shackled together by pairs, viz. two men fasted together by one hand-cuff, being closely fixed to one wrist of each of them, and treated with the greatest severity, nay as criminals." Allen's leg irons, which he estimated to weigh thirty pounds, were clamped "very tight" around his ankles. So restrictive were these irons that he could not lie down except on his back.

This severe treatment of prisoners, according to Allen, was no mere oversight but rather the result of "express orders" given by British authorities.[46]

In addition to the cruelty of his captors, Allen highlighted the strenuous nature of his passage to England, again echoing the captivity narratives of the colonial era which had recounted the grueling march into Canada. Allen told how he and his fellow captives:

> were denied fresh water, except a small allowance, which was very inadequate to our wants; and in consequence of the stench of the place, each of us was soon followed with a diarrhea and fever, which occasioned intolerable thirst. When we asked for water, we were, most commonly, instead of obtaining it, insulted and derided; and to add to all the horrors of the place, it was so dark that we could not see each other, and were overspread with body lice.

Allen was careful to highlight how, despite these conditions, he not only survived but managed to maintain his commitment to the American cause, just as Rowlandson and Williams had held fast to their British and Christian ideals in the face of French and Indian captors generations before. In the face of the near constant threat of being hanged as a rebel, Allen resolved to "exhibit a good sample of American fortitude . . . [and] that if a cruel death must inevitably be [his] portion, [he] would faced it undaunted." In adopting the style of the traditional captivity narrative, Allen's account brought together two significant components of the American efforts to deal with the crisis of identity brought on by the war with Britain. Allen simultaneously provided a story of redemption and a model of behavior in the face of a "haughty and cruel nation." Allen's success inspired others to follow his lead.[47]

The only other narrative published as a book during the war was John Dodge's *An Entertaining Narrative of the Cruel and Barbarous Treatment and Extreme Suffering of Mr. John Dodge during his Captivity of Many Months among the British*. Appearing only a year after Allen's account, Dodge's tale likewise condemned British cruelty and recounted his own trials in the face of such brutality. In many ways, however, Dodge presented a more complicated narrative than did Allen. In addition to the cruelty he experienced as a prisoner, Dodge was careful to narrate his loss of property and wealth at the hands of his captors on numerous occasions. Dodge also suggested that Native Americans in the Ohio country might serve as allies in the cause of Independence. Such a suggestion marked a complete reordering of the traditional captivity narrative. In Dodge's account, Native Americans had become potential allies in the face of the threat created by the savage British.[48]

Dodge's attitude toward Native Americans marks the beginning of a shift in the traditional form of the American captivity narrative. Even as these stories of captivity and a "savage other" helped to define an emerging American identity during the Revolution, the nature of the narratives themselves began to evolve. In the years immediately following the Revolution, the traditional Puritan narrative, accounts of patriotism or faith in the face of a "savage other," was joined by frontier narratives of acculturation. While the traditional accounts of suffering at the hands of an enemy would continue to play a role in defining and articulating American identity, most notably in U.S. interaction with the Barbary States of North Africa, stories of frontier captivity took a decidedly different tack.[49] Throughout the Revolution prisoners' accounts had defined American identity by what it was not, but following the Revolution, narratives of Indian captivity began to portray the frontiersman as the "archetypal American and mediator between civilization and the wilderness."[50] Richard Slotkin points to John Filson's "The Adventures of Col. Daniel Boone," published in 1784, as the earliest and most influential expression of this new identity. In this new style of frontier narrative, American identity is not defined in opposition to a "savage other" but described as a product of acculturation in which the American captive, never relinquishing white cultural superiority, learns the skills of his captors and gains their respect. In the end, the captive emerges from his trial as "part-Indian," wearing a hybrid identity that maintained the best of the civilized world while it provided a skill set that enabled the American to subdue the natural world as well.[51]

Although Slotkin argues that the Boone narrative marks the beginning of this shift, Dodge's narrative provides the earliest evidence of this evolution of the American captivity narrative. While the majority of Revolutionary tales of captivity mirror the traditional Puritan narratives, in which the captive emerges from an ordeal at the hands of a "savage other" firmly committed to his or her faith or country, Dodge's account of redemption offers a hybrid between the traditional narrative and the emerging frontier narrative. Much of Dodge's narrative focuses on his suffering at the hands of his British captors, but his description of his relationship with Native Americans in the Ohio country in the earliest days of the Revolution and his recognition of the role of an Indian guide in his return home is an early step toward the new frontier narrative. Although far from a complete rejection of traditional captivity narratives, Dodge's story of his captivity constructs a frontier identity not unlike that explained by Slotkin.

In the description of his life before captivity, Dodge seems to embody the American frontiersman. Born in Connecticut, he migrated to the Great Lakes region in 1770 and settled in the village of Sandusky on the shores of Lake Erie. Engaged in frontier commerce, Dodge spoke several Indian languages and presented himself as a trusted business partner of the Native groups in the region. He described his new home as "about half way between Pittsburgh and Detroit, where I carried on a very beneficial trade with the natives, until the unhappy dispute between Great-Britain and America reached those pathless wilds, and roused to war Savages in no ways interested in it." Dodge claimed that a number of the Ohio country tribes had responded positively to American overtures for peace and "took up the hatchet" only after the British spread "evil reports" among the tribes in the Great Lakes region that the Americans "were going to murder them all and take their lands." As part of the British efforts to undercut American presence in the region, Dodge was taken from his home on January 15, 1776, and brought to Detroit, where he was held for nearly three years. Dodge argued that he was arrested and detained by the English because of his high level of acculturation to the Native American cultures in the Ohio country.[52]

With his capture, Dodge's narrative reverted to a more traditional narrative form. He described his treatment at the hands of the British much as Allen did his own, labeling his captors "inhuman" and barbarous and calling them "savage adversaries." When Dodge arrived in Detroit, British officials informed him that he would most likely be executed and then was "hurried to a loathsome dungeon, ironed and thrown in with three criminals, being allowed neither bedding, straw or fire, although it was in the depth of winter, and so exceeding cold, that [his] toes were froze before morning." Dodge pointed out that not only was he threatened with execution but his British captors also refused him a fair trial. They denied his requests for a hearing, stating that they were "not obliged to give any damn'd rebel a trial."[53]

Living under the constant threat of execution and extreme conditions, Dodge "at last drove almost to despair . . . told [his jailor Philip] De Jeane to inform the Governor [he] was readier to die at that time than [he] should ever be, and that [he] would much rather undergo his sentence, than be tortured in the dreadful manner [he] then was." De Jeane ignored Dodge's request, leaving him to suffer in his cell and eventually to succumb to illness. Dodge explains, "The weather had been so extreme cold, and my legs had been bolted in such a manner, that they were so benumbed, and the sinews contracted, that I had not the least use of them; and the severity of my usage had brought on a fever." Fearing that he might die in captivity during his illness, British officials eventually transported Dodge to better housing and allowed a doctor to tend him. After a period of convalescence, however, Dodge was returned to his cell and once again placed in irons.[54]

British officials eventually transported Dodge to Quebec in the spring of 1778 and confined him to a prison ship. In August of that year, when many of Dodge's fellow captives were returned to the United States as part of a prisoner exchange, Dodge was simply paroled and prohibited from leaving Quebec. When he inquired into the reason behind his prolonged captivity, Dodge was told that orders had come from authorities in Detroit insisting that he not be freed for fear of his "damn'd deal of influence with the Indians." Finally in October of that year, when his parole expired, Dodge hired an Indian guide and made the monthlong trek from Quebec to Boston, where General Horatio Gates received him and recommended Dodge to Congress as "having some matters . . . worthy of their hearing." Dodge's return home, a wilderness trek led by an Indian guide, was a final comment on the brutality of his British captors. In the colonial captivity narratives the Indian-led journey through the woods away from British settlement was the opening of the ordeal. For Dodge a wilderness journey alongside an Indian guide marked his return to freedom. This upending of the traditional narrative structure underscored a larger point of his narrative. So far had the British fallen that Native Americans, once feared as a "barbarous other," had come to be potential allies. Dodge concluded his narrative by leaving to "the world to judge whether I have not a right to revolt from under the dominion of such tyrants." Dodge's conclusion represented a hybrid of the old and new styles, contrasting his journey to freedom alongside an Indian ally, with the unrelenting cruelty of his British captors.[55]

The success of these narratives inspired other literary indictments of British cruelty, including Philip Freneau's *The British Prison Ship*, first published in 1781 by the same publisher who had printed Allen's captivity narrative. The arc of Freneau's poem echoed that of Allen's and Dodge's narratives, relating the fate of Americans brought low by the savagery of British captors and ultimately turning to thoughts of a future American victory. Freneau began his poem with a description of the beauty of the American merchant ship *Aurora*, crafted "with wonderous skill, and excellence of art," as it sailed from port in Philadelphia. It was not long, however, before the ship fell prey to the "ungenerous Britons," who descended like "famish'd wolves" to take this "gay ship" and her crew captive. In stark contrast to the veneration of the *Aurora*, Freneau described how the British "knaves, subservient to a bankrupt throne," forced the ship's crew into the "dark hulks" of the British prison ships, "rotten and old, replete with sighs and groans," in New York. Once transferred to these vessels, the proud crewmen of the *Aurora* were given only "putrid water" to drink and "mouldy bread," along with "the flesh of rotten swine," to eat. Those who took ill were transferred to the *Hunter*, a "slaughterhouse, yet *hospital* in name." The only medical treatment was then provided by a Hessian doctor, who was "not chief Physician" but rather "master o'er the murdering tribe." In response to such treatment of Americans, who had "in Freedom's sacred cause allied," Freneau called on his fellow citizens to "a just resentment shew, and glut revenge on this detested foe." Ultimately, Freneau had no doubt of an American victory and announced to his British enemies, "The years approach that shall ruin bring your lords, your chiefs, your desolating king, whose murderous acts shall stamp his name accurs'd."[56]

Freneau's poem provided a compressed accounting of British cruelty toward American prisoners throughout the war. As the reprinting of Rowlandson's and Williams's narratives had done in the earliest days of the war, the narratives of Allen, Dodge, and Freneau related stories of suffering and redemption that helped define and give meaning to the Patriot cause.

Stories of captivity and a "savage other" helped Americans make sense of the turmoil engulfing the Revolution from its earliest days. As Nathan Fiske's *Historical Discourse Concerning the Settlement of Brookfield* demonstrated, Americans could easily find a historical precedent for the type of threat they faced in the stories of their forebears' suffering at the hands of French and Indians adversaries. Delivered in 1775, Fiske's sermon, along with the captivity narratives of John Williams and Mary Rowlandson, provided historical guideposts for Americans as they navigated the end of their colonial existence. Building on these historical foundations, Americans quickly found parallels to Williams's and Rowlandson's stories of suffering in the brutal captivity of their countrymen in British prisons. These stories of captivity simultaneously highlighted American vulnerability in the face of British power and the virtue of the Patriot cause in the dark, menacing shadow of

British cruelty. Part of the success of this effort stemmed from the indiscriminate nature of captivity. Any American caught standing against the British could be imprisoned, and almost any American who had experienced British captivity found a willing audience for his story of cruelty, suffering, and survival. These tales of captivity, whether books, official testimony before Congress, or newspaper reports, all served to unite the American people and help articulate and define the cause for which they fought. Any American could be taken captive, so any American could join the debate about the nature of Independence. In the half-century that followed the Revolution, as Americans continued to process of their self-definition, stories of captivity and vulnerability played a critical role in shaping the nascent political culture.

CHAPTER 2

"The More We Are Treated Ill Abroad"

The Continental Congress, Public Opinion, and American Captives in Algiers, 1783–1787

IN MAY OF 1785, newspapers throughout the United States published a letter demanding tribute of "one hundred thousand pounds of their money, thirty thousand pounds of their most costly manufactures, and forty of their most beautiful and virtuous damsels, not under 12, nor above 18, descended from honest parents, free from mole, blemish, or latent imperfection." The letter was signed by "Al Koraschi Ebnallad, sovereign and supreme Dey of Algiers, Lord of the Algerine territories and the Atlantic Ocean." According to the dey, the Americans having withdrawn "from a subjugation to their masters," the English, were now obligated to provide for the protection of their own ships traveling along Mediterranean trade routes. If the Americans failed to deliver the requisite tribute, the dey threatened, he would "let loose [his] corsairs upon them." Despite the publicized threat, the U.S. government failed to reach terms with the North African nation and soon found itself at war. Within three months of the publication of the dey's letter, two American ships, the *Maria* and *Dauphin*, carrying a total of twenty-one crewmen, fell prey to Algerian corsairs. These captured Americans were carried to Algiers and sold into slavery until sufficient funds could be raised to purchase their freedom.[1]

Mere months after the end of the American Revolution, rather than celebrating their freedom from English tyranny, Americans had to contend with the capture of the *Maria* and *Dauphin* and acknowledge the harsh realities of Independence and the loss of the protection of the English Navy. While a focus on the captivity of American prisoners during the War for Independence had helped assure the American people of the righteousness of their political cause, the capture of the twenty-one American sailors and failure of the Continental Congress to win their release highlighted the tenuous nature of American liberty and the weak position of the new United States in the Atlantic world.

Despite this vulnerability and in some ways because of it, the experience of American sailors and news of their travails as reported to the American public played a key role in defining both nationality and nationalism in the early United States.² With the United States facing this insecurity in the Atlantic world, a growing number of Americans took an increasing interest in the Confederation government and American foreign policy. As a number of scholars have noted, the Algerian crisis was one of a number of foreign policy issues that raised questions about the security of the new nation.³ This need for security became "one of if not the primary reasons for constitutional reform in the 1780s, with the Constitution in many ways forming an international institution" that helped solve two diplomatic crises, "that amongst the units (states and regions) of the Confederation and that amongst the units of the Confederation with foreign powers."⁴ These parallel insecurities helped direct public opinion in favor of a stronger federal government, ultimately leading to the ratification of the U.S. Constitution.

If the suffering of American prisoners during the Revolution had stoked nationalism in the face of a British "other," the growing sense of American insecurity in the Atlantic world likewise fueled a nationalist demand for greater protection of Americans' hard-won liberty. In October 1785, anticipating the impact of these foreign threats to American liberty, American secretary of foreign affairs John Jay noted that the frequent abuse of U.S. citizens by foreign powers in the Atlantic compelled Americans to "unite and consolidate" at home for their defense overseas.⁵ This consolidation manifested itself, in part, as a growing number of conversations about how best to secure American liberty in a hostile environment. This chapter explores how the capture of the *Maria* and *Dauphin* highlighted American vulnerability in the Atlantic world and drew an expanding number of Americans into an increasingly democratic discussion about America's place in the world. Ultimately these conversations of an increasingly engaged citizenry increased pressure on the Confederation government to strengthen U.S. security and protect Americans abroad and facilitated the push toward constitutional reform.⁶

During the Revolution, daily confronting the realities of a military conflict with England, Americans generally agreed that a federal government was needed to deal with the challenges of national defense and foreign relations. On the whole, there was also agreement that a federal government, rather than the states, might better manage the western lands of the United States. Beyond these issues, however, the states could not agree on which powers they ought to grant a national government and which powers they ought to reserve for themselves. With this quandary in mind, the framers of the Articles of Confederation had intentionally limited Congress' power to secure quick ratification of the governing document so that this new government might negotiate and win foreign aid in the cause of Independence.⁷

Under the Articles of Confederation, many Americans understood the relationship between the states as a "firm league of friendship" that allowed each state to retain "its sovereignty, freedom, and independence" and as a collective effort to create a more perfect union among independent sovereignties. Given such an understanding of the relationship between the states, many people in the United States recognized that American Independence would not mark the beginning of a golden age of international relations. The creation of the Articles had itself been a recognition of the complex nature of the relationship between the individual states themselves and between the United States and the greater Atlantic world. These rivalries and conflicts at home and abroad defined and shaped the diplomatic agenda of the new nation. With the evolving nature of these relationships, the initial diplomatic challenges faced by the former British colonies were not seen, in and of themselves, as cause for alarm. The cooperation between the states during the Revolution in resisting British tyranny provided evidence that shared devotion to liberty and enlightened self-interest might ultimately provide a foundation for a "perpetual union" under the Articles of Confederation. Despite this initial optimism, the structure of the Confederation government severely limited Congress' ability to effectively lead the nation and jeopardized the future harmony of the states and the standing of the nation in the world.⁸

The failings of the Articles were driven home as a number of international issues emerged to threaten Americans' recently won liberty. On the western frontier, the ongoing British occupation of strategic forts encouraged various Native American groups to perpetuate or renew their resistance to American expansion. In 1784, Spanish officials in Louisiana limited American access to the Mississippi River. On the other side of the Atlantic, American merchant vessels soon found themselves vulnerable to capture by the North African states of Morocco and Algiers. All these problems reminded Americans of just how significant international relations were to the survival and longevity of the United States.[9]

While the British and Spanish threats to the frontier were significant in their own right, the capture of American sailors and their subsequent sale into slavery seemed the most direct challenge to American liberty. The plight of the North African captives highlighted the underdevelopment of the national economy, the lack of respect for the United States shown by European nations, and the inability of the American government to protect its citizens overseas. Just as the suffering of captive Americans had galvanized many citizens to support the cause of Independence during the Revolution, the threat of North African captivity led a growing number of Americans to take an active interest in international affairs. The capture of the *Maria* and *Dauphin* suggested that the young United States might not survive long as an independent nation and possibly slide back into a British orbit, if something was not done to protect American sailors in the Mediterranean. Increasingly, it seemed that if Americans were to realize the lofty promise of the Revolution, a greater number of citizens had to take an active role in national and international politics. Consequently, the Algerian capture of the *Maria* and *Dauphin* led a growing number of Americans, driven largely by fear that their newfound liberty was being undermined in the larger Atlantic world, to engage an expansive public debate over how best to deal with the Barbary threat.[10]

The North African states of Algiers, Tunis, Tripoli, and Morocco, which Europeans collectively referred to as the "Barbary States," first came into existence with the spread of Islam across the North African coast and into the Iberian Peninsula from the Arabian Peninsula in the seventh century.

Over the following eight centuries, these small states on the edges of the Mediterranean world employed a mix of trade and piracy (or privateering) to sustain their economies. Following religious dictate, Barbary privateers sailed against Christian nations that failed or refused to negotiate a treaty with the Barbary States. Once captured, Christians were sold into slavery in the Muslim nations. By the late fifteenth century, however, with the success of the Spanish expulsion of Islamic power from Iberia during the final stages of the *Reconquista*, the small Barbary States faced the wrath of the emergent and powerful Spanish Empire. Burdened with harsh economic regulations imposed by the Spanish, privateering came to dominate the economy of these states. By the middle of the sixteenth century, the Barbary States of North Africa fell under the control of the expanding Ottoman Empire.[11] Saddled with the tribute demands of the Turks, corsair raids on European coastal towns and the capture of European vessels in the Mediterranean quickly became the heart of the North African economy. For the Barbary States, seizing the ships of "infidels" was their best means of survival.[12]

Although commonly referred to as "pirates" by their enemies, the Barbary ships might more properly be referred to as "privateers" or "corsairs." While many of these ships were privately held, they operated with the sanction of the Barbary governments, a relationship lending their activity a measure of legitimacy that the term *pirate* denies them. The practice of privateering, a practice employed by the United States throughout the American Revolution, was recognized as legal by states throughout the world until 1856, when privateering was abolished under the Declaration of Paris. It was on this premise that the Barbary States, primarily Algeria and Morocco, sailed the Mediterranean in search of wealth. These states considered themselves free to attack any state with which no treaty existed or that they deemed to be in violation of an existing treaty. Following these practices, the Barbary corsairs, which, at their peak, numbered around 150 vessels, struck at European ships in the Mediterranean throughout the sixteenth through the eighteenth centuries. These raids supplied the Barbary States with both treasure and captives. The crews and state governments split the spoils of the raids, while captive crewmen were put on the auction block and sold into slavery throughout North Africa. Captives with few skills often ended up laboring in the quarries or shipyards. Seamen trained in a skilled trade were often taken to cities, where they worked at their craft. Those sailors who converted to Islam were able to return to sea as crewmen aboard the Barbary corsairs. Officers on the captured vessels were frequently placed on parole, reflecting similar European practices, provided they paid a monthly allowance for their limited freedom. Often times, a foreign consul would be required to provide a surety, and if an officer fled, the consul would be held financially responsible.[13]

Under this system, the city of Algiers grew into one of the most prominent cities in the Mediterranean, with a population nearing a hundred thousand, larger than Genoa, Marseilles, or Barcelona. The success of the Barbary corsairs was not unchecked, however. In the latter half of the seventeenth and into the eighteenth century, the British and Dutch fleets were sent to the Mediterranean to guard against the Barbary threat. Although both England and the Netherlands continued to pay tribute to the North African states, they did so out of convenience rather than an inability to destroy the Barbary corsairs. For the European powers, the threat of the Barbary States was best managed through a series of yearly tributes to maintain safe passage for their ships. Thus, by the time the United States achieved Independence, the power of the Barbary States was on the wane. Their declining status made them that much more dangerous to the United States. With neither the money nor the naval force to challenge the Barbary States, the United States found itself in a vulnerable position in the Mediterranean region.[14]

The first incident involving the United States and the nations of the Barbary Coast occurred when a Moroccan corsair seized the American ship *Betsey* in 1784. The Moroccan action, despite appearances, was not an act of war; rather it was an effort to facilitate diplomatic relations between the United States and Morocco. During the Revolution, the Moroccan sultan was among the first to recognize American Independence. Morocco had begun to receive American vessels in port two months before the French established diplomatic relations with the United States in 1777 and had granted American ships most-favored-nation status. Despite these diplomatic measures, the new American government had failed to negotiate a formal treaty with Morocco. By 1784, frustrated with a lack of American response, the sultan had ordered the seizure of an American ship. Once the sultan had secured Congress' attention, he informed lawmakers that neither the crew nor the cargo aboard the *Betsey* would be sold and that once a treaty had been negotiated, he would release the ship.[15]

The subsequent conflict with Algiers was not so easily resolved and consequently presented a much greater threat to the stability and development of the United States. When Algerian corsairs seized the *Maria* and *Dauphin* in the late summer of 1785, the vessels and their crew were taken as prisoners of war. The ships and their crews enjoyed none of the protection that the sultan of Morocco had offered the crewmen aboard the *Betsey*. Although the Moroccan crisis was resolved with relative ease, the crisis in Algiers was a formidable challenge for the United States. Most significant was that the capture of American sailors represented a direct threat to American liberty, especially in contrast to the security enjoyed by British sailors. Unlike the captive American seamen, any detained British sailors, who had been mistaken as Americans, quickly regained their freedom under the terms of the British treaty with the dey of Algiers. For American sailors in North Africa, the gains of the Revolution, rather than securing their liberty, left them vulnerable to capture and slavery. As one American sailor observed, they had become "victims of independence."[16]

The Continental Congress was quick to recognize the vulnerability of American vessels in the Mediterranean following the Revolution. As early as the spring of 1784, the American government commissioned Benjamin Franklin, Thomas Jefferson, and John Adams as "ministers plenipotentiary" to negotiate safe passage for American vessels in the Mediterranean. At the heart of the effort was simply regaining the protection that American vessels had enjoyed under the British Empire. Although the American ministers secured assistance from both France and the Netherlands, the protection of U.S. commerce in the Mediterranean was nowhere near the security that American ships and sailors had enjoyed before the Revolution. Eventually, the American ministers in Europe dispatched agents to establish diplomatic relations directly with Morocco and Algiers. Negotiations with Morocco proceeded smoothly and were the only early success in dealing with the Barbary States. The Moroccan treaty provided American vessels with a bit more security in the Atlantic and even opened the door for both Spanish and Moroccan assistance in negotiations with the other Barbary States. Despite this initial success, the ever-changing diplomacy of the Mediterranean world reversed some of the American gains when, in the summer of 1785, Portugal concluded with Algiers a new treaty that allowed Algerian vessels access to the Atlantic.[17]

The revived Algerian threat laid bare the fundamental weakness of the United States under the Articles of Confederation. As Thomas Jefferson observed in the earliest days of the crisis, the United States was left with three options: payment of an annual tribute; "compelling a peace by arms"; or "abandoning the Mediterranean carriage to other nations."[18] Jefferson argued that the best course of action was to refuse any demand for tribute. He contended that the United States ought to stand firm and, unlike the European powers, which paid tribute to secure safe passage in the Mediterranean, to establish security for Americans "by war." Such an action, Jefferson believed, "will procure us respect in Europe . . . and I think it the least expensive." Despite Jefferson's enthusiasm for such a solution, few Americans shared his desire for a military solution.[19]

In his response to Jefferson, Adams acknowledged that "great and weighty considerations" might support Jefferson's favored solution but doubted that "our States could be brought to agree in the measure." Adams reasoned, "We ought not fight them at all, unless we determine to fight them forever." Without widespread support, the United States was ill-prepared to engage in any such long-term conflict. Adams explained: "This thought is I fear, too rugged for our People to bear. To fight them at the Expence of Millions, and to make Peace after all by giving them more Money and larger Presents than would now procure perpetual Peace Seems not to be Economical." For Adams, two powerful reasons recommended negotiation over armed conflict. First, the American people, having recently suffered through the American Revolution, were in no condition to undertake another war. Second, the cost of a war would be far greater than anything the United States government could afford, even if it struggled to pay the cost of a negotiated tribute. Adams concluded that in the immediate future, "neither Force nor Money will be applied," for under the Articles of Confederation, "our States are so backward that they will do nothing for some years." He sensed that many Americans preferred the third option, "to give up all Ideas of Navigation and naval Power" and leave the United States "at the Mercy of Foreigners." Given such a disposition, Adams admitted to Jefferson, "Your Plan of fighting will no more be adopted than mine of negotiating."[20]

Although many Americans shared Adams's sense of despair, U.S. Secretary of Foreign Affairs John Jay saw a potential benefit in the Algiers crisis. Possibly recalling the unifying effect of the prisoner experience during the Revolution, he imagined the conflict with Algiers rallying Americans again. In a few years, Jay would use such external threats to great effect to argue in favor of the new Constitution during the ratification debates. To his understanding, the American experience of ill-treatment abroad profoundly impacted the American public as the young nation wrestled with its vulnerability in the Atlantic world. The Barbary and other attacks seemed nothing less than an existential threat to the United States.[21]

As the American diplomats lamented their limited options because of a weak central government, American sailors plying in the Mediterranean dealt with the reality of the Barbary threat. In the face of potential capture, American ships attempted to hide their ports of origin from would-be captors. In the summer of 1785, the *Connecticut Journal* reported that "several American trading vessels [have] lately eluded the rovers from Algiers, by hoisting English colours." Under the looming threat of attack by Barbary vessels, American sailors found that independence from England hindered their freedom on the seas rather than helped it. While American attempts to hide their identity under a false flag was successful at first, before long the Algerian ships began to stop any vessel bearing the Union Jack and demand to see proof of their port of registry. The threat of capture became a reality when Algerian xebecs seized the *Maria* and *Dauphin* off the coast of the Iberian Peninsula in the summer of 1785.[22]

By autumn of that year, a letter from a merchant in the Mediterranean, published throughout New England, announced, "A Brig from Boston to this place, laden with flour and lumber, has . . . been carried to Algiers." Before long, news of the capture spread as far as South Carolina, where the reports of Americans sailors in captivity were deemed "alarming." These early reports were soon confirmed by the prisoners themselves in letters describing the conditions they faced in their captivity at Algiers. The prisoners' letters made their way to the United States by way of Richard Harrison, the American consul at Cadiz, Spain. Harrison, following the requests of the captive sailors, passed their letters along to the Continental Congress and to numerous American newspapers. The first letter he forwarded to the United States included an introduction stating that the communication was "of so interesting a nature, that the printers are all requested to republish it." The document, signed by the captains of the captured ships, Richard O'Brien and Isaac Stephens, began by reminding all readers that the prisoners held in Algiers were "the subjects of the United States of America" and that they had been "left in a state of slavery and misery, the severities of which are beyond your imagination." The notion that Americans could be sold into slavery ran contrary to the principles of the Revolution. These American sailors had been deprived of the very privilege—their liberty—for which the Revolution had been fought. Furthermore, the captives were quick to point out, "If we do not make some terms, our trade is ruined." The American sailors in Algiers recognized that by linking their personal fate to that of American economy, their calls for redemption might have an even greater impact. In closing, O'Brien and Stephens noted that they hoped their story of suffering and the threat to the U.S. economy would serve "as warning to all Americans" about how vulnerable their liberties were in a hostile world.[23]

There was little question that the Mediterranean was vital to American trade and to visions of an American trade network. Thomas Jefferson estimated that prior to the Revolution the Mediterranean had been a market for "one sixth of their wheat and flour, and one fourth of their dried and pickled fish." Thomas Barclay, the U.S. consul general at Paris, wrote in 1786 that the Mediterranean trade was "absolutely essential to the commerce of our country."[24] The Mediterranean trade was especially critical given that American ships, following the Revolution, had been limited in their participation in the European trade networks, due largely to British efforts to curtail the trade of the United States. Although American consumers resumed the importation of British goods almost immediately after the conclusion of the American Revolution, the United States found itself excluded from the "interdependent multilateral trading system" that crisscrossed the Atlantic between North America, the West Indies, and Europe.[25] The New York Chamber of Commerce observed that "all Europe did indeed desire to see us independent; but now that we are become so, each separate power is desirous of rendering our interests subservient to their commercial policy."[26] Prior to the Revolution, much American trade was directed to supplying British interests in the West Indies with food stuffs. So with the British closure of this market and much of the rest of Europe to American goods, the Mediterranean market was one of the few readily accessible to American ships.[27]

Faced with the Algerian threat in the Mediterranean, John Jay recommended that Congress encourage "the American merchants who traffic in Spain, Portugal, the Mediterranean and to the Madeiras and Canaries, to employ none but Vessels well armed and manned."[28] Despite Jay's warning, Congress was unable to offer much in the way of protection, having disbanded what passed for an American navy during the Revolution. With the Barbary threat to American ships, crews were hard to come by and insurance rates for American ships sailing in the Atlantic more than doubled.[29] Rufus King, a member of the Continental Congress, noted that "it is difficult to persuade our seamen to navigate unarmed vessels on those seas where Barbary corsairs cruise," the consequence of which was that American merchants had turned away from American vessels and had begun to "charter foreign vessels which are protected from the Barbary cruisers to carry our produce to market."[30] As news of the crisis spread, the realities of the postrevolutionary economy were driven home. Even as the deficiencies of the domestic economic policies of the state legislatures was becoming increasingly clear, the loss of another market to American goods would only deepen the economic recession faced by the new nation.[31]

Despite the direct impact of the crisis in Algiers on the American economy, members of Congress found themselves unable to act. The federal government's inability to levy taxes and the weak American economy left Congress without much recourse to address the crisis. Any attempt to negotiate for the release of the hostages might have encouraged further seizures of American vessels and driven up ransom demands, thus making American ships all the more vulnerable. With a seemingly unresponsive government, the American captives began to rely on foreign powers for assistance. The American prisoners' requests for foreign aid validated the low opinion of the United States many Europeans held.

Charles Logie, the English consul at Algiers, was the first European official to whom many of the American captives turned. Logie, whose father had been the Swedish consul in Algiers a half-century before, began his career in the British navy before being named British consul general in Tangiers, Morocco, from 1772 to 1782. Logie was appointed British consul to Algiers in 1785. His experience in and family connection to the region seemed to make him the perfect candidate to serve in the Barbary States. Most significantly, Logie was one of the few European representatives who could speak to Barbary leaders without an interpreter. His understanding of the region and fluency in the language enabled Logie to secure parole for the officers of the captive American ships, and with Logie's assistance, Captain Richard O'Brien of the *Dauphin*, Captain Isaac Stephens of the *Maria*, and Captain Zachariah Coffin, who had been a passenger aboard the *Dauphin*, sent their first letters back to the United States. The three paroled captives encouraged others working to secure their freedom to "write to the British Consul on the subject"; they were certain that Logie "will give you every information respecting us, and how matters may be accommodated with America." Just as American ships had sought protection from the Barbary corsairs under the British flag, so too were the captive Americans forced to look to the British Empire for assistance.[32]

The punishing conditions of the Algerian prisons compelled some captive Americans to deny their U.S. citizenship. Eleven of those aboard the *Dauphin* and *Maria* claimed British citizenship and, working closely with Logie, petitioned King George III of England to intervene on their behalf. These eleven crewmen claimed to be "his Majestys subjects Taken under American colours and at present miserable slaves at Algiers." They had been "captured in the Month of July 1785 On Board the ship Dauphin of Philadelphia . . . and Schooner Maria of Boston."[33] All eleven crewmen claimed to have been "obliged" to serve under American colors by circumstances beyond their control. Despite their claims and Logie's assistance, the British government failed to secure their release.[34]

Whatever the veracity of the claims of these eleven sailors, they had good reason to attempt establishing their British citizenship. The Americans' task of feeling their way through diplomatic relations with the North African states stood in stark contrast to the skill of the European governments, such as the British and French, that had been redeeming captives for generations. In the spring of 1786, a group of English citizens captured while traveling on a Portuguese ship and initially "obliged to work very hard for the first two months of their captivity" yet apparently possessing better proof of citizenship than those men aboard the *Maria* and *Dauphin*, were eventually released "on making it known that they were subjects of England."[35] Other European captives found relief in the form of the Mathurins. This religious order, formally known as the Order of the Holy Trinity and Redemption of Captives, had been formed in the twelfth-century to ease the plight and negotiate the redemption of Christian captives sold into slavery in North Africa. American newspapers reported on these efforts, noting that in 1785, "313 French captives" had been "redeemed this year from Algiers, by the Mathurins and the Fathers de la Mercy." The successful redemption of these French captives stood in stark contrast to the efforts of the American government.[36]

The failure of the American government to redeem the captives was not for a lack of trying. Even before the capture of the *Maria* and *Dauphin*,

Jefferson and Adams had been authorized by Congress to establish peace with the North African states and appointed John Lamb of Connecticut as the American agent to Algiers. Lamb's appointment had been based on the recommendation of Samuel Huntington, the lieutenant governor of Connecticut. Huntington noted that "Lamb is a Gentleman of Fidelity and Mercantile knowledge" and that he was "well acquainted" with the Barbary Coast, "having made several voyages to those parts before the late war."[37] Although his appointment predated the dey's seizing of the American vessels, Lamb did not arrive in Algiers until March 1786, more than seven months after the incident. In light of the new circumstances, Jefferson and Adams instructed Lamb to attempt redeeming the prisoners if it could be done for less than two hundred dollars per man. Jefferson seemed keenly aware of the importance of securing the freedom of the sailors to the stability of the young United States, noting in his instructions to Lamb, "The motives which lead to [these efforts] must be found in the Feelings of the human Heart ... for these Sufferers who are of our own Country, and the obligations of every Government to yield Protection to their citizens, as the Consideration for their Obedience."[38]

Even as Jefferson attempted to convey the importance of these negotiations to Lamb, he and Adams reported back to Congress that their communications with the Algerian ambassador in Paris suggested that Lamb faced an uphill battle in dealing with the dey:

> We took the liberty to make some inquiries concerning the grounds of their pretensions to make war upon nations who had done them no injury. ... The Ambassador answered us that it was founded on the laws of their Prophet, that it was written in their Koran, that all nations who should not have acknowledged their authority were sinners, that it was their right and duty to make war upon them wherever they could be found, and to make slaves of all they could take as prisoners and the every Musselman who should be slain in battle was sure to go to Paradise.[39]

The Algerian ambassador went on to inform the American commissioners that the first member of the corsair crew to board the captive vessel was rewarded with an extra slave and that as the Algerian vessels approached their intended victim "it was the practice ... for each sailor to take a dagger in each hand and another in his mouth and leap upon board which terrorized their enemies that very few ever stood against them." Following this conversation, Adams and Jefferson were convinced that the cost of redeeming the American captives would be far greater than they had initially anticipated.

The two commissioners expected that the demand might be so steep that there was "but one possible way that we know of to procure the money, if Congress should authorize [them] to go to the necessary expense and . . . borrow it in Holland."[40]

Traveling from Barcelona, Spain, Lamb arrived in Algiers on an American-owned ship flying a Spanish flag in March of 1786. It was not long before Adams's and Jefferson's fears were realized. The dey, having been presented with Lamb's offer, "would not speak of peace." Faced with this resistance, Lamb, like the American prisoners, turned to the European consuls in Algiers for assistance, reporting a great deal of support from his European colleagues. Both the French and Spanish consuls readily offered help, but it was Logie who received him "as an old friend." Richard O'Brien reported that Lamb lodged with Logie during part of his time in Algiers. Despite this assistance, Lamb knew that the release of the American captives could only be secured with a substantially larger sum of money. Having met the with the dey on several occasions, Lamb left Algiers in May of 1786 ostensibly to secure the necessary funds to purchase the freedom of the American sailors and establish peace between the United States and Algiers.[41]

News arriving from the Mediterranean in the summer of 1786 led many in the American public to question the future of their republican experiment. Even before word of the capture of the *Maria* and *Dauphin* reached the United States, there had been reports that American sailors had been flying the Union Jack to hide their identity and avoid capture. Following the seizure of the American vessels, news of the American seamen's reliance on the British consul at Algiers underscored an almost neocolonial existence for the United States in the Atlantic world. This sense of vulnerability was only strengthened as news of Lamb's efforts in North Africa first appeared in the American press that summer. Newspapers throughout the United States reported that he had gained audience with the dey "but to no purpose; more money must be had than is yet allowed by Congress to effectuate peace and you may depend that the Algerines will cruise against us."[42] Such news must have frustrated those following the events, for despite the efforts of Congress and the American commissioners, American sailors were still held in Algiers and the seas remained unsafe for American travel and trade. Amplifying these feelings of frustration were reports from the captive Americans, who declared Lamb to be a less than-satisfactory negotiator. Richard O'Brien noted that if the job had been left "in the hands of a qualified statesman" rather than in Lamb's control, the situation would have been much more quickly and easily resolved.[43]

Publication of the prisoners' critique of the American negotiator sparked the first widespread public debate about how best to resolve the crisis in North Africa. While initial coverage of the condition of the captives in Algiers had drawn widespread sympathy, the criticism of Lamb precipitated the first public defense of the government's response to the North African crisis. Appearing in the *Massachusetts Gazette*, "Centinel" defended Lamb. Centinel began his response by questioning the authenticity of the letter that had "appeared (under the Philadelphia head) in some of the papers, said to have been written by a sea Captain, a prisoner at Algiers." Rather than simply accepting the charges of incompetence against Lamb, Centinel remarked that "a correspondent, who is perfectly well acquainted with that gentleman's character, wishes the publick opinion may be suspended, until something of more validity than the charge of an anonymous letter-writer is exhibited against him." Centinel's defense and his effort to sway "the publick opinion" suggests growing interest in and awareness of the topic. By the summer of 1786, the crisis in Algiers had grown beyond a closed debate within the corridors of the American government into an open discussion in the "publick."[44]

The debate that emerged surrounding Lamb's efforts was a stand-in for a larger concern about the effectiveness of the American government. Despite John Adams's belief that the American people preferred to "lay themselves ... at the Mercy of Foreigners" in dealing with the Barbary States, the growing public debate over the American captives in Algiers suggested just the opposite. A growing segment of the American people were becoming party to an expanding debate about the obligations of the federal government. The perception of Lamb's failure, as Centinel had observed, played an important role in shaping "publick opinion." The crisis in Algiers and the widespread news coverage served as a national focal point for concerns among Americans about their own security in the years following the Revolution.[45]

Lamb's failures also underscored the increasing worry of many Americans concerning the role of the British consul in the region. Logie's efforts on behalf of the American captives received special notice both in England and in the United States. An article that initially appeared in the British press and was eventually republished in the United States reported that Logie had "clothed several of the American captives, who were almost naked; and, in behalf of the colonies at large, has used all his interest, though in vain, with the councils of Algiers, respecting the demands for the ransom of American slaves." Having highlighted the benevolence of the British official and the inability of the United States to take care of its own citizens, the article continued: "A dispute betwixt Great Britain and America . . . cannot be considered as a matter of great consequence to this country. The friends of Americans here may bluster as they please, and talk of *retaliation* on our shipping, but the Americans themselves well know, that they are not strong enough to retaliate on any nation on earth that possesses a naval power." That assessment of American weakness was not only an indictment of the U.S. inability to inflict damage on any British interest but also to stand up to the "naval power" of Algiers, a "power" that the English navy could destroy with minimal effort.[46]

Americans responded to the news that the British consul had played a large role in assisting the captives with unease, and the report highlighted concerns about the weakness of the government of the United States. Aside from the attack on American honor that had accompanied the British report, New York merchant David Provoost questioned the intentions and character of the British consul. Provoost recounted his own travails while trading in North Africa. One morning, while on business in Tangiers in 1775, he and his two companions were seized by a "troop of Moors" and accused of trespassing. After their capture, the American merchant "soon found that we were indebted for this inhuman treatment to Charles Logie, esquire, who at that time resided there, as consul to his Britannic majesty. This man, from a whimsical antipathy he had imbibed in the early stages of the war, against the Americans, determining to vent his spleen whenever an opportunity offered," had gone to great lengths to prove that Provoost and his companions had violated the law of the land. "Thus I was, by Logie's tyrannical procedure, without being guilty of even a shadow of an offense," Provoost wrote, "not only conducted a prisoner through Barbary, ill-treated by Negro soldiers, and had money extorted from me to pay them, but subjected to many consequent embarrassments and inconveniences from my detainment."[47] Given his past experience with Logie, Provoost suspected that Englishman's initial kindness to the Americans may have been motivated by more sinister designs. Furthermore, Provoost contended that the United States would "never have been troubled by the Algerines had not the British set them on with the ungenerous view of distressing America to satiate her malice. . . . For accomplishing this diabolical purpose they could not have used a better engine or more willing agent than Mr. Logie, who would rejoice to see all the sons of freedom on this continent chained to gallies and our fairest maidens locked up in Algerine seraglios."[48] Provoost's description of the British consul suggested all the more reason for the United States to redeem its captives as quickly as possible. Leaving the prisoners at the mercy of foreign consuls further weakened the U.S. position abroad, leaving American citizens subject to the diplomatic intrigues of foreign powers. The captives themselves confirmed Provoost's characterization of the British consul: "Consul Logie, treated us with indifference, which, I assure you, is much to his discredit; and I was happy when relieved from a dependence so humiliating to Americans."[49]

Provoost's analysis led him to a conclusion that stood in stark contrast to Centinel's defense of Lamb. Rather than calling for a suspension of public opinion until all of the facts were known, Provoost called on the American people to act. He argued that they and their government shared some of the blame for their present situation: "We who are not in fetters but breathing the sweet air of freedom, do we seem to be touched with the relation of the calamities incident to the dismal situation of these unfortunate captives—our fellow creatures, our countrymen? No!" Such delay, Provoost believed, was the result of the "mistaken idea" that the captives were "civilly treated." Yet "humanity exclaims that something ought to be done for these unhappy men. . . . If the Congress or the legislatures of the several states do not take up this matter seriously, *individuals ought and surely will*." While Provoost reserved much of his scorn for British actions, he also voiced concerns that his fellow citizens and the government had failed to act in their best interest. Provoost expressed certainty that once the full nature of the suffering endured by the American captives was understood, the American people would not stand idly by.[50]

Provoost's criticism of Congress and state legislatures embodied a growing sense that Americans had to act to release their fellow countrymen detained in Algiers. This call to action was, in many ways, a validation of Jay's expectation that Americans would come together in the face of a foreign threat. The merchant's attack on Logie, who represented a return to dependence on England, was intended to arouse the American people. If the American government could not secure the release of the American captives and end the backsliding toward dependence on England for protection and diplomacy, the American people should to take matters into their own hands.

Provoost's summons came at a time of growing agitation and frustration among the American people. The inability of the new American government to redeem the captives in Algiers and secure safe passage for American vessels in the Mediterranean resulted in a widespread unease about the safety of all American citizens at home and abroad. Writing from New York, Louis Guillaume Otto, comte de Mosloy, the French *chargé d'affaires* in the United States, observed that "the hostilities of the Barbarian corsairs have made a great sensation in America."[51] Throughout the country, Americans began to worry about the fate that might befall family members traveling abroad. George Mason feared that Algerian corsairs might capture his son John if he were to travel to the Mediterranean, Hyram Faris of Annapolis worried for his brother's safety en route to Amsterdam, and even Thomas Jefferson advised his daughter Polly to delay her trip to Paris for fear of her capture.[52]

Most notably, rumors circulated throughout the colonies that the celebrated American diplomat Benjamin Franklin had been taken captive by Algerian corsairs as he returned to the United States from Europe. The atmosphere of heightened tension brought on by the Barbary danger was elevated even more by the press. One journalist sarcastically noted: "The editors of news-papers find, that nothing contributes more to the sale of their merchandize in this city than paragraphs respecting Dr. Franklin; at one time they put him to death by fever . . . on his passage; at another they send him a captive to Algiers. . . . Such anecdotes answer their purpose as well as if they were true." Despite such rumors, the article went on to reveal "that our respectable and valuable friend is safe arrived at Philadelphia."[53] The unease at home and the news of Americans in captivity sold newspapers throughout the states. The sense of insecurity kept the American people focused on national and international events and increasingly made clear the need for broader public efforts on behalf of their captive countrymen.

By the summer of 1786, the tenth anniversary of American Independence, reports on the Algerian threat ran alongside coverage of celebrations. American papers reported that "the Algerines are very formidable at sea" and that "six stout frigates have already sailed from port. . . . The largest of the above frigates mounts 44 guns, and they are exceeding fine vessels, built upon European principle, and are manned with numerous crews of resolute fellows, who are daring, and fight desperately." These reports also predicted that "unless the United States can find means to make peace with the Dey, whose imperious demands are very exorbitant, their trade up the Mediterranean and other parts of Europe will be annihilated."⁵⁴ A decade after declaring their independence, citizens of the United States were far from secure about their place in the world. The crisis in Algiers left many Americans questioning the power of their government to protect their liberties.

That same summer, "Benevolus" echoed Provoost's call for the American people to act. Writing from Philadelphia, Benevolus argued that because the federal agent sent to Algiers had failed to achieve peace, "it is high time that the inhabitants of the country should immediately proceed to redeem those unfortunate men who have fallen into the hands of those barbarians." The need for the people to act was made only more apparent by the fact that "the French, the Spanish, and other nations by charitable contributions every year ransom numbers of their countrymen who became captives to the piratical states." Given these successes, could "America, that boasts a greater degree of liberty and purer religion fall short in humanity and compassion for fellow citizens now groaning in slavery?—Slavery the more insupportable as their former condition was free." Benevolus challenged those "opulent" Americans who had benefited from their liberty to take up a collection and promote a subscription to redeem the American captives whom the government had been unable to liberate. His letter was followed with a postscript from the publisher calling on every "son of liberty who is blessed with a feeling heart" to give his full attention to the collection of relief for the captives in the face of Congressional failures and impotence.⁵⁵

In April 1787, Hannah Stephens, the wife of captive sailor Isaac Stephens, petitioned Congress to redouble their efforts to secure the release of the American sailors not only for the sailors who faced the "horrors of Algerian slavery" but also for the families they left behind. Hannah herself had been "left with little . . . to support her and their small helpless children." Without the aid of her husband, they had "long since been reduced to the necessity of seeking Alms or perishing." Following the receipt Stephens's letter, Congress instructed Jefferson to continue diplomatic efforts to achieve peace.⁵⁶

Frustrated with direct diplomacy, Jefferson looked for assistance from the Mathurins, the French religious order, which had been so successful in securing the release of hundreds of Frenchmen over the years. With Congressional approval, Jefferson secretly funded the religious order, hoping that its long-standing relationship with the dey of Algiers might enable it to negotiate the release of the American captives.⁵⁷ Despite these efforts, the dey was slow to negotiate, and the violence of the French Revolution brought a quick end to the Mathurins's efforts to negotiate a settlement shortly after Jefferson had secured their assistance.[58] With the failure of the Mathurin gambit, Congress became increasingly frustrated with negotiation efforts. By 1787, members of Congress calculated that the cost of redeeming the captives would exceed fifty thousand dollars.[59] That fall, Congress went so far as to consider an impost on seamen's wages to raise funds for prisoner relief. In the course of the debate, however, a number of representatives pointed out that such a policy was impossible to apply, for such taxation was beyond the power of Congress under the Articles of Confederation.[60]

Even as the discussion of captive redemption occupied Congress, tensions in the western United States still demanded their attention. In late July of 1787, a letter from the governor of Virginia informed Congress that "in the course of last summer the inhabitants of Kentucky were compelled for their own preservation to commence expeditions against the Indians on both sides of the Ohio" and that the state of Virginia had covered all the expenditures of the expeditions.[61] As Virginia sought assistance to supply and reinforce western settlers, Congress debated the federal government's role in overseeing relations between the state of Georgia and the Creek and Cherokee nations.[62] The threat to American security on the nation's western boundary required as much attention and, on occasion, as much financial support as did the threats in the Atlantic world. Lacking adequate funding (despite loans from various European nations and the state treasuries of Virginia and New York), Congress found itself unable to protect American citizens both on its Atlantic and western frontiers. The Congressional impotence under the Articles of Confederation left the body unable to redeem the American captives in Algiers.

Throughout the spring and summer of 1787, calls for the American public to take action crescendoed. Among these challenges was one issued by the pseudonymous "Humanitas." The writer asked how it was that Americans who enjoyed the fruits of liberty could neglect their fellow countrymen languishing in Algiers. Because of this neglect "those who had once lived in affluence, and under a government of liberty and independence, are now at the will of a merciless tyrant, dragging out a miserable existence in the worst of slavery." Furthermore, Humanitas noted, the unfortunate captives could not rely on Congress or the state government for their freedom:

> It is not at present in the power of Congress to raise a sum sufficient to effect the purpose. Other concerns (though perhaps not of greater magnitude) must be provided for; foreign debts are to be paid, the expences of the late war, the

inability of Congress to discharge their engagements, and a thousand other circumstances, render it impracticable, nay impossible for them to effect so desirable an end. To what source then are the unhappy sufferers to look for their liberty? Congress have it not in their power, the Legislatures of the several states are unable.

According to Humanitas, the American people themselves bore the responsibility to redeem their fellow countrymen trapped in slavery: "If every one in these states were to pay but six pence each, enough would be raised to ransom twelve or fourteen freeborn Americans, from the savage oppression of a barbarous tyrant." If such an effort were to be undertaken, Humanitas had no doubt that "the females . . . would contribute largely, and set an example of genuine liberality" in order to aid "those brave men who have fought for the liberty which is now enjoyed." Humanitas argued that once such an effort was begun, the spirit of the American people would remedy the inadequacies of their government.[63]

By June of 1787, the newspapers of Philadelphia ran advertisements for the very type of action that both Benevolus and Humanitas had called for. The advertisement promised an evening of entertainment for the "Relief of our Fellow-Citizens enslaved at Algiers." The evening, held at the "request of many respectable Citizens," was to consist of "a poetical address, composed for the occasion," followed by a concert both "vocal and instrumental," and "the whole will conclude with an elegant vaud-ville."[64] The "poetical address," later appearing in papers as far-flung as South Carolina's *Columbian Herald*, called on Americans to note well that the captivity of the American sailors was "the shame of nations and the source of tears." The source of this suffering was "the Barbarous triumph of Algiers . . . and friends to freedom, languishing in chains." These Americans trapped in slavery were the very people "whose patriot toil gave independence to their native soil. Lost in the vicissitudes of fate, call on the country to repay the debt."[65] Faced with a government that could not redeem its captive sailors, private citizens, through the medium of the theater, had begun to take action by the summer of 1787.

The inability of the young American government to redeem the crews of the *Maria* and the *Dauphin* represented a failure to live up to what Thomas Jefferson had labeled a part of the "the obligations of every Government."[66] As the

American captives suffered in Algerian slavery, unease about the future of the nation led many U.S. citizens to question the slow and uncertain diplomacy of the federal government. In response to its failures, a growing number of citizens joined a national discussion about how best to resolve the Algerian crisis, eventually moving to take matters into their own hands. Yet, as frustration grew over the government's failure to redeem the captives in Algiers, news of Shays' Rebellion in Western Massachusetts and of the Constitutional Convention began to draw national attention away from the sailors held in North Africa. News of the Constitutional Convention, described as an "illustrious body of patriots and heroes," offered hope to some Americans that a restructured government might be better suited to the task of establishing a secure place for the United States in the larger Atlantic world and obtaining the freedom of their fellow countrymen. From New York, "Harrington" conveyed the feelings of many citizens when he noted that an effort at government reform headed by "the immortal Washington" created the possibility that "America may yet enjoy peace, safety, liberty and glory." Such a change was welcome, he noted, for "under the present weak, imperfect, and distracted Government of Congress, anarchy, poverty, infamy, and SLAVERY await the United States."[67] While the constitutional gathering of "patriots and heroes" offered hope of a more secure future for the young nation, it did not mean an end to popular engagement in American politics. The debate between Provoost and Centinel over how active the American people ought to be in efforts to redeem captive Americans abroad was simply the beginning of a larger debate about the role of the public in foreign affairs. In the decades that followed the ratification of the Constitution concerns about the place of the United States in the larger world (and the fate of captive Americans) would serve to draw a growing number of citizens into an increasingly vitriolic public sphere.

CHAPTER 3

"A Speedy Release to Our Suffering Captive Brethren in Algiers"

The Washington Administration and the Challenge of Public Opinion

IN A LETTER addressed to George Washington in September 1788, the captain of the American ship *Dauphin*, Richard O'Brien, requested that the president-to-be "lay before the Congress of the United States [their] truly Lamentable situation of Slavery." O'Brien informed Washington that he and his crew had suffered an "uninterrupted scene of griefe and misery . . . surrounded with the pests and contagious distempers" for past three years and now requested that the newly reformed government of the United States make all possible efforts to secure their release. O'Brien and the captive sailors at Algiers recognized that the national government under the Articles of Confederation had lacked the funds to make arrangements for their release, "but now . . . that it hath pleased God that the new Constitution of a future government is formed and Ratified by the United States [the] humble petitioners hoped that [their] situation will be taken into Consideration so that ways and means will be adopted for [their] Restoration from slavery."[1]

O'Brien's letter was followed shortly by another from Mathew Irwin, the owner of the *Dauphin*. Drawing on the efforts undertaken to aid the captives in the 1780s, Irwin wrote Washington to request that he ask the American people to take up a collection to help pay for the prisoners' release. In response to Irwin's proposal, Washington explained that while the American minister in the court of France, Thomas Jefferson, "has in view, among other objects, the redemption of these unfortunate men ... I am not satisfied that it would be proper, as you suggest, for me to begin or bring forward a subscription among the merchants and others in the maritime towns of this country, to raise a fund for delivering these unhappy men from their state of bondage." Despite the clear public interest in their captive countrymen, Washington believed that this complex diplomatic issue was best left to government officials, rather than the intervention of the American people.[2]

Initially, Washington's efforts to limit public involvement in the redemption of the American captives were widely supported by the members of his administration and of Congress. Yet the emergence of a bitter partisan divide and of a growing participatory nationalism during Washington's first term greatly complicated these efforts. In 1793, when Algerian corsairs seized nine more American vessels and their crews, the issue of North African captivity became a critical component of the nascent partisan divide and stoked popular interest in international affairs. Responding as they had to the failure of the Confederation government to redeem the captives in Algiers, many people in the American public again demanded greater action, even suggesting that private efforts to redeem the captives be undertaken if the new government could not free them. Supporters of the Washington administration sustained their opposition to any private campaigns, arguing that these efforts were an outgrowth of the "self-created societies" which were a threat to the stability of the young republic. By way of contrast, the emerging Republican opposition deliberately embraced the active participation of the American people in the redemption of the Algerian captives. In fairly short order, the debate over Algiers became one of the center pieces of a larger debate about the contours of the American political system. The opposition Republicans were the first to recognize the political utility of harnessing national insecurity to advance their policies, but the Washington administration would also come to embrace the engaged, but insecure citizenry.[3]

In the earliest days of the conflict with Algiers, Washington's reluctance to engage the public in efforts to redeem the captives was shared by a wide range of American officials, including Secretary of State Thomas Jefferson. Although Jefferson had initially hoped that a military solution to the crisis might be possible, he was quick to recognize that such a response was not immediately feasible for the young nation. Moving toward support of a negotiated settlement, he suggested that a feigned indifference and secret diplomatic efforts might be the best course of action Early attempts at negotiation experienced several setbacks with the unexpected deaths of the first two ministers, John Paul Jones and Thomas Barclay, but eventually seemed to make headway as Jefferson began secret discussions with the Mathurin order, only to be derailed by the outbreak of the French Revolution.[4]

The effort to keep the public from becoming involved in negotiations with Algiers was part of a larger belief held by George Washington and many in his administration, especially those who would go on to become members of the Federalist Party, that public sentiment ought not play a role in politics outside elections. Washington himself went to great lengths to demonstrate that the role of the president was to lead the nation in both a political and cultural sense. On the issue of politics and public opinion, Washington "often declared that government must act in accord with the interest of the people, but this view did not mean immediate response to popular will." Culturally, Washington utilized a great deal of pomp and etiquette, even aloofness, to create and cultivate respect for the office of president among the people.[5] Washington's efforts to define the role of the president as above the whims of public sentiment proved to be one of the foundations for the rise of factions in American politics during the 1790s.

Washington's election to the presidency had provided the hope that American politics might rise above faction, but acrimonious debates over Secretary of the Treasury Alexander Hamilton's fiscal policy and the French Revolution soon shattered any such notions. Before long Washington himself became "a strong partisan of the views of the Hamiltonian Federalists."[6] The result was something of a disconnect between the Washington administration and the people at large, for even as he sought to minimize the role of public sentiment in government, the American people continued to actively debate national issues. In August of 1792, the French minister plenipotentiary Jean Baptiste de Ternant noted that "the newspapers are filled daily with articles either defending or bitterly attacking the new federal government, as well as the actions of its principal agents, and each party seeks thus to win the approaching elections." The Italian-born friend of Thomas Jefferson, Philip Mazzei, remarked that the American people "seek to inform themselves upon public affairs because they find it to their interest. The progress made by the American people, since the beginning of the Revolution till now, in the matter of reasoning upon this sort of affairs is really astonishing."[7]

One of the clearest manifestations of the active popular interest in American politics in this period was the emergence of the Democratic-Republican societies, the very groups that the Washington administration had denounced as dangerous self-created organizations. Sparked in large part by the perceived promise of the French Revolution, these societies opposed many Washington administration policies. Found from Vermont to South Carolina, these groups were made up of a wide cross-section of the American population ranging from farmers and sailors to doctors and lawyers. They questioned federal policies, and encouraged the American public to keep abreast of current issues and monitor government activities. Domestically, the heart of the societies' distaste for the Washington administration was the fiscal policy of Secretary Hamilton and the elitism of the some members of the federal government. On the international level, the Democratic-Republican societies were horrified at Washington's unwillingness to support the French against the English and Dutch. Such actions, the society members charged, not only left an American ally in the lurch but were taken against the will of the people.[8]

As the members of the Washington administration had foreseen, Democratic-Republican societies and their Republican allies in Congress recognized the power of the popular movement supporting the Americans in Algiers and were quick to embrace it. This campaign to end the crisis in Algiers, while utterly contrary to the Federalist model of American government, represented the heart of Republican philosophy. According to Madison, a republic, "in order to effect its purposes, must operate not within a small but an extensive sphere."[9] When operating in this "extensive sphere," the people of the republic were better able to develop a common vision and, through this "public opinion," to "set bounds to every Government," this practice being "the real sovereign in every free one." A broad-based effort to redeem American captives in Algiers may not have been exactly what Madison had envisaged, stretching the bounds of his "extensive sphere" to the shores of North Africa, but this crisis eventually pervaded much of public debate in America.[10]

The capture of nine more American vessels in 1793 served to undermine the Washington administration's argument that the federal government could redeem the captives in Algiers on its own and breathed new life into the public efforts on behalf of the sailors. The publication of the names of the ships and their crews in newspapers around the nation created a new sense of urgency to redeem the captive Americans. Joining the *Dauphin* and *Maria* were the *Polly, President, Minerva, Jay, George, Olive Branch, Hope, Jane,* and the *Minerva*. In addition to listing the captive ships, the papers warned, "There are Cruisers at sea, and more fitting out in quest of Americans."[11] After eight years of negotiations, with four of those years under the new American government, efforts to make peace with Algiers had not only failed to recover the American sailors from captivity but had allowed the capture of nine more ships. Once again, American sailors found themselves sold into slavery and scattered about Algiers.[12]

From captivity, Richard O'Brien played on this renewed attention to American sailors detained and enslaved at Algiers, addressing the American people directly in a letter published in newspapers and magazines throughout the United States. O'Brien noted that he had "repeatedly for these five years past forewarned the United States of the impending danger" of failing to come to terms with Algiers. "Americans in general," he noted, "put little confidence in the assertions of a poor victim captive; but now find that they contained the truth." Now, according to O'Brien, the dey would not even receive the American ambassador "either to make peace or redeem the American slaves; that he had been soliciting the Americans to come and make peace with his regency for three years past and they had treated his propositions with neglect and indifference." Consequently, the dey had "captured ten [eleven] sail of Americans, and like to take many more." O'Brien's frustration was clear from the tone of his letter and the capture of the additional American ships convinced many Americans that his exasperation was justified. Although the creation of a new government in 1789 had offered some hope that the fate of the American captives at Algiers could be left to the government to negotiate, by 1794 many Americans had again come to question the ability of their government to resolve the crisis on its own.[13]

This growing agitation resulted in a clear partisan divide over how best to respond to the renewed Algerian threat. Echoing President Washington's desire to resolve the issue without interference from the broader American public, many in the Federalist majority sought to limit the public's access to information—for instance, closing Congressional galleries to the public in all sessions that took up the "Algerine business." In contrast to Federalist hopes for secrecy, Republican members of Congress repeatedly forced a vote on the issue of the closed galleries and often included news of Algiers in the circular letters that they sent to their constituents. The Congressional debates and the circular letters were emblematic of the differences between Republican and Federalist visions of the importance of public access to information. While Federalists were loathe to share any intelligence on the issue of foreign affairs and believed that such matters were the purview of the government rather than the general public, the Republicans moved in the opposite direction. The commitment to openness on the part of many Republicans was highlighted in the body of their open letters to constituents, which commonly related news of foreign affairs in the years before the War of 1812.[14]

The president and Congress soon found a citizenry that was ready to act in support of the captive Americans with or without the assistance of their government. A wave of letters and petitions calling for more vigorous federal action began to inundate the national capital. More than one hundred ship captains and owners called on Congress to enact an embargo "until such time as we can pursue our business with safety."[15] Wives of the sailors themselves called on Congress to act, "praying that measures may be taken for procuring the ransom, or relief from slavery of their husbands and other citizens of the United States who are now in captivity at Algiers."[16] Three weeks later, the "citizens of the towns of Norfolk and Portsmouth . . . in the state of Virginia" called on Congress to "adopt such measures as, in their wisdom, may be deemed most expedient and effectual to obtain redress for the vexations and spoliations committed on the commerce of the United States . . . by the citizens and subjects of other foreign countries."[17] At a meeting in Augusta, Georgia, concerned citizens called for the creation of a committee to coordinate a financial program for the relief of Americans in Algiers. This resolution was forwarded to Congress and published in newspapers throughout the nation. In Savannah, crowds of people flocked to the courthouse and called on the members of the House and Senate to adopt "such measures as Congress may think proper . . . in order to obtain redress for the many insults and injuries committed on the American flag and commerce."[18] From the American frontier came "a memorial of the Representatives of the People in the United States, South of the River Ohio," which "was presented to the House and read, praying that such measures may be adopted as deemed most expedient and effectual . . . for the releasement from slavery of such of the citizens of the United States, as are now in captivity at Algiers."[19]

From New England, a concerned citizen, who identified himself as

"Benevolence," wrote to Secretary of State Edmund Randolph calling for a general collection to be taken up on behalf of the captive Americans. Echoing Matthew Irwin who wrote a half-decade earlier, Benevolence noted that he was writing "upon the principle of compassion" and called on President Washington to issue a proclamation urging the American people to take up a collection on behalf of the American sailors in captivity. Such a proclamation, Benevolence argued, would "touch the feelings of mankind" and build on a growing desire to ease "the sufferings of our citizens among the Algerines." Benevolence had seen evidence of this powerful sentiment in his travels around New England. Farmers throughout the region were willing to contribute to the cause, none pledging less than a dollar. Benevolence himself promised ten guineas.[20]

The diverse origins of these letters and petitions revealed the hold of the Algerian crisis over the United States. Concern for the captive Americans spread from the coastal towns and cities to the interior of the United States and even to the territories "south of the River Ohio." In New York, the *Daily Advertiser* proclaimed that "it is not the merchant and sailor only who are interested in the war with the pirate of Algiers." The effects of the crisis extended to every level of American society. The American people, far from retiring to their insular communities in the years following the ratification of the Constitution, continued to follow national and international events and make their voices heard when they believed that their interests and ideals were at stake. Issues ranging from personal liberty to economic interests and national pride made the crisis in Algiers an issue of interest to every region of the United States, and provided a national issue that sparked popular debate.[21]

Efforts on behalf of the captive sailors did not end with petitions to Congress and letters to the president. In Philadelphia, the national capital, numerous groups emerged to deal with the situation. One such group unanimously adopted a proposal to seize the ships of nations that had captured American vessels and demanded reimbursement for any losses incurred because of illegal seizures. Another collection of interested citizens called on the federal government to undertake "the most expeditious and the most effectual measures (which appear to have been too long postponed) to procure reparations for the past; to ensure safety for the future; to foster and protect the commercial interests; and to render respectable and respected among nations of the world, the justice, dignity, and power of the American Republic."[22] A committee was also created to "superintend the collection, management, and distribution of the fund contemplated to relieve and redeem those unfortunate citizens belonging to the port of Philadelphia, [who are] captives of Algiers." This committee went so far as to appoint local supervisors to oversee and encourage donations in the various wards of the city. The organization of such groups suggested the level of commitment of many Americans to aiding the captive American sailors.[23]

In April of 1794, the publishers of the *Columbian Centinel* in Boston noted that they had "the satisfaction of acquainting our readers that Messrs. Dominick, Terry, and Co. have advanced the sum of Three Thousand Dollars for the maintenance of the unfortunate captives at Algiers, which sum they gave without any security or indemnification—so generous an act, it is to be hoped, will not go long unrewarded."[24] In Rhode Island, concerned members of the community placed for sale "to the highest bidder . . . 2000 acres of LAND."[25] Those who had offered it for sale promised to keep no more than "half a dollar per acre, and whatever it will fetch more, shall be applied to the relief of the Americans in captivity at Algiers." If the land sold for a reasonable market price, the article commented, "it will afford a relief of *ten thousand* dollars." In Philadelphia, a sermon, originally written and delivered in German, was republished for an English-speaking audience: "The object of this sermon is two-fold—the first he expects that the contents of it will be of benefit to the soul of every man who will read it with attention—The second is, that the whole amount of the sale of this sermon is intended by him for the benefit of the poor American captive in Algiers, wherefore he expects that this sermon will be bought by every charitable American who can read and understand German." The money was to be remitted to "the managers of the 'Society for the relief of American captives in Algiers.'" While citizens from across the United States urged their government to action, other Americans were unwilling to wait for the government. In Boston, Providence, and Philadelphia, concerned citizens worked to aid in the efforts to redeem the American sailors.[26]

The activities of these groups proved a partial success when they managed to redeem three American prisoners in late 1794. George Smith of the *Maria* and William Patterson of the *Dauphin*, both of whom were captured in 1785, and John Burnham of the *Hope*, captured in 1793, were freed as a result of these private or nongovernmental collections. While the government continued to debate the best course of action, the efforts and the charity of these privately organized groups returned three captive Americans to the United

States.²⁷ Another three years would pass before the rest of the captive sailors would enjoy their freedom.

In addition to the nongovernmental collections solicited on behalf of the captives, there was a cultural dimension to these redemption efforts. Throughout the country, poems elegizing the American sailors in captivity began appearing in magazines and newspapers. On the stage, theater productions dealt with the theme of captivity by restaging older plays that reenacted North African captivity and premiering new works created in response to the crisis in Algiers. One of the first poems addressing the subject was actually part of a play that dealt with the same topic. The epilogue of Susanna Rowson's *Slaves in Algiers* was published in the "Poet's Corner" of the *Independent Gazetteer* in July 1794. Rowson's epilogue called on the benevolent spirit of the American people and reminded them of the power they held to bring freedom to the captives in Algiers. She declared, "What rap'trous joy must the poor captive know, Who freed from slav'ry's ignominious chain, views his dear native land and friendship again." The American people, according to Rowson, could bring "rap'trous joy" to their fellow citizens held captive in Algiers by working to secure their release.²⁸

Another poem, *The American Captive—An Elegy*, published widely throughout the United States, related the story of a lost love. The poem told of a young sailor enslaved in Algiers whose suffering was made all the more intense by the memory of his Julia. The captive tearfully remembered his home and his love. "Once I, Columbia, dwelt upon they shore, and the glad strains of joy and freedom joined," but then he was taken captive by "the hell-hounds of Algiers, the dreadful fauchion glitter'd in each hand." Despite the valiant efforts of the crew, they found themselves overwhelmed and "the vigor of a freeman's arm was vain, in vain man's sacred rights and country plead; around our limbs they fold the galling chain—See, O my country! You'r brave freemen bleed." The poem attempted to give a human face to the anguish in North Africa. Presenting the captive sailors as once-joyous citizens now suffering at the hands of "hell hounds," the poem summoned Americans to support the cause of the Americans held in Algiers.

In addition to describing the plight of the prisoners themselves, the poem depicted the anxiety and pain of family members left behind. The author writes, "There my fond father and mother live and sorrowing mourn their son's unhappy lot; thousands for ransom cheerfully they'd give—but Poverty surrounds their weeping cot." Left behind was also his "lovely Julia . . . fair as the beauty of the dawning morn." Sadly, the captive found himself far from his family and "happy cultur'd fields" and "cooling shade" of "Columbia." Instead of his happy home, the captive had been made a prisoner among the "screaming calls" and "dismal dread" that marked the land of Algiers. The poem concluded with exhorting American citizens to remember their humanity and patriotic virtue and go to the aid of their captive countrymen:

> Ah! Cruel country! Can my groans and pain
> Make no impression on they callous heart?
> Does not the glow of Sympathy remain?
> Does not Humanity its sigh impart?
> Art thou the land where Freedom rears her throne,
> Where conquered WASHINGTON, where WARREN bled,
> Where patriotic Virtue, and where Valor shone,
> And where oppression bow'd her guilt-stain'd head.[29]

Playing on many of the same themes as Rowson's epilogue, *The American Captive* sketched a personal story that hung a human face on the suffering of the captives in Algiers. The American people should remember their heritage and fulfill their obligation as citizens to redeem the suffering captives. To do otherwise would shame the land that claimed to be the very seat of "Freedom" herself.

Meanwhile on stage, American theater companies applied their own interpretations to the Algerian crisis. Nowhere was the vigor of public interest in the captive American sailors more apparent than in American theaters. The crisis in Algiers came at a time of transition in the American theater. According to Heather Nathans, theaters in the Early American Republic operated on unstable ground. During the colonial and revolutionary period, many venues or halls had been closed down by public decree condemning them as an un-republican symbol of excess and luxury. As the nation began to stabilize following the Revolution, American theaters began to reemerge as public institutions. To secure both funding and public support, theaters in the 1790s seized on captivity as a theme that would neither "offend their wealthy Federalist patrons, nor . . . turn the tide of popular political sentiment against the theater."[30] The threat of the pirates of Algiers was a theme that seemed to resonate with the largest possible audience, alienating neither the public nor theater patrons. In 1794, theaters in Boston, New York, and Philadelphia ran English playwright John Brown's *Barbarossa, Tyrant of Algiers*. Although the play had been written nearly a half-century earlier, the theme of Algerian tyranny was all too real to Americans in 1794. Based loosely on the history of Algiers, the play recounted the story of Barbarossa, a Turkish sea captain who helped the Algerians drive out Spanish invaders, only to turn on the Algerians once the Spanish had been defeated and seek to rule the state himself. In conjunction with the production of *Barbarossa*, Mathew Carey of Philadelphia published *A Short Account of Algiers*, which contained a history of the region. Both on stage and in print, Americans confronted a history of tyranny in Algiers.[31]

By December of 1794, a new play, *Slaves in Algiers, or, a Struggle for Freedom*, by Susanna Rowson, replaced *Barbarossa* as the play of choice presenting theatergoing audiences with a vision of American captivity in Algiers. Even as it was performed on stages throughout the United States, Rowson's script appeared in book form at the price of twenty-five cents. The play, highlighting American virtue, depicted an escape by American captives in Algiers from two villains, Muley Moloc, the dey of Algiers, and Ben Hassan, an English Jew who had become a Muslim renegade. Rowson portrayed the American captives as the embodiment of American virtue in the face of Algerian tyranny. In the story, the two female captives, Rebecca and Olivia, resisted the advances of the Muley Moloc and Ben Hassan, clinging to their American identity. In so doing, both the two women set an example for the Muslim women around them. Presented with an Americanized worldview, the Muslim women eagerly accepted this new perspective. One comments that "it was [Rebecca] ... who taught me, woman was never formed to be the abject slave of man.... She came from that land where virtue in either sex is the only mark of superiority—She was an American." As Americans worried over the fate of their fellow countrymen in Algiers and the fate of their nation as a whole, Rowson offered a reassuring message: even in a state of slavery at the hands of a tyrannical ruler, Americans could cling to their republican virtue and retain their political identity. American identity could defend itself regardless of place, condition, or enemy.[32]

The success of these plays led to a productive fusion in the relief effort. In addition to presenting plays that dealt with the captivity crisis, American theaters also assumed a direct role in the relief efforts, offering benefit shows almost immediately after news of the captivity of the nine American ships reached the United States. Theater companies across the nation donated part of their profits to relief funds established for the American captives. In

Philadelphia, the New Theatre "generously and humanely propose[d] appropriating the profits arising from [its] . . . entertainment, towards mitigating the sufferings of distressed brethren at Algiers." The *Gazette of the United States* praised these donations as "an offer so noble and philanthropic" that the New Theatre "justly merits the thanks and approbation of the citizens of Philadelphia."[33] Newspapers throughout the country published reports of the theater's efforts, noting that in one night, it managed to take in "1230 dollars—the clear profit probably about 900."[34] In South Carolina, "the sum of two hundred and fifty six pounds two shillings and sixpence sterling, was the amount of the benefit night at the Theatre in Charleston."[35] The *American Minerva* lavished praise on the efforts of Boston's Federal Street Theater: "We shall not attempt a panegyric on Mr. Powell, for his benevolence in this measure—the 'recording angel' has placed in the archives of Heaven; and the prayers of the captives, whose cup will be sweetened by the act, will to him be more than ample recompence. The sum collected amounted to Nine Hundred Dollars."[36] In New York, the Old American Company began performing *Barbarossa* "for the RELIEF of the American captives in Algiers." Becoming more than a symbolic link with the captives in Algiers, the American theater began to take an active role in raising money to aid the captive sailors.[37]

While the ordeal of the American captives was being played out on stage, the emerging Democratic-Republican societies embraced the cause of the American sailors as part of their political agenda. In Baltimore, a local Republican society resolved to "do everything in its power for the relief of the unfortunate American suffers at Algiers," following the reading of a petition from Richard O'Brien on behalf of the captive Americans. At New York's City Hall in March 1794, "a very numerous meeting of our true republican fellow-citizens assembled . . . to express the sincere joy they felt at the recapture of Toulon, and other happy success of our brave and generous allies, the citizens of the French Republic." From there they paraded to the house of the French consul, where the celebration continued. "During the repast . . . patriotic Toasts were drank," including one to "our captive brethren in Algiers; may the protecting hand of our government be speedily extended to their relief." The toast was met with "9 cheers." The failure of the Washington administration to redeem the American sailors became a political weapon that the Republican societies could deploy to discredit Federalist rule.[38]

Other less partisan groups also took up the cause of the imprisoned Americans. On St. Patrick's Day, the Shakespearean Society of Boston held a celebration in remembrance of the people of Ireland who, during the Revolution, "were uniformly friends to American liberty and independence." After the dinner, numerous toasts were given; among them was a call for the celebrants, enjoying in their festivity, to remember their "brethren in slavery and in chains—and may the public spirit of Americans speedily wipe off the stain of permitting their fellow countrymen so long to continue captives in Algiers."[39]

Celebrations of the revolutions in the United States and France also offered occasion for an acknowledgment of the suffering of the American captives. In Charleston, South Carolina, the Fourth of July, normally "a day with festive mirth and good harmony," was concluded with a series of toasts offered by the Cincinnati and Revolutionary Societies, including a remembrance of "the American captives at Algiers: may their bondage soon happily terminate, and be never experienced by any more of their fellow citizens."[40] In Baltimore, the storming of the Bastille in Paris was celebrated by the "Baltimore Washington Rifle Company, at the house of Capt. Resse," where the toasts called for "a speedy release to our suffering captive brethren in Algiers, and an entire civilization or extermination of the Barbary corsairs."[41] Regardless of the cause for the gathering or of the political affiliation of the group, the plight of the American sailors in Algiers was commemorated at solemn and festive events around the nation.

Just as plays on behalf of the Americans in Algiers offered an opportunity for new American voices to be heard, so too were these toasts a growing public participation in the national debate over their countrymen incarcerated in Algiers. As David Waldstreicher has noted, "Anyone who proclaimed a toast, cheered one, or discussed it was a participant in both ceremony and criticism." In addition to highlighting issues for the audience at such celebrations, the toasts were often reprinted in newspapers throughout the country, expanding the power of a single evening's gesture. Local festivities, including the toasts, were part of a local effort on the part of individuals to participate in a larger national dialogue. While those who attended these gatherings or even those giving the toast lacked the standing of an elected member of the federal government, these public forums and the subsequent transmission of these toasts through the press offered these citizens a voice that could inform and shape national policy. By remembering the captive Americans, these toasts put pressure on both the American government and its people to restore their countrymen to liberty.[42]

Although the pressure to act was keenly felt by all members of Congress, the response to this pressure had a distinctly partisan character. Congressional allies of the Democratic-Republican societies advocated allowing the public access to debates over the crisis in Algiers. The Federalists, who saw the Democratic-Republican societies as a threat to the United States, worked to limit that public access and preferred dealing with the crisis without the aid of private citizens. A closely divided House supported a Federalist approach to the crisis in Algiers, closing all sessions engaging the issue to public viewing. This policy, however, did not go unchallenged. On several occasions, Republican members of Congress sought to overturn the House rule that limited public access to these discussions. Republican opponents to the closing of the galleries spoke out against "mystery in government" and noted that "it was the business of the House at all times to favor publicity, and it ought not be in the power of any individual to shut out the constituents of Congress but for the strongest of reasons." Despite these Republican demands for greater transparency, an effort to amend House rules failed by a single vote.[43]

The closed sessions came to an end only after the Federalists believed they had crafted legislation that might resolve the crisis in Algiers. A Republican member of Congress, Anthony New of Virginia, leaked news of this impending legislation to his constituents in January 1794, informing them that "by some it is thought, that a . . . fleet to force a peace from Algiers" is sufficient "to protect commerce and assert our national rights; and votes have passed in the House of Representatives for these purposes."[44] With this legislation in place, the House finally lifted the ban in early February. This rule change opened the way for the Federalists to officially unveil their plan, a military solution, to terminate the crisis in Algiers. The legislation called for "a naval force, to consist of four ships of 44, and two ships of 20 guns each, be provided for the protection of the commerce of the United States against Algerine cruisers." Federalists believed such a force would "be amply sufficient to protect the commerce of the United States against the Pirates of Barbary." Characteristically, the Federalists allowed the public into the galleries only after reaching a solution that, they believed, would solve the issues at hand.[45]

Federalist supporters of the legislation argued that a military solution was the only sure way to end to a crisis. They noted that almost a decade of negotiation had not only failed to redeem the crews of the *Maria* and *Dauphin* but had also led to the capture of nine more American ships. Ironically, it had been Thomas Jefferson who had first called for a military solution when Algerian corsairs seized American ships in 1785.[46] Now it was the Federalists' turn. The Republicans, despite Jefferson's earlier support for military action, were less enthusiastic about the planned use of force in the Mediterranean. Pointing to the federal response to the Whiskey Rebellion, Republicans feared that such military power might be turned against the American people. James Madison thought the money might be better spent to pay Portugal to defend American shipping against the Algerians, while New Jersey congressman Abraham Clark worried that the creation of a navy was the first step in a massive enlargement of U.S. military forces and an unchecked expansion of federal power.[47]

In addition to the fears voiced by Madison and Clark, Congressman John Page of Virginia declared his opposition to the bill on a more practical level: "I cannot think that any measure we could adopt would be more grateful to our rivals in the commerce at which we are aiming, than an attempt to equip and keep in pay a naval force." Page argued that the price of a navy would only grow once the United States became involved in a war with "the Barbarians of the East on their own element." He elaborated that "a considerable part of our constituents would prefer having their proportion of the sums which may be found necessary to purchase peace, or to redeem unhappy captives," to the "warlike naval equipments proposed in the bill." The United States, in building a navy and expanding its military might, contended Page, would be abandoning the 'pacific disposition which it becomes an infant republic to cherish." Beyond the needs of the nation as a whole, Page commented that he dreaded "the consequences of . . . a report [on an American navy] reaching the ears of those who hold our unhappy countrymen in chains . . . . Should the report of our naval armament reach the tyrant of Algiers, immediate death might be the consequence to some of the miserable prisoners, additional chains, and perhaps dungeons become the lot of the others." The best course of action for a young republic in this situation to pursue, according to Page, was to appropriate a fund "for the redemption of unfortunate captives; and the ransom negotiated so, as to appear to the Regency of Algiers, as the result of private contributions and not as arising from an Act of the United States. If this could be done it would be far less expensive than the equipment of the 6 frigates; or the annual tributary payments, and would excite no jealousy at home or abroad." Although the legislation for the creation of the navy passed, Page's criticism struck a chord with many in the American public.[48]

As critiques of the new legislation began to appear in the American press, supporters of this legislation refused to let them go unanswered. In a letter first published in the *Philadelphia Gazette*, "Warren" called on the "reasonable Citizens of the United States" to support the legislation and to willingly pay the requisite taxes. He opined, "Beware my fellow citizens, of those persons amongst us who excite you against a government which is straining every nerve to protect you against your enemies. . . . If you see *new comers* clamoring against taxes and inflaming you against the government, you may justly suspect some sinister design." Warren argued that such criticisms were a threat not only to domestic stability but to the nation's very liberty:

> If when danger threatens from abroad, we are disunited at home, what will become of our independence?—rouse therefore, let every man contribute his share towards the defense of his country and reprobate those who, under the cloak of patriotism, are sapping the foundations of that excellent government, without which we shall soon fall prey to internal feuds and foreign invaders. The man who at this critical moment withholds his contributions, & thereby exposes the United States to ruin, shews clearly that while he pretends to patriotism, he is nothing better than a selfish interested person, worthy of public execration.[49]

According to Warren, Americans could best secure their liberty through faith in their government and support of federal policy. Failure to support the government, both in their sentiment and payment of taxes, would lead to internal division and ultimately foreign invasion.

In arguing against the direct involvement of private citizens in foreign affairs, Warren was clinging to an older model of civic discourse in which the authoritative few spoke to the people and discouraged a larger public dialogue. Warren's more traditional world view was echoed in the *American Minerva* and the *Gazette of the United States*. The newspapers published a piece that called on the American people to put their faith in the federal government and refrain from participating in any of the popular clubs that were attempting to influence public policy. "We think it a duty at all times to state *facts;* and warn the public of dangers," the author reasoned. "We have repeatedly noticed in speculation the attempts of certain violent men and popular associations to *dictate, direct,* or in some measure, to *influence* the proceedings of government. We must now relate a *fact* that sets the danger of such attempts in strong point of view." The article went on to argue that "soon after it was known that the Algerines had made prisoners of a number of our

American seamen, [the] government took the most effectual measures, and the most liberal means were provided to redeem those unfortunate men." The blame for the failure of these efforts was placed squarely on the "misjudged and ill-timed benevolence of our own citizens, who by various means, have been endeavoring to raise money for the same purpose by voluntary contributions." Such actions, the author contended, led the dey of Algiers to believe that no price was too high—that the American people would meet all his demands. As a result, the government had been forced to keep its negotiations "*private*, [and] this led people to suppose no measures had been taken to redeem the wretched captives and their humanity called for benevolent aid." Such an appearance, however, was the creation of a "misguided zeal of some" and a "sinister view of others" that perpetually embarrassed "or wholly thwarted the operations of government. The mischiefs arising from this constant popular interference with the legislative and executive powers of government are innumerable." Having chosen their representatives, the people must be satisfied that their government, acting with "the *best* means of information," was developing the appropriate policy. This system breaks down when people enter into "private clubs, transient associations, formed and acting on *partial* or *inaccurate* statements or facts, [and] undertake to direct and control the measures of the government. In short, they elect men to do business and then do it themselves, without means of knowing whether their steps are right or wrong." If Americans were unwilling to trust the government and "have no confidence in our executive; if he is not permitted to manage negotiations, entrusted to him by the constitution and laws of the United States; we may as well dissolve the government at once and 'every man to his tent, O Israel.'" Most significantly, "if Americans could have restrained their intemperate zeal, and let government conduct the business, our brethren in Algiers might probably have been, by this time, restored to their country." The author of the article did not doubt the good intention of Americans, but all they had done, "by those private aids," was "to thwart and perplex government." Finally, if the people of the United States wished to see the captives in Algiers freed and to see the American government continue to serve the best interest of the people, they should, "with great unanimity, reprobate all clubs formed to *influence public measures,* and consider them as unconstitutional and dangerous."[50]

Mirroring "Warren's" assessment of the situation, many officials in the federal government argued that any nongovernmental efforts on behalf of the captives were misguided. Even Jefferson, in the earliest days of the crisis, had sought to limit public participation in the measures taken to redeem the captives, fearing that such actions would only encourage the dey to increase his price. Acknowledging the diverse nature of the groups attempting to aid the captive sailors, opponents of private clubs argued that whatever their intention, their activities only served to undercut American foreign policy. Public opinion, many Federalists believed, had no place in government policy and operations.

Despite Federalist hopes that the American people would be satisfied with the creation of a navy, nongovernmental efforts only grew in the months that followed. Sparked in part by the actions of the American diplomatic corps, the second half of 1794 saw the height of private campaigns on behalf of the captives in Algiers. In June, the *City Gazette and Daily Advertiser* reported that at a celebration of the "President of the United States . . . at Lisbon [Portugal] in the house of our minister there . . . a subscription of 1000 dollars was completed for the relief of citizens of the United States in captivity in Algiers."[51] Later that summer, John Pintard, the American consul at Madeira, announced to the American Marine Society that he would donate the profits from the sale of wine to members of the society to the relief of their "unfortunate fellow-citizens who are in captivity at Algiers."[52]

Even with military preparations underway, not all Federalists opposed the movement to raised money to redeem the captive sailors. David Humphreys, U.S. minster to Portugal, was one of the greatest foils in Federalist efforts to quiet public contributions to the redemption of the sailors. Secretary of State Jefferson had appointed Humphreys as the lead agent in the Algerian negotiations following the deaths of the first two appointees to head the talks, John Paul Jones and Thomas Barclay, in 1793. Humphreys, a member of the Connecticut Wits, had served as Washington's aide during the Revolution and had accompanied him to Mount Vernon after the war. In 1785, he had traveled with John Adams, Thomas Jefferson, and Benjamin Franklin to report on the state of affairs in Europe. Following his appointment to Algiers, Humphreys worked through a number of channels to gain an audience with the dey. Despite several attempts, Humphreys never managed to meet with him to negotiate the release of the captives. Frustrated, Humphreys challenged official policy. In late 1794, he wrote directly "to the People of the United States of America," calling on them to help fund the relief of the American prisoners in Algiers:

> My dear Fellow Citizens, the Plague, that terrible scourge from Heaven now rages in Algiers. Our fellow citizens, at work with crowds in the marine by day, and confined in prison at night are much more exposed than persons who are at large to fall amongst its first victims ... [conditions were so bad for the American prisoners that] death may at last be deemed less dreadful by the miserable remnant of survivors, than dereliction and despair. [Therefore] however wise or proper the policy might formerly have been to decline ransoming our citizens from slavery at Algiers, until a peace could be negotiated with that Regency; at present, it appears to me, the principal political reasons on which that policy was founded have ceased to exist.[53]

Humphreys, the appointed U.S. representative to Algiers, questioned the diplomatic course being pursued by Congress and the president. He suggested that the quickest way to bring an end to the crisis was through a national lottery. Such a collection ought to take place to provide for the ransom of the American prisoners, "or if there should be any insuperable objections to that measure—it is to be hoped that the individual states will grant particular lotteries for the purpose. . . . *Citizens of the United States of America!* You have it in your power to rescue your forlorn fellow citizens from a premature death, which without your intervention in their favour, seems inevitable." Published widely throughout the United States, Humphrey's plan drew tremendous support among the public. Although neither the federal nor state governments seriously considered the idea of a lottery, many citizens viewed Humphreys's letter as official sanction of nongovernmental efforts to redeem American captives.[54]

Secretary of State Edmund Randolph, Jefferson's successor in that office, faced the delicate task of reigning in the stampede caused by Humphreys's plea without alienating either him or the supporters of the national lottery. In an attempt to limit public response, Randolph reported that the Humphreys's lottery was unnecessary as the government had already set aside $800,000 to secure the release of the captives. Such assurances from the government, however, did little to quell the popular uprising. Humphreys's letter only fanned the flames of public interest that had been ignited as early as 1785.[55]

Indeed, tremendous public support of a national lottery erupted. In late November 1795, a letter in the *Salem Gazette*, signed "Essex," noted that "the address . . . conveys so much *sympathy, philanthropy, virtue,* and, I may add, *pity,* that I doubt whether there is one of the addressed but what joins with me in approbating a theme that sets my soul on fire."[56] For many,

Humphreys's letter offered an opening for the American people to display their true character—their republican virtue. With the semiofficial sanction from Humphreys, Americans across the United States made plans to collect contributions to redeem the American captives in Algiers. When Washington called for a day of national thanksgiving in February 1795, those who had been working to redeem the captive sailors made use of the occasion. Following his announcement, newspapers throughout the United States issued an elaborate "plan of a continental contribution for the relief of our American Brethren in captivity at Algiers." The collections were to be forwarded to "the Treasurer of the Union at Philadelphia to be by him appropriated to the purpose aforesaid." The request for the collection reminded Americans of the names of the ships that had been seized and urged Americans to "transport yourselves in idea, to the City of Algiers; leave behind you the tenderest charities of life . . . fancy that you are prisoners, in chains, condemned to life long toil . . . goaded to labor by the uplifted scourge . . . and unrelentingly confined with the subjects of pestilential disease." The organizers of the national collection asked how Americans could "forget the greatest of all possible calamities, which rests on the wearied heads of [their] fellow citizens." The American people must not ignore the ordeal of their captive countrymen. "We are convinced, by a thousand examples," the organizers declared, "that the sons of Freedom are forever prompt to relieve the wretched." The authors of the plan called on Americans to make "the 19th day of February 1795 . . . a day never to be forgotten in the annals of philanthropy . . . for this was the day which gave liberty, happiness, domestic joys to all the American Captives in slavery at Algiers."[57]

As if to underscore the need for the people to contribute to the relief of the American captives, newspapers throughout the country republished a letter from John Lamb, who claimed that his efforts to redeem the American captives had failed because the American government had been unable to supply him with enough money to obtain their release. Lamb's letter, dated 20 January 1793, emphasized the need for the American people to become involved in the affairs of government. If Lamb was to be believed, the only way to redeem the American captives was through ransom, which the government could not afford on its own. Successful redemption of the prisoners was truly in the hands of the American people.[58]

While no member of the federal government directly refuted the endeavor to connect the day of thanksgiving with a national collection, covert maneuvers to subvert the charitable enterprises began almost immediately after the publication of the call for a national collection. The most prominent feature of these countermeasures was a series of reports that suggested a possible settlement in Algiers. These reports centered on Humphreys's return to Newport, Rhode Island. It was further suggested that he was on his way to Philadelphia to meet with President Washington. While the reasons for Humphreys's return were unclear, it was rumored that he carried with him "important communications to THE PRESIDENT," which, it was believed, might "unfold some interesting intelligence of the captives at *Algiers*."[59] Such reports, however, were unfounded for Humphreys had returned only to receive instructions on how to proceed, having failed to receive any direction following his initial rebuff from the dey.[60] The motivation of these reports may have been the belief that Humphreys's return to the United States portended an end to the conflict with Algiers, but it may also have been an indirect attempt to subvert the national collection. The premature announcements of peace were corrected shortly after the day of thanksgiving. A retraction ran in several newspapers: the information that supposedly "came from the government" and stated that "there are very favourable prospects, that a Peace with Algiers will be concluded," did not actually come from any official source. No such peace was imminent.[61]

Despite the reports of a settlement, which may have undercut the thanksgiving collection slightly, supporters of the effort continued to advertise their cause in the days leading up to the collection. A meeting of one of the aid societies in Marblehead, Massachusetts, recommended to local ministers that they "distinguish the approaching day of public thanksgiving, by a contribution to the relief of our American brethren, who are at this moment dragging the chains of slavery at Algiers, that city of bondage and of death."[62] A letter from William Penrose, captain of the captured ship *President*, was published in several newspapers. He wrote: "The Dey hath given permission for any person to come forward on the part of the United States to effect the redemption of the Americans in captivity in this place. Nay, he even fervently wishes to be upon good terms with America." The belief that the Dey was willing to negotiate may have served as encouragement, suggesting that donated funds could be put to use immediately. Penrose, however, went further to argue, "If something is not done soon we may as well give up every idea of liberty, and sink under the pressure of the most abject and cruel slavery." He added that such a fate could not be possible as "America, the freest country upon earth, [could not] suffer her citizens, who have fought and bled to establish & secure that liberty, to languish out a miserable existence in chains and the most abject slavery." With the opening provided by Humphreys's letter, supporters of the collection idea rushed to take full advantage of the situation.[63]

Ministers throughout New England threw their support behind the national collection. On the Sunday before the day of thanksgiving, Isaac Story delivered to his New London congregation a sermon entitled *A Discourse . . . as Preparatory to the Collection, on the National Thanksgiving, the Thursday Following, for the Benefit of Our American Brethren at Algiers*. Story informed his listeners "that a small sum from each hand would accomplish [the captives'] redemption." With that in mind, he asked his congregants to "consider the felicity, of which their ransom will be productive." If his audience were "sincere friends of [their] country . . . and would experience the consolatory assistance of the holy spirit in a dying hour," he urged them, "open your hearts, and open your hands to these deserving objects."[64] Samuel Seabury, the Episcopal bishop of Connecticut and Rhode Island, responded enthusiastically to the call for contributions: "I do most fervently recommend it to you, brethren, beloved in Christ, to have such a contribution made in all the Episcopal congregations." Furthermore, Seabury hoped that this "good work of mercy" would be repeated "among Christians of all denominations in the United States." Although Federalists downplayed the need for a national collection, the call for a private undertaking to redeem captive Americans in Algiers spread in the press and rang from the pulpit throughout the United States.[65]

In the weeks that followed the day of thanksgiving, reports from around the Northeast declared the collection a success. *Dunlap's American Daily Advertiser* in Philadelphia enthused: "We hear from Berwick that the Rev. Mr. Thompson . . . has stirred up the pure minds of his congregation to contribute liberally, and we wait with impatience to hand the names of some very philanthropic individuals to their admiring countrymen. Many other religious societies have also voted to contribute on this charitable occasion." One Bostonian "generously gave FOUR THOUSAND DOLLARS," a sum sufficient to procure the redemption of a master.[66] In Maine, reports of "the late Thanksgiving day" noted that "in Thomastown, 106 dollars were collected. In Cushing on that day and since, they have collected about 60 dollars." And at a town meeting in Warren, it was reported that $100 had been collected. "We had not a rich man in the town, and yet 10 dollars came from one hand."

In "the little plantation of Maduncook," a handsome sum had also been raised. The town of Bristol was reported to have collected between $200 and $300, while the towns of "Waldoborough, Union, and some other places" have scheduled their collections for an April meeting. The activities were so widespread that in Portland, Maine, "the society of *Friends*" took up a collection in support of the captives, and in Albany, New York, a Dutch Reformed congregation collected $130. These collections suggest the energy with which many Americans responded to the call to aid the captives in Algiers. Even as Congress officially laid out plans for a military solution, the American people organized on a national scale to resolve privately what their new government had been unable to do on its own.[67]

Despite the Washington administration's initial hope to keep efforts to redeem the American captives at Algiers out of the public view and despite Federalist denunciations of "self-created societies," by the middle of Washington's second term the Federalists could do little to stop a growing public interest in national and international affairs. Following a new round of Algerian attacks on American vessels in 1793, a renewed interest in the American hostages in Algiers created a multitude of private relief efforts. The wide-ranging debate on how best to redeem their fellow countrymen played a significant role in shaping the dynamic that was emerging between the newly created federal government and the American people. Even as the Federalist members of Congress sought to bring an end to the debate by legislating a military solution to the crisis, a growing number of concerned citizens, responding to what they saw as an inability of the new federal government to secure the release of the captives, continued their movements to raise funds for their release.

As early as the spring of 1794, hoping to appease the public outcry, President Washington requested that Secretary Hamilton explore the acquisition a foreign loan that the U.S. government could use to secure the release of hostages in Algiers. Although the eighty-five captive sailors who survived Algerian captivity would not return to the United States until February 1797, diplomatic negotiations and the payment of $1 million in gold, not the threat of an American navy, secured their release. Some officials in the federal government tried to tamp down the involvement of the American people in the

Algiers controversy, but many American citizens continued to speak out in the press, on the stage, in the taverns, and in the streets. While many members of Congress and the Washington administration favored the application of military power, growing public pressure and private collection efforts ultimately led Washington to purchase the freedom of the American captives detained in Algiers.[68]

Through petitions, letters, newspapers, and even the theater, Americans demonstrated that they would not be silent when they believed their government was not living up to its responsibility to protect citizens overseas. From the captive sailors themselves to members of Congress, almost every sector of American society played some role in the debate over Algiers. Numerous groups emerged to raise funds for their fellow citizens trapped in captivity and slavery, hoping to demonstrate the depth and strength of the American character, especially in a crisis. Members of Democratic-Republican societies, recognizing the power of the public campaigns to redeem the captives in Algiers, were quick to adopt the cause as one of their own, championing the voice of the people frustrated by the inaction of the Washington administration. Members of Congress also came to recognize the power of this movement. Republican congressmen sought to facilitate citizen participation by opening government proceedings to a wider audience. Even the many Federalists, who were initially opposed to the public efforts, eventually recognized the power of a motivated and active citizenry. That acknowledgment prepared the Federalists for the fight over the ratification of the Jay Treaty a year later. As historian Todd Estes has suggested, the debate surrounding the Jay Treaty "altered the entire political system within which the nascent parties operated." In the many ways, this political shift was rooted in the political culture that emerged during the Algerian debates beginning as early as 1783.[69]

The crisis in Algiers demonstrated that many Americans would not be shut out of public debate in the young United States. Federalist members of Congress could not silence the people; the growing public pressure to act forced the hand of the Washington administration. In making their voices heard, these citizens not only set the terms of the debate but steered the American government to a negotiated rather than a military settlement. The Algerian crisis revealed that in the face of the federal government's inability to resolve an international threat to American liberty, an engaged and active citizenry would emerge to help overcome the challenge. The lessons of the Algerian crisis were not lost on either the Federalists or Republicans. In the two decades that followed. both parties worked to portray themselves as the greater defender of American security abroad. In the face of ongoing threats from North Africa and Europe, Federalists and Republicans continually staked out increasingly nationalist positions in an attempt to harness public opinion in support of their political agenda in the decades that followed.

CHAPTER 4

"Millions for Defence, but Not a Cent for Tribute"

Debate and Public Sentiment during the Tripolitan War, 1801–1805

WHEN NEWS OF renewed hostilities with Tripoli reached the United States in early 1801, Federalist newspapers up and down the Atlantic coast called for war, declaring, "Millions for defence, but not a cent for tribute."[1] A Federalist editorial in Massachusetts argued that "the recent demands of the bashaw of Tripoli must excite a general emotion of indignation in this country." It was, according to these Federalists, absurd for the United States to continue paying for peace with Tripoli, a nation that had "outrageously disgraced" the American flag and was now "insolently" demanding a new tribute. Furthermore, "their injustice is as capricious as it is extravagant." The result of Tripoli's threat is that "our commerce is insecure and our citizens exposed to slavery upon every fresh wish of avarice, or new whim of almost unbound insolence." Annual tribute might have made sense "when we first agreed to make them presents," for "we were without a ship of war." Now, however, the United States kept "a naval force competent to wipe away the ignominy which lies upon us, to press their insolence, to prevent our commerce becoming their prey and at least induce them to keep within some bounds in their villany."[2] While the Federalist response to the renewed threat in the Mediterranean fit with the long-standing debate over how best to deal with the Barbary States, it was also an effort to remain relevant in the realm of domestic U.S. politics.

With the party facing a new political reality in 1801, Federalist support for a military solution to the renewed threat against American shipping in the Mediterranean was simultaneously a patriotic gesture and political expedience. The Federalists' bellicose rhetoric was part of an initial plan to maintain its political presence despite the party's serious losses in the election of 1800. Believing that president's political ideology would prohibit a military response, the Federalists staked out a strongly nationalist position on how the Jefferson administration ought to respond to the Tripolitan menace. The minority party hoped that this nationalist rhetoric would garner public support and paint the Jefferson administration as weak on American security abroad.

Although unfamiliar with being the minority political party, the Federalists were no strangers to the power and significance of public opinion. In the mid-1790s, a number of Federalists began to recognize public demonstrations of support for government (at the time Federalist) as legitimate activities. Building on this recognition, Federalist officials employed public opinion to great effect during both the ratification of the Jay Treaty and the XYZ Affair.[3] During the Jay Treaty debates, Federalists employed George Washington's widespread popularity to harness public sentiment and drum up popular support for what had initially been an extremely unpopular treaty. The effort to ratify the treaty marked an important turning point in the Federalist understanding of politics in the young United States and demonstrated a measure of flexibility in Federalist political culture.[4] During the XYZ Affair, the Federalists employed tactics that echoed those of their successful campaign to ratify the Jay Treaty. Following the release of the documents proving French demands for cash tribute, Federalists organized meetings around the country to express public approval of the Adams administration's policies and actions. Throughout the spring and summer of 1798, public messages of support and Adams's responses to those letters filled American newspapers. These exchanges "invited every feeling citizen to participate with the commander in chief in the affective field of patriotism."[5]

Despite the initial popularity of the Adams administration's efforts in the Quasi War with France, the passage of the Sedition Act undercut much of this earlier popularity and served to radicalize the opposition press.[6] Federalist successes were soon undone by a radicalized opposition and political infighting within the party leading to Adams's defeat in 1800. With Jefferson's election to the presidency, the Federalists found themselves in a novel position, that of the minority party. Although the Federalists have been categorized as "a party in search of an issue" after 1800, the hostilities with Tripoli initially seemed like the issue around which the Federalists could rebuild. Doubting Jefferson's ability to resolve the crisis with Tripoli, the Federalists hoped they could once again employ public sentiment to defeat their political rivals and return to national power.[7]

Contrary to Federalist expectations, however, Jefferson did offer a military response to the Tripolitan threat. Walking the line between ideology and pragmatism, as he would throughout much of his presidency, Jefferson balanced the Republican vision of a limited federal government with public demands for military action. Dispatching a small squadron of frigates to the Mediterranean with orders to protect American commerce against the threatened attacks, the Jefferson administration hoped that this show of American force would "awe" the bashaw into negotiating a settlement without having to go to war.[8]

Despite both Federalist and Republican hopes that the Tripolitan crisis would provide a quick and decisive means of gaining political advantage and boost American self-confidence, the United States found itself entangled in a prolonged and costly conflict with the North African state. The up-and-down nature of the four-year conflict in the Mediterranean served as one of the most enduring challenges of Jefferson's first term, with both Federalists and Republicans attempting to muster public opinion behind their version of events. As Federalists adapted to their new political standing, this debate was a touchstone for their opposition to Jefferson and the Republicans and for their efforts to refashion and reestablish their political identity. For Republicans, the conflict with Tripoli became a test of the administration's commitment to its party ideals, limited government in particular. By the end of the conflict in 1805, Republicans could claim both a military and political victory. Despite the political success that the end of the war provided the Republicans, Jefferson's initial decision to try remaining within the bounds of his presidential authority by ordering only a limited expedition likely led to the conflict going on far longer than it might otherwise have. This lack of a quick victory in North Africa resulted in a four-year public debate over U.S. operations in the Mediterranean as both parties sought to claim the mantle of "defender of American security." The Federalists used their experience during the conflict, including a number of smaller political victories, to begin developing strategies with which to challenge the Republican majority over the course of the next decade.[9]

The United States Senate ratified the first "treaty of perpetual peace and friendship between the United States of America and the Bey and subjects of Tripoli, of Barbary" in early 1797 as part of a wave of settlements with the Barbary States. For the next three years, more concerned with the threat presented by revolutionary France, the Adams administration would fulfill the policy of tribute to appease the North African states.[10] By 1800, however, the policy of appeasement had become increasingly difficult for the United States to maintain. In the face of these challenges, a number of Americans, including the president's son, began to question the wisdom of continuing to pay tribute in exchange for safe passage in the Mediterranean.

Writing from Berlin in January 1800, John Quincy Adams remarked to Secretary of State Timothy Pickering that the American relationship with the Barbary States "appears to deserve the peculiar attention of the government" and may be in need of some revision, as the security of American vessels in the Mediterranean under "any treaty with the Barbary powers must be precarious." Making matters worse, argued the younger Adams, was that this tenuous security had been achieved at "an expense so much more considerable than had ever before been applied to that purpose by any European power."[11]

As if to emphasize Adams's point, even as he expressed his reservations about the growing demands of the Barbary States, the dey of Algiers forced the U.S. frigate *George Washington* to transport tribute to the Ottoman sultan under an Algerian flag. Although the American captain, William Bainbridge, initially resisted the dey, the vulnerability of his ship and crew in the Algerian port left him little choice but to comply. In a series of letters, which were reprinted in the American press at his request, Bainbridge explained the rationale behind his decision, especially citing a fear of the "loss of property & slavery of our Citizens." Despite his explanation, the captain concluded, "I cannot help observing that the event of this day makes me ponder on the words *independent* United States."[12] Writing from Tunis and echoing Bainbridge, William Eaton remarked, "Is it not somewhat humiliating that the first United States ship of war which ever entered the Mediterranean should be pressed into the service of a pirate?"[13] Despite the initial public support for the settlement with the Barbary States in 1797, by 1800 many in the United States were questioning whether capitulating to the demands of the Barbary

States was the best means to protect American security in a larger Atlantic world.

Shortly after the humiliation suffered by the crew of the USS *George Washington*, Tripoli increased its demand for annual tribute. When the Americans refused, the bashaw expelled the American consul and chopped down the flagstaff outside the U.S. consulate. If the United States failed to pay the increased tribute, the bashaw declared, Tripoli would resume cruising against American ships in the Mediterranean. In March 1801, with Americans still reject the Tripolitan demand, the bashaw made good on his threat, ordering Tripoli's corsairs to seize any American ships they came across.

Although renewed hostilities with Tripoli officially began just before Jefferson's inauguration to the presidency, the subject of American relations with the Barbary States had served as fodder for the presidential campaigns the previous fall. Republicans, responding to attacks on Jefferson's piety, questioned Adams's faith, pointing to the eleventh article of the 1797 treaty with Tripoli and noting that Mr. Adams "has made a treaty with the Bey of Tripoli (an *infidel* and *piratical* state) in which he declares, that the constitution of the United States is, in no sense, founded on the Christian religion."[14] More directly, Republicans denounced the Federalists for high levels of federal military spending with little to show for the outlays, noting that despite the growing size of the American naval forces, the United States was still "subjected to the spoliations of foreign cruisers" and paid "an enormous tribute to the petty tyrant of Algiers." Jefferson promised to bring an end to this system of tribute and establish a system of free trade.[15]

Federalists were quick to dismiss Jefferson's vision of a new Atlantic world as naïve, arguing that the "philosopher of Monticello" lacked the resolve to defend American interests abroad. They contended that evidence of Jefferson's timidity could be seen on a number of occasions, including his flight at the first sign of a British invasion when he was governor of Virginia during the Revolution and later his opposition to the expansion of American naval forces during his two presidential administrations. Jefferson's resistance to military spending and Republican arguments in favor of limited presidential powers led Federalists to conclude that Jefferson lacked the mettle to engage in an armed conflict with the Barbary States. When Tripoli began to cruise against American ships shortly before Jefferson's inauguration, the Federalists believed that the Tripolitan threat could be used to their political advantage and gleefully declared "millions for defence, but not a cent for tribute."

Occasionally appearing alongside copies of Bainbridge's letters from Algiers, in which he questioned the independence of the young nation, the Federalists's bellicose rhetoric quickly created a test for the new president.[16]

It is important to recognize, however, that domestic politics were only one of the motivating factors in the demand for a resort to American arms. David Humphreys, in his final days as the U.S. minister to Spain, saw the Jefferson administration's response to the Tripolitan threat as a critical moment in defining the United States' position in the Atlantic world. In a letter to Secretary of State James Madison, which was reprinted in the American press, Humphreys advised that answering Tripoli's demands with armed force would ultimately benefit the United States. "To chastise that haughty but contemptible power," he explained, "which now dares first to insult us by its aggression would certainly serve, not only as a salutary example to the other piratical states, but it would produce an almost incalculable effect in elevating our national character in the estimation of all Europe."[17] Humphreys was not alone. From North Africa, James Cathcart and William Eaton, the American consuls in Tripoli and Tunis respectively, echoed Humphreys's view that this new Barbary threat represented a chance for the young nation to prove to the world the strength of its military arms and national character. When Madison suggested that the American consuls might look to Sweden for assistance in negotiations with Tripoli, Cathcart countered that such an arrangement would be entirely unacceptable. Instead, the United States ought to make an independent stand against the North African state; such action would tend "to establish a national character" but only if it was undertaken "without the assistance of any of the powers of Europe."[18]

Writing from more practical concerns, twenty-three "Masters" of "American vessels lying in the port of Barcelona" petitioned the president for "protection against any depredation that might be attempted on them." The need to protect these vessels was made abundantly clear by the "feelings which are yet alive of the sufferings of our Fellow Citizens when under that worst of degradation, *Slavery*, a repetition of which is now threatened." These petitioners looked "to their Government for aid and protection, against a ruthless band of a barbarous enemy, to whose Tyrannic grasp, upwards of three hundred Citizens of the United States (now waiting to return to their families and friends) would be exposed, if they attempted to leave this port."[19]

In the context of these wide-ranging pressures to act, the Federalists called for war. Their hope was that staking out a bellicose and deeply nationalistic position—"Millions for defence, but not a cent for tribute"—would expose the new president as a false champion of American security in the larger Atlantic world.[20] Jefferson, however, surprised the Federalists by pursuing a military option to address the Tripolitan threat, albeit on a limited scale. Within a few weeks of his inauguration, the president ordered a squadron of three frigates and a schooner outfitted for service in the Mediterranean. Despite this prompt action, he was more circumspect in giving the order to sail. Before dispatching American forces to the Mediterranean, the new president carefully examined the constitutionality of this naval deployment in consultation with his cabinet. A majority encouraged an aggressive response. Although the president did not have the constitutional power to declare war without Congressional approval, the majority reasoned, the fact that Tripoli had already declared war on the United States "bound [Jefferson] to apply the public force to defend the country." The lone dissenter from this broad interpretation of the president's authority came from Attorney General Levi Lincoln, who suggested a more defensive approach. In his view, the American squadron should be instructed to "repel an attack on individual vessels, but after the repulse," it should "not proceed to destroy the enemy's vessels generally."[21] Although Jefferson had long believed that a military solution was the only real means to end the Barbary threat, he sided with Lincoln. The president ordered the squadron to limit its engagements to repelling or punishing those vessels that attacked American ships and not to pursue Tripoli's corsairs or take them as prizes.

The limited nature of the American response was underscored by Jefferson's letter to the bashaw written less than a week after the meeting with his cabinet. Jefferson offered the Tripolitan leader "assurances of friendship" and a "sincere desire to cultivate peace and commerce" between the two nations. The president acknowledged that the United States had dispatched a squadron to the Mediterranean, but he hoped that its "appearance will give umbrage to no Power." The purpose of the naval expedition, Jefferson explained, was "to superintend the safety of our commerce there, and to exercise our seamen in nautical duties."[22] Although the president had pursued a military solution to the Tripolitan threat and confounded the expectations of his political adversaries, he had done so in a way that allowed him to remain true to his understanding of the constitutional limits of his presidential authority.

While Jefferson had gone to great lengths to square his policy with his ideology, the Federalist press portrayed the order to use military force without

Congressional approval as political hypocrisy and a radical departure from Republican ideology. Surprised by Jefferson's willingness to deploy federal military power, the Federalists pursued a new tack to pummel the president. The opposition press now declared that although Jefferson had given the order to dispatch the American ships to the Mediterranean, he would never "have been able to send a squadron to chastise the Tripolitans" without the development of an American navy under the Adams administration. Worse hypocrisy still, the Federalists argued, was that Jefferson and the members of his party had vehemently opposed funding the buildup of a U.S. naval force during the previous administration. Without Federalists' efforts and the defeat of Republican obstruction, "must we not have submitted to become their tributaries, or their slaves? No thanks are due the democrats, that the United States has such a squadron to send." According to these Federalists, any success that might come of the military expedition to the Mediterranean ought to be a credit to Federalist foresight rather than Jefferson's leadership.[23]

Federalist "Locke" was more direct in his criticism of Jefferson's hypocrisy. He argued that the administration's military response, while a policy the Federalists had initially supported, represented a violation of the Republicans' long-stated principles. Jefferson and the members of his party had once condemned the power of the presidency as a threat to American liberty but were now ignoring the very constitutional boundaries they had once defended. Locke wrote: "What are we to think of all this? Either that their sentiments changed, or that their zeal for the liberties of their country was false and hollow; or that they will justify any power provided it is possessed by themselves." The only defense against Jefferson's clear power grab was, according to Locke, the U.S. Senate, which must "'correct the procedure' of the President." Jefferson's pragmatic response to the crisis in Tripoli, initially intended to undercut Federalists' clamor for war, left them only ideological grounds for their attack.[24]

Despite Federalist charges of hypocrisy, early reports of the U.S. squadron's arrival in the Mediterranean gave Americans cause for optimism. Writing from Madrid, Spain, in a letter widely reprinted in American newspapers, David Humphreys declared, "Nothing could have been more opportune for the protection of our commerce than the arrival of this force." Without an American naval presence, Humphreys argued, the nascent conflict with Tripoli might likely "have produced the most disastrous consequences" with Tripolitan vessels "capturing the property of our merchants to an amazing amount, and making slaves in great number of our citizens." Instead, with the deployment of a military force against the renewed Barbary threat, American trade "will never again be left in the same defenceless and exposed situation." The American response stood in stark contrast to the many European states that had lost their carrying trade at the hands of Barbary corsairs. Humphreys declared, "No occasion could be more favorable than the present for encouragement of the American spirit of industry and enterprise in that quarter." The American response, he hoped, would be an example for all of Europe.[25]

Humphreys's optimism at the arrival of the American squadron was soon validated. Within days of entering the Mediterranean, the U.S. schooner *Enterprise* engaged the corsair *Tripoli*. The *Enterprise*, flying a British flag, hailed the Tripolitan vessel and inquired into the nature of her activities. When the Tripolitan crew revealed that they were in search of American vessels, the crew of *Enterprise* revealed its true identity and opened fire. After a three-hour battle, the *Tripoli* surrendered, "she having 30 men killed and 30 wounded." Of the *Enterprise*, Lieutenant Andrew Sterrett reported, "We have not had a man wounded, and we have sustained no material damage in our hull or rigging." Sterrett and his crew stopped short of seizing the vessel outright, recognizing the limits imposed by their orders. Instead, the victorious Americans threw the enemy weapons overboard and left the vessel little more than a floating hulk.[26]

The victory was more than Jefferson could have hoped for. The president had gambled that an American victory in Tripoli could be obtained on the cheap with a limited naval response, and his policy appeared to be working. This early success undermined much of the Federalist attack on Jefferson's military solution. As news of the *Enterprise*'s victory reached the United States in November 1801, both Federalist and Republican newspapers celebrated Sterrett and his crew for having "manifested the truest spirit, and sustained the greatest efforts during the engagement."[27] The victorious crew, the newspapers noted, "are entitled to encomium for their valor and good conduct."[28] Some pundits in the Republican press sought to make as much political hay from the victory as possible. In Stonington, Connecticut, the Republican-leaning *Patriot* chided as foolhardy those who had doubted the president's response to the Tripolitan threat and remarked: "How chagrined must the poor creatures feel, when they read that the haughty spirit of the Barbary powers has been reduced by this same squadron . . . . What will the Feds find to grumble about now?"[29] The president himself promptly joined the celebration of American arms, congratulating Sterrett in a personal letter that was soon reprinted in the press. Jefferson proudly commented on "the high satisfaction inspired by your conduct in the late engagement" and declared that Sterrett had "shewn to [his] Countrymen, that that enemy cannot meet bravery and skill united."[30] Regardless of their political affinity, all Americans could agree that the success of the *Enterprise* was a moment of national pride.

This moment of celebration highlighted the partisan nature of the ongoing debate over the Tripolitan threat. From a political perspective, the actual implementation of a Tripolitan policy was almost a secondary concern. To many leaders in Washington, the key debate was who deserved credit for securing American freedom and liberty in the Atlantic world. The Federalists' initial insistence on war was as much about discrediting the president as about an actual desire for a military response to the Tripolitan threat. When Jefferson called the Federalists' bluff on their demand to spend "millions for defence," the Federalists, rather than applauding the president's military actions, attributed any success to John Adams's foresight, not Jefferson's chosen course. The *Enterprise*'s victory, however, left little room for political bickering, for no American could doubt the symbolic power of the moment.

The victory also marked a shift in Jefferson's Tripolitan policy. Despite his initial reservations, the president used the opportunity to advocate an expansion of the American military presence in the Mediterranean. Although his initial response reflected reservations about the constitutional limits of his authority to dispatch American vessels to the Mediterranean, Jefferson had long preferred the policy of military force to quash the Barbary threat. Even before news of Sterrett's victory had arrived in the United States, Jefferson had expressed his desire for a more aggressive response in a letter to Secretary of State James Madison. "I am an enemy to all these doceurs, tributes and humiliations," the president wrote, and "I know that nothing will stop the external increase from these pirates but the presence of an armed force, and it will be more economical and more honorable to use the same means at once for suppressing their insolencies."[31] By December 1801, thanks in part to the Federalist expansion of the navy under Adams and the public support for such operations following the victory of the *Enterprise*, President Jefferson was finally able to push for a full-scale naval expedition to the Mediterranean.

The call for expanded action came in his first annual message to Congress in early December 1801. Jefferson began by highlighting Sterrett's success as "a testimony to the world that it is not a want of [bravery] that makes us seek their peace; but a conscientious desire to direct the energies of our nation to the multiplication of the human race." Despite this naval victory, Jefferson continued, the fact that the Americans were prohibited from taking "any defeated vessels as prizes" left them at a disadvantage. Playing on the bipartisan celebration of the *Enterprise*'s victory and striking a nationalistic tone, Jefferson called on Congress to consider "authorizing measures of offence," so that the American forces might be "on an equal footing with that of its adversaries."[32] Within two months of Jefferson's request, Congress passed "An Act for the Protection of the Commerce and Seamen of the United States, against Tripolitan Cruisers." Although not a formal declaration of war, the legislation removed the constitutional limits on the president's power to deploy offensive military force against the North African threat.[33]

In the wake of the *Enterprise*'s victory and congressional passage of the act to protect the "Commerce and Seamen of the United States, against the Tripolitan Cruisers," the Federalists adjusted their political message once again. Although some Federalists had initially criticized what they viewed as Jefferson's hypocrisy in sending a naval squadron to the Mediterranean without Congressional approval, the minority party made a complete about-face by 1802. Following the president's request for greater leeway in tackling the Tripolitan threat, leading Federalist Alexander Hamilton now attacked the president for having moved too cautiously at the outset and for issuing orders that had prevented the *Enterprise* from taking the *Tripoli* as a battle prize. Writing as "Lucius Crassus," Hamilton questioned Jefferson's strategy of putting constitutionality ahead of national safety. In his review of Jefferson's decision to limit the American force to defensive operations even after Tripoli had declared war on the United States, Hamilton argued, "We are presented with one of the most singular paradoxes ever advanced by a man claiming the character of a statesman." Jefferson's reading of the limits of presidential power in the case of Tripoli, was "repugnant to good sense" and "inconsistent with national security." The president's hesitation had "cast a blemish on our national character." Hamilton's "examination" walked a careful line between praising the success of Sterrett and his crew and criticizing the president for depriving the *Enterprise*'s brave men of a full victory. Although Hamilton's attack represented a shift in tone, the fundamental message remained the same: the United States would be more secure under a Federalist president than under Jefferson's leadership. Throughout the Tripolitan War, Federalists and Republicans jockeyed to portray themselves as the true defenders of American security abroad.[34]

By the spring of 1802, following a string of political and military successes, the Jefferson administration believed that an end—once and for all—to all Barbary tribute might be in sight. Secretary of State James Madison ordered James Cathcart, the expelled U.S. consul to Tripoli, to "stifle every pretension or expectation, that the United States . . . will make the smallest contribution . . . as the price of peace." Had Cathcart been able to negotiate such a settlement—peace without tribute—the relatively untested United States would have achieved more than any European power had been either willing or able to accomplish in the centuries-old engagement with the Barbary States. Such complete victory would have fundamentally undermined any Federalist efforts to cast doubt on Jefferson's ability to defend American interests abroad. Despite this optimism, the early successes in the Tripolitan conflict were soon overshadowed by a series of defeats, and although the Jefferson administration would ultimately claim victory in the war with Tripoli, it would be more than a decade before the United States was able to secure peace without tribute in North Africa.[35]

Even as Madison issued instructions to Cathcart to stifle talk of even the smallest tribute, a Tripolitan corsair seized the American merchant ship *Franklin* sailing from "Marseilles with an assorted Cargo for the West Indies." The nine-man crew was kept in chains on board their captors' ship for nearly a month before their delivery to Tripoli. Once deposited, the crew was sorted by nationality. Almost as soon as the men landed in Tripoli, the non-American crewmen were liberated by their respective governments. By the end of July 1802, "two officers and one Seaman" who were British subjects and "two more that were foreigners" found themselves at liberty to leave Tripoli. The remaining men, four Americans including Captain Andrew Morris, would remain in Tripolitan hands for several months.[36]

The first rumors of the *Franklin*'s capture arrived in the United States in September by way of American merchant vessels recently arrived from Marseilles. And the first official report came from Richard O'Brien, who was stationed at Algiers. O'Brien's circular letter confirmed that a Tripolitan corsair had passed through Algiers and that the vessel had "in her possession the American brig Franklin, capt. Morris of Philadelphia" O'Brien, in addition to reporting the vessel's capture, took the opportunity to comment on the naval blockade, lamenting that "we have not a few more of our frigates and light cruisers in this sea, to be a fleet of reserve, and give more effectual security to our commerce and citizens, and to destroy this new system of the Corsairs of Tripoli."[37] Shortly after the publication of O'Brien's report came a second account from William Eaton in Tunis. More dire than O'Brien's description, Eaton's account explained that upon arriving in Tunis, the American "brig and Cargo were put up at public auction in the city; but the master and the crew, nine in all were destined for Tripoli."[38] As these letters were reprinted in newspapers around the country, the celebration of the *Enterprise*'s victory began to give way to a new wave of frustration and uncertainty.[39]

Reaction to the *Franklin*'s capture immediately assumed a partisan tone. Expanding on O'Brien's lament that the blockade had not done more to protect American vessels, Federalists relaunched their criticism of Jefferson's handling of the crisis and the effectiveness of the blockade. One Federalist newspaper directly challenged the celebratory reports of the *Enterprise*'s success a year earlier. The administration believed that the blockade had improved America's reputation in the eyes of nations around the world, but the author declared, "We are much at a loss as to know where to find them." The Federalist dissenter sarcastically inquired, "Is it France, is it Britain, is it Spain, or Algiers, Tripoli and the whole host of Barbarians that so highly respect us?" Rather than improving American standing in eyes of Europe, the Federalists argued, the blockade led other nations "to avail themselves of our feeble and short-sighted policy."[40] The *New York Gazette* focused on the crewmen themselves, noting that "the poor fellows captured in the brig Franklin must curse that system of ECONOMY which lays up in dock our ships of war, while they are dragging the chains of slavery in Tripoli." To Federalist critics, the capture of the *Franklin* was proof of Jefferson's weakness—his inability to secure American liberty abroad.[41]

One of the greatest expressions of frustration with the seeming ineffectiveness of the blockade came from the *Franklin*'s captain, Andrew Morris. His letter, addressed to James Cathcart, was also widely reprinted in the American press. The letter ran with an introductory header declaring that "it contains information which imperiously demands the consideration of our government." Morris began by noting that there was no need to describe the difficult conditions he and his crew faced in their detention, for Cathcart and, by 1802, many Americans were "well acquainted with the conduct of these Barbarians towards the unfortunate that falls into their hands." Morris bluntly expressed his frustration with the failure of the U.S. blockade to protect his vessel and crew: "I cannot pass over the disappointment in not meeting with any of our vessels of war off Cape Bon, a place that the great necessity of guarding must appear evident to every naval commander." Worse still was that after his capture, the Tripolitan vessel in which he was held was anchored within sight of an "American frigate, who never made the smallest effort to obstruct our progress." Morris concluded with a warning to all American captains and crews and a call for the greater and more-effective protection of American shipping in the Mediterranean. "It was," the captain of the *Franklin* noted, "the sanguine assurances that I had from several quarters of the impossibility of their cruisers to get out that lead me to sea without convoy or arms." He hoped that his capture would serve as a warning and "prevent any more falling into their hands and excite our vessels of war to more vigilance.—And I must repeat to you the great necessity for one or two vessels being stationed off Cape Bon."[42] Although not addressed directly to the American people, Morris's letter confirmed to a national audience the validity of Federalist criticism of the porous blockade and underscored the need for the U.S. Navy to operate more effectively and aggressively to terminate the Tripolitan depredations on U.S. shipping.

The loss of the *Franklin* and the attacks that followed certainly dampened the Jefferson administration's optimism in the wake of the *Enterprise*'s success. Jefferson himself seemed somewhat chastened by the loss of the *Franklin*. While the president had begun 1802 by calling for a complete end to any Tripolitan tributes, his message to Congress in December took on a far-more-muted tone. He admitted the challenges facing the nation in the Mediterranean during his address and noted that "the shallowness of [the Tripolitan] coast and the want of smaller vessels on our part has permitted some cruisers to escape unobserved; and to one of these an American vessel unfortunately fell prey." But he did little beyond acknowledging the loss of the *Franklin*.[43]

In the Republican press, the administration's supporters did their best to put a positive spin on the turn of events. The pseudonymous author "Coriolanus" declared Jefferson's "mild and interesting" report stood in stark contrast to the analysis of the "wanting men" who read the message with "a jaundiced eye, and being disposed to view every act of the administration thro' a false medium, they censure indiscriminately, and insultingly call it the language of fear and pusillanimity." Rather than giving into those "wanting men," Coriolanus remarked, the president had instead addressed the Congress in a tone "consistent with the mildness of our national character." Such a definition of American character marked a significant retreat from the vision of a nation that had humbled the "haughty spirit of the Barbary powers" only a year earlier.[44]

Although Jefferson made little mention of Mediterranean affairs in the body of his message, the administration released with the presidential address a series of communications from the American consuls in North Africa intended to counter Federalist criticism. The reports from James Cathcart, Richard O'Brien, and William Eaton, reprinted collectively in the December 22 issue of the *National Intelligencer* and separately in a variety of other papers, countered disparagement of the administration's policies and operations in North Africa. Written from Algiers, O'Brien's reports demonstrated the speed with which American officials had responded to the capture of the *Franklin*. The letters from Eaton and Cathcart suggested that American military presence in North Africa was meeting with greater success than the critics would allow and that, with the application a bit more energy, the United States might bring an end to the Tripolitan threat.[45]

On the issue of prisoners, O'Brien detailed his negotiations to secure the release of the *Franklin*'s crew. Although at the time of his writing, he had not yet redeemed his captive countrymen, by 1802 O'Brien understood well the nature of negotiations surrounding Barbary captivity and moved quickly to free the American captives. With the dey of Algiers serving as a middle man, O'Brien bought the crew's freedom for $5,000, a payment made to the dey, who transported the sum to the bashaw of Tripoli as a variety of lavish gifts. At the urging of the dey, the bashaw offered peace at the price of $120,000, $30,000 of which would go to the dey. Although not authorized to negotiate a peace settlement with Tripoli, O'Brien believed the bashaw's pitch a promising start.[46]

The communications from Cathcart and Eaton, which the administration included with the annual message, presented the possibility of American victory and a final settlement with Tripoli as an attainable goal. One of the included letters from Cathcart, dated May 10, 1802, declared that "the Bashaw of Tripoli seems disposed to enter into a treaty with us." The reports from Eaton went even further. In a letter dated December 13, 1801, the American consul at Tunis reported that, among the people of Tripoli, the war with the United States was "very unpopular" and that they "were ripe for a revolt: they waited for nothing but succor." The citizens of the North African nation, Eaton reported in his letter, "clamor against the madness and oppression of their chief, say he makes war on his friends to the destruction of their little commerce, takes plunder to himself, and in the issue reduces them to starvation."⁴⁷ In addition to serving as a counter to Federalist attacks, these letters and the decision to release them to the American public highlight how chastened the administration was by the turn of events in late 1802. Although the early success had provided some hope that the United States might finally bring an end to the Barbary attacks, Jefferson's shift in tone and the publication of these documents suggested a return to a more pragmatic approach to the conflict with Tripoli.

The need for the administration to temper its initial optimism increased as the conflict dragged on. Rather than quickly subduing the Tripolitan threat with an economical naval force, Jefferson and the nation were becoming embroiled in the long-term conflict that John Adams had predicted more than a decade earlier, when he advised against a military response to the Algerian threat.⁴⁸ Indeed, Tripoli's shallow-draft vessels successfully skirted the American blockade by navigating the shoals. Avoiding direct conflict with U.S. warships, the smaller Tripolitan vessels maintained a steady supply of food and ammunition to their besieged country. Even before the capture of the *Franklin*, U.S. commodore Richard Dale acknowledged that if the blockade was to succeed, "it will be absolutely necessary to have three or four Gun boats" constructed specifically to "prevent all small craft from going in and coming out."⁴⁹ By the spring of 1803, the secretaries in the Jefferson administration who had voted unanimously to pursue a military solution to the Tripolitan threat two years earlier changed course and voted unanimously to "buy peace of Tripoli."⁵⁰

The vote to purchase peace was accompanied by a shakeup in the leadership of the American naval force in the Mediterranean. Following an official review of Richard Morris's conduct as commodore of the American squadron, he was removed from his post for "not being competent to the command of a squadron" and replaced by Commodore Edward Preble.⁵¹ Arriving in late 1803, the well-respected Preble, who had served during the American Revolution as a lieutenant and in the Far East as a captain, was determined to enforce the US. blockade of the Tripoli harbor. From aboard the USS *Constitution*, Preble ordered the officers in his seven-ship squadron to run down any Tripolitan vessels that attempted to outflank the blockade along the shoals. Preble believed that if properly enforced, the American blockade could produce a favorable peace with Tripoli by the following spring.⁵²

Despite Preble's optimism, the prospects for a peace benefitting the United States continued to sink when, during the pursuit of Tripolitan cruisers, the American frigate *Philadelphia* ran aground in late 1803. Trapped on the shoals and soon surrounded by enemy vessels, the crew of the *Philadelphia* struck its colors. The loss of the 307 American sailors, who were imprisoned in Tripoli, and the *Philadelphia* itself, which was recommissioned *The Gift of Allah,* were devastating blows to Preble's hope for a quick victory. In a letter to Secretary of the Navy Robert Smith, Preble declared: "This affair distresses me beyond description and very much deranges my plans of operation for the present. I fear our national character will sustain an injury with the Barbarians.—Would to God, that the Officers and Crew of the *Philadelphia* had one and all determined to prefer death to slavery." However much Preble was crushed by the loss, the bashaw was emboldened by his victory. With 307 American captives and an American naval vessel under his control, the Tripolitan leader raised his price for peace and demanded a ransom of $1,000 for each captive sailor.[53]

The capture of the *Philadelphia* handed the Federalists with a fresh crisis with which to bludgeon the Jefferson administration's handling of the conflict with Tripoli. As news of the loss arrived in the United States, the Federalists immediately revived their long-standing criticism that the war was being fought on the cheap and that Jefferson had failed to protect Americans overseas. "The present administration boasts loudly of its wisdom, as well [as] economy," the *Newburyport Herald* reported. "But the loss of the frigate Philadelphia, is a poor comment on either. Had there been a single tender in company [of] that frigate, we should not have to deplore the fate of above Three Hundred of our countrymen in slavery. *Now the mischief is done.*"[54] Other Federalist attacks echoed Preble's own assessment of the capture as a poor reflection on national character. One Federalist paper labeled Jefferson the leader of a "weak and pusillanimous administration" and castigated his failure as U.S. commander in chief. To the Federalists, the capture of the *Philadelphia* was a clear sign of a spineless president and weak nation.[55]

With the Federalists denouncing Jefferson as "weak and pusillanimous" and questioning the security of the American people, the Republican press quickly came to the president's defense. The Newburyport, Massachusetts, *Political Calendar* stated, "Every citizen of the United States will view the loss of this vessel as a national calamity, and everyone, who has the common feelings of men, will most seriously deplore the unhappy condition of his fellow citizens, who, in consequence of that loss are placed in captivity among the rude barbarians of Tripoli." Given the uncertainty of their fellow countrymen held captive in North Africa, Republicans were outraged by the Federalist assault. The Newburyport paper continued: "That party malevolence should undertake to lug in the loss of the *Philadelphia* as an evil which might have been avoided is indeed truly ridiculous. To think of charging it to the account of the President is malicious, is despicable. A mere accident; an accident which no man could possibly foresee, much less prevent." Additionally, the Republicans taking up the Federalist message, "Millions for Defence, but not a Cent for Tribute," argued that once this "mere accident" occurred, Jefferson had moved quickly in shepherding through Congress legislation authorizing the construction of a fleet of ships and gunboats suited for combat in the shallows off Tripoli.[56] As had been the case following the capture of the *Franklin*, the defeat of the *Philadelphia* became fodder for another round in the long-standing debate about which political party was best suited to ensure American security in the larger Atlantic world.

The depth to which the issue of security, liberty, and freedom played a role in this debate was encoded in the very language employed by both Republicans and Federalists in their discussion of the imprisoned crew of the *Philadelphia*. Members of the Jefferson administration were careful not to refer to the captives as "slaves." In formal gatherings and in the press, Republicans spoke of the crew as "our brothers in captivity" or "our captive brethren in Tripoli." In contrast, the Federalists eagerly pointed out that the bashaw of Tripoli had made slaves of American sailors; their tragic fate was the result of the president's failed policies in the Mediterranean. The *Boston Gazette* reported Federalist toasts to "our brethren in captivity at Tripoli" and the hope that "their country's sympathy" might "break their chains." Federalist poetry lamented the crew of the *Philadelphia* as "the slave of slaves" and "brave men . . . doom'd to slavery's chain." The choice of descriptors for the captured crewmen revealed the depth of the partisan divide over American security in the Atlantic world during the Jefferson administration. To the Federalists, Jefferson's foreign policy had set the nation on a path to weakness, slavery, and insecurity, leaving the nation vulnerable to the whims of barbaric pirates.[57]

The political windfall that the capture of the *Philadelphia* provided the Federalists was short-lived, however. Within a month, reports of a daring nighttime raid and destruction of the *Philadelphia* replaced the coverage of its loss. The operation took place on February 16, 1804, when, aided by reports of the harbor layout from William Bainbridge, the imprisoned captain of the *Philadelphia*, First Lieutenant Stephen Decatur snuck into Tripolitan waters aboard a captured ketch. Decatur and his seventy-man crew, having practiced their raid aboard the USS *Constitution*, moved swiftly to place their charges and set fire to the captured vessel. Before long, the flames had reached the stored powder, the explosions wrecked and burned the ship. Decatur and his sailors escaped the harbor with no one killed or injured.[58]

Suddenly, the terrible loss of the *Philadelphia* had been redeemed by a story of American enterprise and courage. Republicans seized the moment to savor and celebrate the victory on a public stage. In a letter widely reprinted in the Republican press, Commodore Edward Preble wrote: "I now have the pleasure of informing you of the destruction of the frigate *Philadelphia*, by an action most daring, and perhaps attended with a success as brilliant as any recorded in naval history." The accounts in the American press described Decatur's crew, disguised as Turkish sailors, cruising into Tripoli's harbor and boarding the *Philadelphia* before an alarm could be raised. Once on board the ship, the American crew destroyed the vessel, setting it ablaze and retreating to a safe distance. From there, "they saw the frigate burn to the water's edge, her cables burnt off, and the bottom drift on shore near the Bashaw's castle." What followed, according to an officer aboard the USS *Constitution* was a "scene of terror and confusion in Tripoli" that was "beyond description." The successful raid on the *Philadelphia* was a turning point in the conflict and revived flagging public sentiment over the war. Preble's account, published around the United States, noted that "the importance of this bold and intrepid enterprise, to the commerce of America must be acknowledged very great; but what affords the highest satisfaction is, that we have lost, in this action, not a single man."[59]

Republicans were once again on the political offensive. The *National Intelligencer* had hoped "the gallant conduct of our seamen in the Mediterranean" would instill "one common feeling throughout the land," but it was clear that since "our tars have dared to manifest under the administration of Mr. Jefferson a bravery and enterprise certainly unsurpassed," the Federalists had denied their "measure of applause" for the American success. Their criticisms of the previous month, now seen as a lack of faith in American resilience, were a political liability as Republicans launched a national celebration of Decatur's victory.[60]

Decatur's success enabled Commodore Preble to expand his operations to end to the conflict. Reviving the bold voice that had marked his earliest days in command of the American forces in the Mediterranean, Preble declared: "I have no doubt but we shall be able to dictate our own terms before the last of July. I am preparing to attack his Coasts on every part of it."[61] Even as Preble planned his new wave of assaults, Hamet Karamanli, the brother of the Tripolitan bashaw, requested American assistance in the form of a "loan of forty Thousand Spanish Dollars with Guns Powder &c." with which to overthrow his brother. In exchange for this support, Hamet offered a more-secure peace with Tripoli and all the other Barbary States.[62]

Once again, the turn of events in Tripoli marked a turn in administration policy. Sensing an opportunity to bring a final end to the long-running and costly conflict and enjoying renewed popular support following Decatur's destruction of the *Philadelphia*, Jefferson summoned his cabinet to consider how best to proceed. After careful consideration of all the possible outcomes, Jefferson both endorsed Preble's plan for an expanded assault and offered to supply Hamet's expedition. To advance and support these efforts, Jefferson dispatched what was by far the largest of any U.S. fleet in the Tripolitan conflict under the command of Commodore Samuel Barron. The expedition, assembled and operated at a cost of $1.5 million, was three times more costly than the initial Mediterranean squadron had been.[63] The success of the "gallant" Decatur and his crew had made the Jefferson's administration's attempt to buy peace in the spring of 1803 a distant memory.

Although slow to materialize, Preble's wave of attacks, ultimately supplemented by Barron's fleet, and the capture of the eastern city of Derne by Hamet's force, executed in conjunction with American forces headed by William Eaton, turned the tide of the war in favor of the United States. News of the U.S. naval success began to reach American shores in early 1805. A source "who accompanied our fleet to the Mediterranean" reported that the joint American naval force under Preble and Barron was reported to have "stamped an impression on the Barbary mind, which will not be erased this generation, and has restored the character of our arms to its proper value among neighboring nations." From this same source came extracts of a letter to Barron from a "distinguished commander in the British navy" offering his "congratulations on the services you [Barron] have rendered your country, and . . . in setting so distinguished an example to your countrymen . . . you have done well in not purchasing peace with money." Finally, the source reported: "The pope of Rome expresses himself thus on the subject—'The

American commander . . . has done more for the cause of Christianity, than the most powerful nations of Christendom have done for ages.'"[64]

Faced with this American offensive, the bashaw finally maneuvered for peace. The Tripolitan leader's initial gambit called for the United States to pay $200,000 in return for its captured sailors and an end to hostilities. The American negotiator, Tobias Lear, rejected the offer out of hand. Using the recent successes of U.S. naval forces as leverage, Lear ultimately reduced the American payment to $60,000 in exchange for the return of the captives and, as Lear noted, "not a cent for peace." At home, Republicans celebrated the settlement as a victory. Notably these Republican accounts highlighted the public's role in the success of the negotiations. According to reports, the bashaw had been reading copies of American newspapers acquired by the captives and the news of the effectiveness of the Jefferson administration's Mediterranean tax, levied to aid in the continued prosecution of the war, had discouraged the Tripolitan leader. Faced with such reports, the Republicans argued, the bashaw "saw that the spirit of the American nation was yet unbroken" and realized that he must soon come to terms. For the Republicans, events in the Mediterranean seemed to validate the Jefferson administration's strategy and signaled a victory to the American people.[65]

Throughout the United States, news of the end of the war with Tripoli was cause for celebration and an explosion of nationalism. The *Aurora General Advertiser* concluded that the United States expedition to North Africa was "now closed," and with its successful conclusion, "the nation has excited the esteem and admiration of European nations, and the respect and fear of those Barbary [states]." In Richmond, Virginia, news that the imprisoned crew of the *Philadelphia* had safely returned home elicited a massive celebration commemorating an event "which has given liberty to our own countrymen and glory to our arms."[66] A celebration in Philadelphia included not only the standard toasts but a series of paintings commemorating the American victory. They pictured "in one view the frigate *Philadelphia* wrapt in flames, and the ketch *Intrepid*, (by which this gallant exploit was achieved) bearing off from the scene of glory." Another canvas "consisted of the American Eagle, holding a sword pendant in his talons, and in her a bill a label, with the inscription, 'the gratitude of a country the reward of merit.'—On a roll below it was inscribed, in letters of gold, the Resolution of Congress, voting a sword to Captain Decatur for his gallant conduct in the destruction of the frigate Philadelphia."[67] At a theater in New York, "The Historical Tragedy of

Bunker Hill" was performed along with "TARS FROM TRIPOLI or A Tribute of Respect to the MEDITTERANIAN HEROES." On stage, the victory in Tripoli stood on equal ground with the triumph of the American Revolution. In conjunction with the acquisition of the Louisiana Territory, the victory in Tripoli instilled in many Americans a "renewed sense of mission and destiny."[68]

Federalists, well aware of the turn in public sentiment, joined celebrations of the end to the conflict and tributes to the soldiers and sailors who had risked their lives in the war. But they still criticized Jefferson for failing to achieve a complete victory. Following the capture of Derne, the Federalists argued, the United States was in a far stronger position than the final treaty suggested. If the Jefferson administration had offered greater support to the American forces at Derne, the bashaw himself might have been toppled and the United States might have achieved far more in the war with Tripoli. Federalist dissent, however, was not enough to dampen the national mood of celebration. As Americans marked the final end to the Tripolitan War with celebrations of "our infant navy," which "has thundered along the shores of Africa and reduced to terms tyrants who have spurned the powers of Europe," the Jefferson administration, despite a long and costly conflict, could celebrate a victory over rivals both abroad and at home.[69]

Battered by defeat in the election of 1800, the Federalists struggled to regain their political footing—now as the party out of power. The conflict with Tripoli seemed to provide the Federalists with the opportunity the party needed. As the Jefferson administration debated how best to respond to the renewed Barbary threat, the new minority party staked out a stridently nationalist position calling for a military response to the Tripolitan declaration of war. When the Jefferson administration surprised the Federalists by pursuing such an armed solution, effectively declaring its own nationalistic response and following some initial success with such a policy it seemed that the administration and the nation were on pace for a quick political victory at home and a military win in the Mediterranean. Although this initial success would not last and the war would drag on for years, offering both Federalists and Republicans the opportunity to claim the mantle of defender of American security abroad, the Jefferson administration was ultimately able to claim the victory it thought they had achieved in the earliest days of the conflict.

The American victory in the Tripolitan War was a setback to the Federalists, but their political strategy had been sound. Building on the lessons of the first quarter-century of Independence, both the Federalists and Republicans understood the power that threats to American security abroad had over the American public. While the constitutional settlement had assuaged concerns over the continued unity of the young nation, the American place in the larger Atlantic world was far from secure. Both parties knew that the ability to defend American interests overseas and promote a sense of nationalism would serve them well. For the Jefferson administration, the victory in Tripoli and the acquisition of the Louisiana Territory provided just the type of success that could feed the nascent American nationalism. Yet, despite these victories, the administration's successes were tempered by a continued European threat to the liberty of American sailors. While the Federalists had clearly been handed a political defeat in the conflict with Tripoli, the ongoing threat of impressment became the centerpiece of a new round of partisan conflict as the two parties engaged in a new contest to claim the title of defender of American liberty abroad.

CHAPTER 5

"We Shall Ever Be Prey of the Jealous and Monopolizing Spirit of the English"

Impressment and Party Ideology in Jefferson's Second Term

IN THE SUMMER of 1805, even as Americans anticipated success in the long-running conflict with Tripoli, Republican newspapers throughout the United States announced "with strong feelings of indignation . . . the impressment of our fishermen by the British." The report, initially printed in the *Salem Register,* related the news that "several fishing vessels from Marblehead, Beverly, and Salem, have lately been fallen in with by the English frigate, *Ville de Milan* . . . and had twelve or fourteen of their best men forcibly impressed and carried off to Halifax." Making matters worse, the Massachusetts newspaper reported that "we fear that many others will experience a similar fate" and that "we know not what security they will receive that this practice may not be followed up for the season." Efforts were already underway, the paper reported, to secure the release of these American citizens and "it is said the British Consul residing in Boston, has advised the Admiral on the Halifax station to give up the men." Yet, the *Salem Register* argued, even if the fishermen were granted their release, it would not undo the capture of "*two thousand seamen* taken from our Merchant ships of the United States in less than two years." Additionally, the actions of the *Ville de Milan* suggested that the United States "shall be visited in our very harbors by British cruisers, hunting after their prey." Many Republicans were coming to believe that if the British impressment of American sailors was not soon ended, the United

States ought to "stop all intercourse with Great Britain immediately and let the '*green mountain boys*' march to Canada."[1]

The Republican calls for action following the *Ville de Milan* impressment were part of an increasingly bellicose rhetoric surrounding the issue following the Tripolitan War. While anti-British sentiment was a well-established aspect of Republican Party discourse, the demand for an energetic national response to the external threat represented a departure from earlier Republican ideology. The energy with which the Jefferson administration engaged the threat of English impressment has even led both nineteenth-century contemporaries and twenty-first-century historians to accuse Republicans of exaggerating the crisis for political gain at the expense of the Federalist opposition. Despite this well-established understanding of the British threat to American seamen, a closer examination of the challenge of impressment during Jefferson's second term reveals a far-more-complex story.[2]

The threat of impressment and lingering American vulnerability in the Atlantic became the central issue in a contest for public support between Federalists and Republicans during Jefferson's second term, as both parties articulated and championed increasingly nationalist positions following the conflict with Tripoli. Engaging in such a rhetorical contest pushed both Federalists and Republicans against the boundaries of their traditional ideology. For some Republicans, their exertions to prove their nationalist credentials meant exploring the utility of a vigorous federal response to impressment or the threat of it. For many Federalists, showing their commitment to American security meant softening their traditional pro-British leanings. A number of Federalist newspapers challenged the Jefferson administration to take "such spirited measures . . . as would have been adopted under the *Adams* administration" to protect American sailors, going as far as to suggest that they might support their Republican counterparts' calls to "stop all intercourse with Great-Britain" and launch an invasion of Canada. Despite this posturing, however, these Federalist editors doubted the president would follow through: "this does not happen to be MR. JEFFERSON'S sort."[3] The result of this back and forth was a period of shifting political ideology during Jefferson's second term. In the face of a renewed wave of impressment beginning in 1803 until the eve of the War of 1812, both Federalists and Republicans, sensitive to the power of public opinion, continually shifted their stance on the issue as they scrambled to get ahead of public opinion on what had become the greatest threat to American liberty abroad.

The British threat to American sailors, which would drive ongoing partisan debate, was rooted in the years before the American Revolution, when after the Seven Years' War, North American colonists "carried out spectacular riots whenever press gangs attempted to take seamen on land."[4] Following Independence, American merchant vessels immediately became an attractive haven for deserters from the British navy. Life on board the American ships offered runaway British sailors better conditions and higher wages than they received in service of the king. As the ranks of British deserters swelled, vessels sailing under the American flag became an attractive target for English press gangs. In British ports and on the high seas, American sailors faced the threat of impressment at English hands. While American officials did not deny the right of the British to reclaim their subjects, a common language and little concern for the rights of American sailors led to the widespread impressment of American citizens.[5] The danger represented by these British press gangs only intensified in 1793 when Great Britain went to war with France. The long-running conflict increased the English demand for sailors at a striking rate. British naval manpower grew from 36,000 men in 1792 to roughly 120,000 in 1805. The peacetime incentives that had driven British sailors to American merchant vessels were only magnified by the ongoing conflict with France. By 1805, the British needed an additional 10,000 seamen per year to replace those lost through desertion and death.[6]

The continuing threat of impressment was critical enough to convince both Republican and Federalist members of Congress to act in early 1796. After some debate, Congress approved issuing certificates of U.S. citizenship designed to protect American-born seamen from wrongful impressment by the British. These documents listed the sailor's name, identifying characteristics, and place of birth. Recognizing that these documents alone would not be persuasive enough, Congress also set aside funding for U.S. agents, appointed by the president, who would protect American seamen abroad and to whom captains could report the impressment of their sailors. Ignoring these U.S. measures, the British Royal Navy still routinely seized American sailors, claiming that the doctrine of indefeasible allegiance granted it the right to press into the king's service any person born in the British Isles, regardless of current claims of citizenship. In British eyes, all American sailors, despite

Congressional protections, were treated as royal subjects unless they could definitively prove otherwise.[7]

In 1805, just as tensions in Europe were again reaching a boiling point, Jefferson attempted to restructure American trade relations with England. Emboldened by recent successes in the Mediterranean, the president instructed James Monroe, the American emissary in England, to secure most-favored-nation status, establish trade reciprocity, and negotiate an end to British intrusions on American neutrality—specifically the impressment of American sailors. Despite the American hope for better treatment from the European powers following the victory in Tripoli, both British and French forces continued to claim the right to search American merchant vessels for "deserters" from their respective navies. In the face of a renewed military conflict, neither England nor France could afford to allow their sailors to escape naval service by signing on to American merchant vessels. As a result of the European conflict, sailors aboard American ships faced a near-constant threat of impressment. Although the United States had recently defeated Tripoli, Jefferson knew that the United States could not hope to outgun the British and French fleets. "Under the new law of the Ocean," Jefferson conceded, "our trade in the Mediterranean has been swept away by seizures and condemnations."[8]

As had been the case with other foreign threats to American liberty abroad, news of the British impressment of their fellow citizens quickly captured the attention of the American public. In newspapers, songs, poems, pamphlets, and novels, Americans turned British impressment into a shared national experience. The continuing inability of the federal government under both Federalist and Republican administrations to quash the threat only fueled the determination of the American people. Outraged by British claims that the practice of impressment was justified under the principle of indefeasible allegiance, Americans engaged in a broad discussion of the boundaries and rights of American citizenship. Rejecting indefeasible allegiance, Americans trumpeted and celebrated the notion of volitional citizenship, which envisioned the relationship as a choice rather than an obligation. Threats to this ideal brought the nation together in defense of its freedom and ignited calls for the federal government to act.[9]

Although the Treaty of Amiens between France and England in 1802 offered a brief respite from these attacks, the outbreak of the Napoleonic War a year later revived the threat and marked the beginning of a new round of impressments. Throughout the summer of 1804, American newspapers, both Federalist and Republican, were filled with news of "More Impressment" of and "British aggressions" toward American sailors and included lists of dozens of American sailors who had been pressed into the service of the Royal Navy.[10] In New York, the editors of the *Evening Post* noted, "It is with much pain and concern that we perceive from the morning papers, that this unjustifiable practice has been carrying on and is still carrying on by certain English vessels off the coast." The editor added that the practice was "not merely illegal but in the highest degree indiscreet. Why create animosity between the countries in the period?" They hoped that "when the British captains shall be convinced of their mistake, they will release every impressed American Citizen without a moment's hesitation."[11] Others were less conciliatory toward the British attacks. The *Carolina Gazette* stated: "Will it never cease to be our duty to record British aggressions committed in our harbor?—It would be less unpleasant to repel than record these insolent attacks. It is more agreeable to an individual and honorable to a nation to resist than to suffer indignities."[12] The tone of the coverage varied, but the message was the same: Americans perceived and expressed insecurity in the larger world and unified around a desire to protect the rights of American citizens abroad.

Federalists seized on these recent impressments to denounce the Jefferson administration and its congressional allies. Opposition newspapers excoriated the administration's policies and actions to protect American sailors as "poor, spiritless," and "pusillanimous." To underscore their point, the Federalists dismissed the administration's release of reports from the Lewis and Clark's Corps of Discovery recently returned from exploring the Louisiana Purchase, and remonstrated that Jefferson was "occupied and amused about horned frogs, salt mountains, and prairie dogs" more than with securing the rights of Americans on the high seas. Under Jefferson, they contended, "the miserable Spaniard, who has hardly an existence or a name among the independent nations of the earth, rises into a momentary importance when put in comparison with a government more pusillanimous than his own." In attacking Jefferson's interest in the newly acquired Louisiana Territory, Federalists derided the new acquisition as a distraction from the most significant issues of the day; Louisiana was hardly the grand accomplishment hailed by many Republicans. The "content Magistrate of the Union, who having in his hands the means of protecting our rights looks on with perfect unconcern for month after month, and sees them made the sport, the derision, and the prey of every paltry picaroon that navigates our waters, while he is amusing himself and the nation with knick-knacks and playthings that would disgrace a school boy." The issue of impressment, an insult to American citizens, offered the Federalists an opening to turn the Louisiana Purchase into a political liability that amplified the Jefferson administration's failure to protect the rights of American sailors and to allay resurgent American insecurity.[13]

The Federalist efforts to court public opinion also included portraying themselves as the great defenders of sailors' rights, while highlighting the Jefferson administration's failed promises to protect them from British press gangs. Several Federalist newspapers chided their Republican counterparts for daily lamenting the practice of impressment "as if it still depended on the federalists to find a remedy for the injury." The Federalist editors reminded their readers that it had been "one of the most flattering of the promises made to the people by the democrats, that as soon as they got into power . . . they would soon take measures to stop the impressment of this useful and abused and meritorious class of our fellow citizens." The Democratic-Republicans had not forgotten the plight of their impressed countrymen, but they had failed to take any action. The Federalist newspapers pointed to the recent Democratic tabling of a bill in Congress "providing for the 'Protection of American Seamen'" as direct evidence of the majority party's unwillingness to fulfill its promise to American sailors. Reviving earlier Federalist efforts to paint Jefferson as weak in the face of an external threat, the Federalist partisans closed their comment by noting that rather than defending American sailors, the Republicans "dismantle our infant navy; they dismiss the best commanders, and turn adrift the sailors . . . as if they never intended to fight except when in the act of running away. Such is the philosophical administration of the affairs of a great and powerful nation."[14]

In the face of these Federalist attacks, many in the Republican press tried to outflank their political opponents, calling for a "national" response to the resurgent British threat. All along the East Coast, Republican papers declared that "it is time that we become a little more national," for "we have no hope of a cessation of impressment until some strong and decisive step shall be taken." Faced with a British challenge to the very notion of American citizenship and harassed by Federalist partisans, the party of limited government called for a robust and unified federal response to British outrages. Supporters of such a measure argued that the impressment of American sailors should be treated little differently than the imprisonment of American sailors in North Africa.

"It makes no difference to the mother, the wife or the children, whether the captive in the power of the British or the Tripolitans," one newspaper explained. "Their loss is equally as great and afflicting." Despite traditional party ideology, these Republicans insisted that a threat to American liberty abroad, whatever its form demanded an vigorous national response.[15]

Republicans also sought to diffuse criticism of the Jefferson administration's handling of the British menace by pointing to the Adams administration's mixed record in defending sailors' rights. During the previous administration, Republicans noted, "although the British ministry affected great regard for the [president], it was with the utmost difficulty that the release of a single seaman could be procured, and even after release the unfortunate man was again impressed." Under Jefferson, while "every possible step was taken by government to obtain the freedom of our mariners," and although some had been released, "it is now evident that our applications have been generally evaded." Making matters worse, since the war with France had gotten underway, "*Fifteen hundred* American seamen have been forcibly taken. . . . These are solemn, indisputable *facts* which the federal apologists for the British cannot deny." Many Republicans contended that such aggression could no longer be tolerated and challenged their Federalist opponents to rally behind the president and an aggressive policy toward British impressment. "If the federalists really have the respect which they so loudly profess, for the *honour* of the nation, for the *energy* of the administration, and such detestation of *dependence*," the *Aurora General Advertiser* chided, "they will join in approving any effectual measure for promoting the one and avoiding the other."[16]

Released in 1805, a Congressional report detailing the number of "American seamen who have been impressed or detained on board the ships of war of any foreign nation" supported the Republican account of the scope of the British attacks. The report and subsequent press coverage intensified Republican demands for action: "With such facts before us, there can exist no doubt of the necessity of taking measure for redress; for until some decisive step is taken, we shall ever be the prey of the jealous and monopolizing spirit of the English." If the threat was to be ended, many Republicans argued, much more needed to be done. One Republican organ stated: "The measures yet taken by congress, we do not consider, by any means, as adequate. . . . The insult and injury to our rights and commerce are national, and the punishment should be national also."[17]

The growing bellicosity of the nationalist faction of the Republican Party was only fueled by the news of the HMS *Ville de Milan*'s impressment of a dozen or so American sailors in the spring of 1805—with some Republicans going as far as to demand the invasion of Canada.[18] The aggressive nationalism of these Republicans left the Federalists unsure of how to proceed, resulting in a mixed response from them. Some Federalists immediately challenged this Republican bellicosity, arguing that the impressment of the Massachusetts sailors had been a simple mistake and that "measures have been taken by the friends of the unfortunate impressed men to prove their citizenship." With the issue of the sailors' citizenship resolved, these Federalists noted, the British consul had "given every facility in his power" to "obtain their immediate release." Yet, recognizing any defense of British actions could become a political liability, a growing number of the Federalists began to push back against the British. The more aggressive members of the minority party blamed the Jefferson administration for failing to protect American sailors, even challenging the president to make good on Republican calls for a military response.[19]

By the fall of 1805, Federalist attempts to call the Republicans on their nationalist posturing turned to cries of hypocrisy. Despite the Republican insistence on a military response to the English threat, Federalists sought to remind the public of the long-standing Republican opposition to the development of a respectable and viable American navy. The Federalist editor of the *Boston Gazette* dismissed their political opponents' recent military posturing as "hypocritical" and the Republicans themselves as "time serving sycophants," who "seem to have forgotten, that a few years ago, they joined the cry of those now in office against the former administration, because, as it was asserted, they had introduced an expensive naval establishment." Although the Adams administration had made some progress in establishing an American navy, once in power Jefferson and his administration had "dismantled and sold, or laid up to rot" much of the small U.S. fleet and left the nation's merchant vessels "prey to the unprincipled freebooters of all nations, and our seamen subjected to the insults of every maritime power upon the globe." It was only in the face of the threat of impressment, the *Boston Gazette* charged, that Republicans had now, "with hypocritical pretentions of regard for the interests if their fellow citizens," begun to call for a more aggressive response to the continued threat to American sailors. Only now, the paper argued, "rubbing their eyes after their philosophical slumbers," had the administration and its congressional supporters finally recognized the value of their predecessor's push for an American navy and "fitted out the frigate Adams, calculating probably that her name will at least be respected, and commanding her to go on the coast and see how things are going there." The members of the Jefferson administration, the Federalists contended, "will yet find that not only to preserve their popularity but even to save the country, they will have to follow the footsteps of their predecessors." In the days that followed, the Federalist *Gazette* argued that the Jefferson administration's continued realization of the wisdom of the Adams administration to support a strong national defense would reveal "to the whole community the difference between sound and substance, between measures of permanent and substantial policy, and the superficial arrangement of temporary expedience." In the end, the Federalists contended, American citizens would realize that they had "displaced their real and faithful friends, for mushroom politicians and philosophical theorists." The Federalists, the *Gazette* sought to remind the American people, were the true nationalists.[20]

Federalist charges of hypocrisy seemed to have struck a nerve with some members of the Republican press. Throughout the fall of 1805, a number of Republican editors, in pieces that were widely reprinted, attempted to step back from the calls for war with England. Attempting to walk a fine line between the desire to maintain an image of national strength, while affirming a commitment to their traditional principles of limited government, the editor of the Trenton *True American* published a series of articles that returned to a slightly more traditional Republican position. These New Jersey Republicans challenged Federalist "wiseacres" to find a time since Independence and with Europe at war when the United States had "been more free from insult and aggressions than at present." Was American commerce not "almost cut up by the roots and innumerable instances of disrespect shewn us by foreign powers during the *Washington* and *Adams* administrations?" The reality of the situation, the *True American* instructed, was that "while the European nations are in a state of warfare, America will always be more or less disturbed. . . . This is an evil which we cannot entirely prevent, and for which we can obtain perhaps no complete redress until a state of peace returns." Given the scale of the European conflict, the Republican editors advised that Americans proceed with caution, rather than giving in to Federalist challenges (and their more bellicose Republican counterparts) to follow through on calls to arms. "To plunge headlong into war, because a seaman was impressed, or a ship captured, would be madness in the extreme," declared the Republican editors.[21]

In a follow-up article, the Trenton newspaper challenged the effectiveness of efforts taken on behalf of American seamen during the previous Federalist administrations. Although an American "certificate of citizenship" was supposed to be "as valid as a British certificate to defend us from British tyranny ... the papers [are] despised and torn to pieces. And what greater insults can be offered the independence and integrity of our constituted authorities than this usage?" Despite the efforts of the Adams and Washington administrations to put a stop to impressment, the *True American* contended, the nation's sailors still at risk of mistreatment in foreign waters and lands. Despite the failure of Washington and Adams, the *True American* expressed an "undiminished confidence in our government" and a belief "that steps are taken or contemplated to obtain redress for the high handed and cruel usurpations committed on our flag, our commerce and our citizens." But the Republican paper did not believe that Jefferson ought to rise to Federalist demands for a military response. Instead, as "it cannot be imagined that we shall cope in arms with the tyrant of the ocean," the paper expressed their trust in "the wisdom and energy of our administration" to "devise some means which shall in future prevent the impressment and detention of the innocent and genuine citizens of the United States against the depredations of a power whose only rule of right is strength." Under Jefferson's leadership, they anticipated, just as the nation had "determined to pay no more tribute of money to the unprincipled hords [sic] of Barbary, we trust we shall furnish no more tribute of men to the equally infamous powers of Europe."[22] In responding to Federalist charges of hypocrisy, the *True American* and the Republican newspapers that reprinted its articles struck a balance between an increasingly belligerent nationalism and traditional Republican values.

The *Salem Register* echoed the *True American*'s challenge to the Federalist version of history. Taking issue with the Jay Treaty, the Massachusetts paper declared that while Federalists "dexterously shift the blame from their English friends to our government," they forgot that during the Washington administration, the English had "adjudicated 500 American vessels in '94 and '95," and instead of retaliating, the Federalists "seemed to kiss the rod that whipped them." Rather than stand up for American rights, the Washington administration sent John Jay to London, where he "had the honor to kiss his majesty's hand (or great toe, it is not recollected which) once or twice, and a treaty was the consequence." While merchants might have liked the treaty at the time, the Republicans argued, "they overlooked the commercial disadvantages and restrictions which the treaty entailed upon their country," including a lack of protection for American sailors. Now, a decade later, Jefferson "is doing everything in his power to arrest the mischief, by proper and energetic representation to the British government," to repair the diplomatic blunders of the Washington and Adams administrations, which had "palliated and excused the British" during their time in office.[23]

As Federalists continued exhorting the Jefferson administration to defend American sailors from forced service not only on British vessels but on those of France and Spain as well, the Republican *Newark Centinel* responded to the challenge. "We are willing to admit, for our part, that [not] only England, but France and Spain have molested our commerce to an unjustifiable degree," but the "fact is, the depredations on our southern coasts by French and Spanish privateers, appear to be vessels without commissions, or at least not immediately deriving them from their mother countries." Regardless, the Republican paper stated, "It cannot but be pleasing to every American to hear of the public spirit which is manifesting itself against *all* nations who trespass on our rights as a neutral and independent people." They had no doubt that in response to this public spirit, the administration would "act with vigour and independence toward" the foreign threats. If "remonstrances and petitions fail, let energetic measures be adopted—it can be done without bloodshed—and we look with confidence to the deliberations of the ensuing congress for the adoptions of such measures." All this must be done, the *Newark Centinel* instructed, in defense of "our rights as citizens, and our dignity as a powerful people. Justice demands it—self importance requires it, and the voice of an injured, though patient people call aloud for it."[24]

The politics of impressment only added to the difficult diplomatic circumstance surrounding the issue and added to the pressure on the Jefferson administration to resolve the problem. In early 1806, the administration dispatched Baltimore Federalist William Pinkney to London, where he joined James Monroe in negotiating a new trade agreement with the British government. Impressment was only one of a number of diplomatic issues facing the American ministers, but James Madison made in his instructions to the delegates special note of the urgent need to find "an effectual remedy for this practice" of impressment, particularly given "the growing impatience of the country [suffering] under it."[25] As negotiations got underway in late June 1806, it seemed that both sides were feeling the pressure to develop an "effectual remedy" for the long-standing source of tension between the two nations. Throughout the talks, both British and American officials employed a conciliatory tone, and it seemed that a resolution might soon be at hand. Despite a seeming agreement among the negotiators in London, the Jefferson administration rejected the terms of the treaty, due, in no small part, to the anticipated public reaction to the diplomatic settlement.[26]

At the heart of Jefferson's rejection was the limited British concession on impressment. The British Board of Admiralty refused to revoke the Royal Navy's right to impress sailors on the high seas, imperiously declaring "that as the high seas were extra territorial," other powers had no right to "protect British subjects from the exercise of the King's prerogative over them." In the face of British intransigence on impressment, the American ministers initially declined to proceed, contending that their acceptance of the Board of Admiralty's position would be tantamount to abandoning American rights. The U.S. ministers disavowed any plan that did not allow American ships to protect their crews.[27] British officials eventually convinced Monroe and Pinkney to resume negotiations over trade rights with the promise of a written treaty addendum guaranteeing that "the strictest care shall be taken to preserve the citizens of the United States from any molestation or injury, and that immediate and prompt redress shall be afforded upon any representation of injury sustained by them."[28] Granted such assurances, the American ministers agreed to proceed, believing that they had achieved the spirit of their instructions. The result was a treaty that offered far less on the issue of impressment than the Jefferson administration had requested, but the document promised the Americans a great deal on a variety of other issues, especially trade, and stipulated significant gains over the terms of the Jay Treaty.[29]

It was the failure to end the British practice of impressment, however, that led senior officials in the Jefferson administration to reject the treaty. Although the American delegates believed their negotiations were successful on purely diplomatic grounds, Jefferson and his advisers examined the treaty with an eye toward domestic as well as international politics. On receipt of the document, they "expressed the greatest astonishment and Disappointment," for no clause secured a complete abrogation of British impressment.[30] Although the envoys from the two nations signed the treaty on the last day of 1806 and the terms were indeed a substantial improvement over those in the Jay Treaty, Jefferson refused to submit the agreement to the Senate for ratification. In a private letter to Monroe, Madison expressed part of the rationale behind the administration's repudiation of the settlement. He explained that "the case of impressment consists altogether of thorns" and that the prickly nature of the subject had led the "public mind" to reach "a crisis of sensibility."[31] Fearing the wrath of an outraged public and the inevitability of Federalist attacks, the administration could not accept a treaty, despite favorable concessions on trade, that did not formally end the British impressment of American sailors

The ongoing "crisis of sensibility" in the public mind created by impressment escalated to full-blown public rage following the *Chesapeake-Leopard* affair in late June of 1807. The engagement between the HMS *Leopard* and the USS *Chesapeake* took place just off the coast of Virginia. The incident itself stemmed from the desertion of three crewmen from a British gun sloop *Halifax* docked in Hampton Roads, Virginia, the previous March. The sailors fled to Norfolk where they signed up to serve on the *Chesapeake*. These deserters joined three others from the British frigate *Melampus*. When he received news of the desertions from the *Halifax* and the reports that the men were now on board the *Chesapeake,* the British minister in Washington, David Erskine, appealed to authorities in the Jefferson administration to return the British crewmen. American officials promised to look into the matter, and if the sailors were identified as British subjects, they would immediately be returned to the British service. The investigation led American officials to conclude, however, that all three men in question were American citizens. They were allowed to remain aboard the *Chesapeake*.[32]

When reports of the desertions from the *Halifax* and *Melampus* reached Vice Admiral Sir George Berkeley, the British naval commander at Halifax, he immediately ordered all vessels under his command to retrieve the deserters should they encounter the *Chesapeake* beyond the territorial limits of the United States. Thus, when the *Chesapeake* left port on June 22, 1807, as a part of an American squadron bound for the Mediterranean, it immediately became the target of British vessels in the region. Ten miles off the Virginia coast, the *Leopard* began its pursuit. Although Commodore James Barron, the senior officer aboard the *Chesapeake*, noticed the approaching British vessel, he did not expect anything to come of the pursuit and failed to beat to quarters, which was standard practice when a foreign ship approached. The British vessel trailed the American squadron for much of the day before finally hailing the *Chesapeake*. On coming alongside, British officers informed the Americans of their orders to search for deserters as soon as the American vessel had reached international waters and demanded that the crew muster. Barron refused, declaring that he "had no British subjects on board; that the men in question were American citizens and under the protection of the American flag; and that he should not surrender them." As the British officers returned to the *Leopard*, Barron finally ordered his men to general quarters, but by then, it was too late. Within minutes, the *Leopard* opened fire on the American vessel, which was utterly unprepared for the attack. This initial broadside "killed three men and wounded twenty-three" others, and left the *Chesapeake* disabled. Unable to respond, the American captain ordered the colors struck and surrendered his ship. The British refused to take possession of the vessel itself, for the two nations were not officially at war. But the men at the heart of the incident were immediately taken into British custody. Badly damaged, the *Chesapeake* limped back to Norfolk.[33]

The American reaction was swift and heated as accounts of the incident began to circulate throughout the country. Running under headlines such as "British Outrage," "The Crisis," and "Murder," stories of the events off the Virginia coast turned a simmering frustration over impressment into explosive anger.[34] In Virginia, residents began to prepare for an invasion, with citizens in Norfolk destroying two hundred casks of water intended for British vessels and shoring up their defenses. In Philadelphia, an angry mob unhung the rudder of a British supply vessel. In Charleston, South Carolina, a crowd abused a man who had mocked the public mourning of Americans killed in the engagement.[35] At a meeting of the Rifle Corps of Alexandria, Virginia, the riflemen denounced the British attack on the *Chesapeake* as a "savage and dastardly outrage," and the body resolved that "the tyrannic conduct of the British nation on the ocean has justly rendered her odious among all civilized powers." In the face of this attack, the Alexandria Rifle Corps stood ready "in defence of our national dignity."[36] A "General Meeting of the Citizens of New York, held in the Park," chaired by De Witt Clinton, resolved that "we consider the dastardly and unprovoked attack made on the United States armed ship the Chesapeake, by his Britannic Majesty's ship, the Leopard, to be a violation of our national rights, as atrocious as it is unprecedented."[37] Revelers at a Fourth of July Celebration in Baltimore toasted "the memory of our fellow-citizens murdered by the robbers of the ocean—their blood cries to heaven and millions of freemen are impatient to avenge it. By the God of our fathers we swear!!"[38] A meeting of the citizens of Norfolk, where the incident had begun, resolved "that we view this unprovoked, piratical, savage and assassin like attack upon the Chesapeake with that horror and detestation which should always attend a violation of the faith of nations and the laws of war; and we pledge our lives and our property to co-operate with the government in any measures which they may adopt."³⁹

The Norfolk pledge to "co-operate with the government" embodied uncertainty about what ought to happen next. Although most Americans shared outrage, many also believed that an immediate military response might not be the best course of action. In an article reprinted throughout the United States, "Franklin" declared that "at no period since the establishment of our independence have I witnessed the national resentment equal to what has been manifested in every class of citizen." The attack on the *Chesapeake*, according to Franklin, was part of an ongoing British plan to "oppress our commerce and insult our national dignity." The United States had reached a point where "patience cannot be exerted, nor forbearance exerted." At such a time, when "every bosom swells with indignation, it is natural to ask WHAT CAN BE DONE?" Yet Franklin stopped short of insisting on war.⁴⁰

The Federalist Press seemed mired in the same issues facing their Republican counterparts, simultaneously churning with anger and hesitating from uncertainty about how to proceed. Just as in Republican papers, Federalist editors expressed the deepest levels of outrage over the incident. The *Norfolk Ledger*, "one of the most respectable federal papers . . . said to be particularly under the patronage of the British consul at that city," declared that "the blood of our countrymen has been shed by the hand of violence, and the honour and independence of our nation insulted beyond the possibility of further forbearance."⁴¹ The *Boston Gazette* exclaimed, "The question 'whether our country shall submit to Disgrace, or bravely resist oppression in whatever shape it may appear,' will find no dissentients among Federalists." The editor of the *Gazette* noted that during the war with Tripoli, the Federalists "were the first to declare this sentiment—'Millions for Defence, but not a Cent for Tribute.'" Following the attack on the *Chesapeake*, the *Gazette* remarked, Federalists "unequivocally pronounce; that 'War ought to follow the late outrage in the Chesapeake unless full and ample satisfaction is made." Despite these expressions of anger, the *Gazette*, like many of its Republican counterparts, asked that "in appealing to the world for the justice of our cause, we must be sure that our conduct has been marked by wisdom and prudence—that our endeavors to avoid the calamity, have been earnest and sincere." There was little doubt that the attack on the *Chesapeake* had been a great insult to national honor, but across the political spectrum, Americans questioned the wisdom of a military response.[42]

The uncertainty over how to proceed led many to express support for whatever course of action the Jefferson administration might pursue. Rather than issuing calls for the invasion of Canada or some other sort of military action, as some in the Republican press had done two years prior, even the most excited Americans tended to limit their bellicosity to a "readiness to take up arms in defence of those sacred rights which our forefathers purchased with their blood."[43] Many of the most widely read denunciations of British actions called on Americans to "confide in the wisdom and justice of Jefferson and his worthy associates."[44] At the "General Meeting of the Citizens of New York" held on July 2, 1807, the assembly resolved that the best means for defending the "rights and dignity of our country" was through supporting "our government in whatever measures it may deem necessary to adopt in the present crisis of affairs."[45]

The restraint exhibited in the reaction to the *Chesapeake-Leopard* affair suggested that by 1807, both Federalists and Republicans had few delusions about their nation's naval resources. Despite the calls for war to punish the English, Americans soon realized the limits of their naval power, even in the immediate afterglow of the victory in Tripoli. The continued impressment of American sailors and the attack on the *Chesapeake* made it all too clear that the American success in the Mediterranean had not "excited the esteem and admiration of European nations."[46] In many ways, the cost and length of the American conflict in the Mediterranean, in conjunction with the strength of the Royal Navy, seemed to have tempered the American response to the *Chesapeake-Leopard* incident. While Jefferson did close American ports to British vessels in aftermath of the attack and demand an end to all British impressment of American sailors, he counseled patience in determining the method of response. Reflecting the cautious tone in the American press, Jefferson advised, "We should avoid every act which may precipitate immediate and general war."[47] Despite the initial mob violence following the *Chesapeake-Leopard* engagement, the mood of the nation, although angry, also seemed cautious. In newspapers throughout the nation Republicans declared that they would "recommend a patient waiting for the measures of that man who has never disappointed the just expectations of his country."[48]

The mixed and hesitant American response to the British attack only served to increase the vulnerability of American sailors. Rather than expressing contrition for the unwarranted assault off the Virginia coast, British officials blamed the *Chesapeake-Leopard* affair on the Americans for failing to return the deserters and issued new Orders in Council in November 1807. The new decree required that all vessels bound for Europe from the United States must first pass through Britain to receive a license before proceeding to the Continent. French officials responded to the new British measure by declaring that any ships complying with the new British regulation would be subject to seizure by the French navy. Jefferson countered the multifaceted threat with the Embargo Act of 1807.[49]

Members of the Jefferson administration had believed that the Embargo would protect American property and force both the English and French to withdraw their threats to American merchant vessels, all without engaging either side in a military conflict. While it was clear to Jefferson that France was better positioned to weather the Embargo, he believed that the British navy posed a greater immediate danger to the United States and was therefore willing to take the chance that American actions might lead to a French victory in the war. The Embargo was divisive in the United States from the first, with Jefferson's critics (and even some in his own party) decrying what seemed to be a pro-French policy. Despite these objections, the president managed to convince Congress, dominated by Republicans, to pass the requisite legislation in December 1807. In the end, however, the Embargo represented a tremendous failure of American policy. The policy ultimately had little impact on England, which managed to counter the loss of American trade with the timely opening of Spanish markets. For Americans, by way of contrast, the loss of trade devastated the northeastern economy; business ground to a halt and left the very people the policy intended to protect without a means of income.[50]

Around the country, Jefferson's Embargo shattered the unity that enjoyed during the initial response to the *Chesapeake-Leopard* affair. While Federalist criticisms of the administration were to be expected, the closed session of Congress that had led to the passage of the Embargo Act compelled James Cheetham, editor of the Republican-leaning *American Citizen,* to question the administration's motives. He feared that "the hard hand of a foreign tyrant is upon us, secretly directing our national affairs" and that Jefferson was leading the United States "into the ocean of national degradation and slavery!" Cheetham cited as evidence a letter from "a gentleman of education, great respectability, and talents, who represents one of the most republican counties in this state, who has been an uniform, zealous, and active republican, and who served in the capacity of an ELECTOR, who had voted for Mr. Jefferson." This letter noted that "it appears to be the order of the day to keep everything a mystery, until we are plunged into an unnecessary and disgraceful war, to meet the views and interests of _____." Cheetham speculated that "the blank should be filled up with the word Bonaparte.... Does the reader call for proof that we are at this moment under the secret control and direction of Napoleon? What proof does he want? What proof can he expect?" All that a reader needed to know was to remember "that the doors of Congress were closed." If there were nothing to hide, the editor of the *American Citizen* argued, there would be no need to silence Congress. Instead, "not a member of Congress, of Congress the supreme power of the nation, of Congress the great and immediate guardian of the people, is at liberty to say.... Congress is tongue-tied and hand-tied and the nation is wrapped in *mystery*." The nation's last defense is "the purity and energy of the press. Who at such a time can blame me for stepping forward to save by the locks a drowning people?" The New York Republican's criticism of the Embargo demonstrated how economic interest in the Northeast might ultimately trump party loyalty and that anger against British actions might extend only as far as Americans' purse strings.[51]

Within days, Federalists reprinted Cheetham's call to action. The *Balance* in Hudson, New York, ran the letter under the headline "No laughing matter." The *Spectator* noted that while similar charges had been published in several Federalist papers, they had gone "without commanding sufficient attention. But when these truths are told by one of the most able and ardent advocates of the present administration, surely they will not again be pronounced 'Federal falsehoods.'" Federalists editors pointed out that these charges, coming from a Republican paper, surely "cannot fail to rouse the people of all classes to a sense of the dependent, degraded, alarming situation of our country. If these things are true, that freedom for which our father[s] fought, and bled, and died, is about to be exterminated forever—Let the people 'arise and awake, or be forever fallen.'"[52]

When it became clear that Napoleon was not behind the Embargo, the Federalists shifted their mode of attack, employing humor even as they lamented the devastation the policy wreaked on the American economy:

Q. Why is the Embargo like sickness?
A. Because it weakens us.
Q. Why is it like lameness?
A. Because we can't go.
Q. How is it like fire?
A. Because it consumes our substance. . . .
Q. How is it like broken bones?
A. Because it stops us from going at present, and leaves us cripples hereafter.
Q. How is it like madness?
A. Because we can't reason with it.
Q. If we spell it backwards, what does it say?
A. O GRAB ME!
Q. What is O GRAB ME?
A. The foolish act of a weak administration; a new box of Pandora, containing new plagues.[53]

Others in the Federalist press, sought to court the vote of those Americans most directly impacted by the Embargo. Running under the headline "O don't grab me," a number of Federalist newspapers in New England noted the fact "that pensioners, salarymen, and hirelings, should praise the Embargo, is not strange. They are paid for it. It grabs not them." Those Americans who were suffering were "the laborious farmer, the industrious Mechanic, the hardy Seaman out of employ, and the enterprising Merchant—The ruinous measure *grabs* from them all their earnings, without affording them a prospect of more."[54] Confronted with Jefferson's Embargo, Federalists took up the cause of farmers, mechanics, and sailors, hoping that a populist message in a period of the economic hardships created by federal policy would turn votes in their favor.

Now on the defensive, in some cases against charges from their own ranks, many Republicans attempted to defend the president. They cast Federalists as sympathizers of the British and traitors to American liberty. Building on these efforts, the Jeffersonians worked to revive anti-British sentiment from the era of the American Revolution with carefully orchestrated patriotic displays. In New York, Republican organizers staged a public ceremony to provide a proper burial for Revolutionary-era prisoners who had died aboard the British prison ship *Jersey*. The reburial was necessitated by the tidal disinterment of the skeletal remains that had originally been place in shallow graves in the mudflats of Wallabout Bay. Other efforts included broadsides that encouraged Republicans to vote: "Every Shot's a vote, and every vote Kills a Tory! Do your duty Republicans, Let your exertions this day put down the Kings and Tyrants of Britain." While these efforts managed to secure a Republican victory in the presidential election of 1808, in large part because of the sizable immigrant populations in New York and Pennsylvania, the Embargo remained unpopular in and undercut Republican politicians throughout the Northeast. Before long, many of these northern Republicans joined the Federalist opposition to Jefferson's policy, their defection ultimately leading to its repeal on March 4, 1809. The failure of the Embargo tarnished the final years of Jefferson's presidency in ways he could not have predicted.[55]

The implementation of the Embargo required the recall of the U.S. warships that had remained in the Mediterranean to ensure the safe passage of American trade vessels in the region. With the removal of these vessels, any American ships still engaged in Mediterranean trade became vulnerable to depredation by Barbary corsairs. Recognizing an opportunity, the dey of Algiers declared the United States delinquent in its annual tribute and demanded immediate payment. Although Jefferson had long opposed the practice of paying tribute to the Barbary States, he recommended to Madison, "We had better send to Algiers some of the losing articles in order to secure peace there while it is uncertain elsewhere."[56] Despite the administration's willingness to pay for the safe passage of American vessels in the Mediterranean, three American ships, the *Eagle, Violet,* and *Mary Ann,* soon became victims of Barbary depredations. Almost immediately, the American consul general at Algiers, Tobias Lear, began negotiations for the release of the captive sailors. In striking contrast to any previous American diplomacy with the Barbary States, including the conflict with Tripoli during Jefferson's first term, the United States immediately sued for peace. Lear offered "the amount of two years annuities . . . in cash" for the release of the captive sailors and an end to the conflict.[57] The speed of the American settlement preempted the type of public debate that had occurred in the build-up to the war with Tripoli seven years earlier. Appearing in the press a mere four days after the initial reports of "WAR WITH ALGIERS," news of the American sailors' release noted that the crews had "been treated very well, and no pillage of any kind has been committed."⁵⁸ The international challenges and domestic politics of the previous eight years, culminating with the seeming failure of the Embargo Act seemed to have softened the Jefferson administration's stance on American relations with the Barbary States. The administration's response to this renewed North African threat was a telling indication of just how deeply the Embargo had injured the widespread public support that the president had enjoyed in the days immediately following the *Leopard*'s attack on the *Chesapeake*. By the final year of Jefferson's presidency in a divided nation, the United States would pay for peace.

From the earliest days of American Independence, impressment had ignited the American imagination and united the nation around a long-term British threat to American liberty. Throughout their existence, both Republicans and Federalists worked to channel and manipulate public concern over this danger to enhance their position on the national political stage. Yet a changing political landscape led the two parties to experiment with new policies that reflected a change in their political standing in the first decade of the nineteenth century. These changes fundamentally altered both parties' concept of their place in the politics of the United States.

The end of the Tripolitan War in 1805 motivated both Federalists and Republicans to capitalize on the national mood by calling for an energetic or militant response to British impressment of American sailors, a practice the Royal Navy had resurrected in 1803. For Federalists, challenging the Jefferson administration to enforce a harder line against the British meant moderating some of their traditionally pro-British rhetoric. For Republicans, this meant the further scaling back of the constitutional limits on federal power—very much against the grain of accepted Republican ideology. Despite this activist rhetoric in the immediate afterglow of the Tripolitan War, the limits of the American naval power led many Americans to moderate their calls for vengeance following the *Chesapeake-Leopard* affair in 1807. While almost all Americans expressed outrage over the British attack, both Federalists and Republicans stopped short of demanding war and trusted the Jefferson administration to act in the nation's best interest.

The Embargo of 1807 left the nation paralyzed and restoked partisan fires. As much as the victory in Tripoli had served to boost popular support for the Jefferson administration in 1805, the near-complete failure of the Embargo undercut Jefferson's support both within his party and throughout the nation. Republicans were forced to play political defense, ultimately managing to hold on to their electoral majority but only through great effort. Without widespread popular support and seemingly well aware of their weakened position, officials in the Jefferson administration secured the immediate release of the American crews taken by Algiers in the fall of 1807. A far cry from Jefferson's earlier support of a military response to the Barbary threats, his final act in dealing with the North African states was to buy peace as quickly as possible. Such a resolution stood in stark contrast to the order issued the consul at Tripoli in 1801: "stifle every pretension or expectation, that the United States . . . will make the smallest contribution . . . as the price of peace." Instead, by 1807 Jefferson and the Republicans were too weak and unpopular domestically to reject or ignore the dey's demands for tribute.[59] The realities of American insecurity and politics marred Jefferson's second term in office. The surge of self-confidence that seemed to have defined the much of his first term and the widespread popular support that had come with it dissipated quickly in the face of British impressment and a renewed Barbary threat in his second. Less than a decade after Jefferson took office to the cry of "millions for defence, but not a cent for tribute," the United States once again found itself faced with an overwhelming sense of vulnerability on the global stage—ultimately leading to calls for war.

CHAPTER 6

"Floating Hells of Old England"

The Prisoner Debate and Federalist Opposition to the War of 1812

NOVEMBER 1813 SEEMED an unlikely time for a day of "Public Thanksgiving and Prayer" in Massachusetts. The failure of the U.S. Embargo under President Thomas Jefferson and of Macon's Bill Number 2, the Madison administration's own attempt to end British attacks on American merchant vessels, had once again led the United States to war with England. From the first, the war was politically divisive. Federalists around the country denounced the war as "unnecessary, inexpedient," and "disastrous."[1] In New England, Federalist governors refused to authorize the deployment of the state militias to federal armies. In addition to this political divide, expectations of a brief conflict had been replaced by the harsh realities of a long war for which the United States was ill-prepared. Despite this tumult, Massachusetts governor Caleb Strong issued a proclamation setting aside the twenty-fifth day of November as a day to offer "praise to the Supreme Being, for the gifts of Providence conferred upon us." If the special observance seemed poorly timed or misplaced, the collection of individuals at the home of Isaiah Thomas in Worcester, Massachusetts, was even more so. The guests included Mary Seaver, a widow and frequent visitor to the Thomas home; Charles White, the county attorney and occasional playwright; Henry Bancroft, an American naval officer; and Charles Morris, a lieutenant in the British army and prisoner of war.[2]

Morris was one of ten British officers who had been paroled following their capture by American forces. These officers had enjoyed relative freedom in Worcester and daily expected to receive news of their exchange. All that began to change, however, following the Battle of Queenston Heights. By December 1813 officers on both sides saw their liberal parole replaced by policies of close confinement. With this change in policy, Morris, a little more than a week after sharing a Thanksgiving meal with one of Worcester's most prominent citizens, found himself detained in the town's jail.

The debate surrounding the treatment of Morris and the thousands of other prisoners of war held by both sides during the War of 1812 represented a critical piece of the last legitimate Federalist effort to regain majority status at the federal level. The Federalists had employed a number of tactics to regain the White House and win a congressional majority. They ranged from disparaging the Jefferson administration's handling of the Tripolitan War as too timid to defaming the Louisiana Purchase as an abuse of presidential power. The early missteps in the War of 1812, however, offered the Federalists their best and final opportunity to take advantage of public unease over foreign threats and reestablish control of the federal government.

Beyond simply providing a political opportunity for the Federalists to attack the administration of President James Madison, Jefferson's successor, the debate over the fate of American prisoners embodied and expressed insecurity about the future of the United States. At the heart of this debate lay fundamentally different understandings of the legacy of the American Revolution and the place of the United States in the larger world. For Federalists, the debate centered on the fear of an overly powerful central government drifting toward Napoleonic-style tyranny. For Republicans, the greater threat lay in the stubborn British refusal to respect American rights and the danger and humiliation of a neocolonial existence. This back and forth over the plight of prisoners of war turned on its head the ideological divide between the Republicans and Federalists that had emerged during the earliest years of the Republic. Amplifying a process that had begun during Jefferson's second term, the political jockeying by both parties during the War of 1812 demonstrated a near-complete shift in both parties' traditional ideology. In dealing with prisoners of war, the traditionally states-rights Republicans embraced policies that expanded the power of the federal government while Federalists, who had long supported the expansion of the federal state, vilified the Madison administration's tactics as symptomatic of a power grab that put the United States on the road to tyranny. In turn, Republicans argued that the brutal treatment of American prisoners by the British demanded that the United States rise to the challenge and defend the rights of their countrymen. Regardless of the shifting nature of the debate, the battle over the treatment of prisoners of war during the War of 1812 highlights how American insecurity—persistent and undiminished—about the future of the United States and its standing in the world defined the political culture of the young nation.[3]

James Madison's first term in office was very much shaped by policies that he had helped put in place as secretary of state in the Jefferson administration. Although the Napoleonic Wars had been a boon for the United States in many ways, attacks on American shipping by both the French and English navies left the United States in a vulnerable position. Unwilling and unable to redress the insults militarily, Jefferson and Madison responded with the Embargo Act of 1807, essentially closing American ports to foreign trade. From the beginning of his administration, Madison was faced with the consequences of Jefferson's policy. The Embargo drove the nation into a deep economic depression and rejuvenated the Federalist Party, which led the protest against the disastrous policy. Finally, in May of 1810, Congress replaced the Embargo with Macon's Bill Number 2, which promised to reopen trade with either France or England—whichever nation was the first to normalize trade with the United States—while it reinstated the Non-Intercourse Acts against the other power. Napoleon acted first, promising to lift all restrictions on American shipping to Europe. Suspecting the French promise was little more than a ruse, English officials tried to meet the terms of the bill but requested that the United States impose a nonintercourse policy against all British enemies rather than France alone. After examining the two offers, Congress reopened trade with France, while resuming nonimportation against British goods. Following the passage of this second nonimportation act, relations with the English rapidly deteriorated in the months that followed. With diplomacy buffeted by growing discord, an increasing number of Republicans began to discuss the possibility of war with England. The supporters of the military option argued that war was indeed a serious step but all other alternatives had been exhausted. In a letter to John Quincy Adams, William Plumer of New Hampshire later suggested that "negociation & commercial restrictions failed to obtain redress, [so] submission or war were the only remaining alternatives."[4]

As many Republicans became increasingly convinced that war was the only means by which Americans might redeem their national honor, the long-lamented issue of impressment became one of the focal points of national debate. Within the administration, impressment was seen as "a practice which has so strong a bearing on our neutrality and to which no nation can submit consistently with its independence."[5] At the international level, members of the administration called on British officials to cease the practice of impressment. In a diplomatic dispatch to Britain's Lord Wellesley, which appeared in newspapers throughout the United States, William Pinkney called on England to respect American maritime rights. Responding to the seizure of four American sailors by the British ship *Africa* in the autumn of 1810, Pinkney commented that such attacks demonstrated "an utter disregard of the rights of the American government, and . . . its citizens." Official denunciation of these lawless British actions extended beyond the federal level.[6] Governor John Tyler, in an address to the Virginia Legislature, denounced England as an aggressor against American rights. "America," he stated, had "been continually groaning under oppressions of every sort, and a never ceasing invasion of her national rights ever since her act of Independence," as a result of "adjudications, impressments, and paper blockades." Tyler's speech, quickly reprinted around the country, found a receptive national audience.[7]

The growing criticism of British actions was not solely the realm of government officials. In a widely disseminated letter to the *Boston Patriot*, "Volunteer" declared that the "British defender of the faith" in allowing "impressment" had simply given a new name to "the *Infidel practice of* MAN STEALING." This renaming, Volunteer argued, was "an abuse of language" that "veiled from the great mass of an unscrutinizing nation, the rank offense of its rulers." Although the renaming of this grand offense may have been enough for the people of England, Volunteer elaborated, it could never be enough for the American people. No matter what term was used, American "seamen, the stolen goods . . . are still in possession of the thief; and it is the duty of every man, in whose veins runs a drop of American blood, *to make perpetual claim of our right*--to raise the *hue and cry* against the *felon* 'till we *obtain indemnity for the past and security for the future*." Volunteer concluded his letter urging Congress to act with purpose and force. He recalled that six years earlier, a congressman from Maryland had introduced legislation that would have protected "the personal rights of our seamen," but Congress had failed to pass it. "Had this bill passed to a law, and the defence of our brave tars had been committed to their own hands," he explained, "they would have done justice to themselves and avenged our disgrace."⁸

In another letter to the *Essex Register,* "S" drew parallels between the plight of the American captives in Algiers and that of Americans pressed into British service. "What must the feelings of the American Government be," S surmised, "when they have certain knowledge that more than 3000 natives of these United States have been *impressed,* and are now suffering on the '*Floating Hells of Old England*' such cruelties as would disgrace the national character of the Algerines!" "Algerine slavery is both hard and cruel," but it is "nothing comparatively speaking to British slavery." For evidence of British cruelty one needed to look no further than almost any sailor who had managed to escape the "clutches" of the English. These former captives displayed "their scars, or tell of 'scenes that fill the mind with horror!'" Faced with such evidence, S declared, "It is time the American government should demand the liberation of this invaluable class of our citizens." The time for government action was now, for "many destitute widows have been deprived of their only hope of comfort and support, and many families have been thrown by British tyranny and impressment from a state of comfort and enjoyment, into a miserable existence of penury and want." The British impressment of American sailors, S argued, had eliminated the gains of the Revolution for countless American families. Sailors forced into servitude consigned their families to lives of want. Clearly, according to S, something needed to be done.⁹

As had been the case since the American Revolution, efforts to rouse public opinion against British transgressions were fortified by firsthand accounts of American sailors who had escaped English captivity. Joshua Davis's narrative, which recounted his impressment in the British navy, was published in the spring of 1811 joining the growing attacks on the British practice. In his narrative, Davis recounted his service during the Revolution on board the American privateer *Jason* and his subsequent capture and impressment by British forces. While the narrative followed the standard description of his brutal treatment, escape, and eventual return home, the appendix and a note to his "readers and others" directly engaged the ongoing discussion of British impressment.

Davis's appendix described in detail the "barbarity" of the British officers and the mistreatment of those who failed to follow orders. Those sailors who "prefer to be hung" were taken on deck and tied to and dangled from the yard arm. The victims were "run up until [their] head touches the yard . . . and thus . . . hang for about half an hour," before their bodies were taken down and buried in mud flats at low tide. Those men who did not wish to be hung were often "flogged through the fleet." Those prisoners targeted for whipping were tied to the longboat and received fifty lashes from the boatswain of every British ship in the area. Davis wrote, "If you live through it, you are taken back to your ship . . . but if you die before your receive the complement, you are taken to every ship, and get every lash the Court Marshall [sic] ordered." In one incident witnessed by Davis, a fellow sailor was court-martialed for assaulting an officer. The court "sentenced [him] to receive 800 lashes. The day he was punished, after he had been flogged along side 13 ships, he was bro't to ours. The blanket was taken off his shoulders . . . and the doctor . . . found that the man was dead." Despite the victim's death, the punishment continued and the boatswain applied fifty lashes. Davis concluded the episode: "After this he was carried to two other ships and received fifty lashes at each, and then carried to [the] low water mark, and there buried in the mud." Davis's account underscored the charges of brutality and savagery that newspapers were leveling against the British around the country on a daily basis.[10]

In spite of his rather graphic descriptions of harsh conditions on board the British ships, Davis counseled those Americans who sought to "know the fate of your fathers, husbands, brothers, uncles, cousins, or sweethearts" not to lose hope. For despite the punishing conditions, the lost loved ones may have survived. "Many of them are on board those hellish floating torments," he consoled, "and wish to let you know where they are. They write letters often but it is ten to one whether they ever reach your hands." These letters, according to Davis, were intercepted and handed over to British officers. Once discovered, the authors of the letters were asked "what he meant by sending letters out of the ship, without an officer's consent." With no legitimate excuse, these sailors were left to the mercy of the officer. "If the officer happens to be a Washington, he will tell the man never to do the like again, but if he should prove a Nero, the man [will be] . . . put in irons, until a time is set by the course of inquiry for the writer's destiny and all this merely for attempting to let his friends know his unhappy situation—There are nine Neros in the British navy, to one Washington." Davis's message of hope was tempered by the notion that those Americans who survived were under the command of "Neros," who might force them into chains or any one of the other brutal punishments Davis had described.[11]

Davis's account echoed earlier captivity narratives in highlighting British and Barbary cruelty toward American captives. Like that of earlier narratives, the goal of his and other accounts was to spur Americans to action. These narratives exhorted Americans to stand strong against the British for a host of reasons. British impressment and subsequent cruelty suggested that Americans had failed once again to protect the gains of the American Revolution. In seizing American sailors, the British had revealed themselves to be little better than the Algerian pirates. Above all else, the failure of Americans to bring closure to the practice of impressment left their fellow countrymen to suffer in captivity. As had been the case in the Revolution and throughout the conflicts with the Barbary States, these stories of captivity were a call to action for the American people.

Citing these many violations of American rights at sea, many Republicans pushed for the United States to declare war on England. A number of Federalists, despite a traditionally hawkish approach to external threats, resisted this bellicosity, questioning the case put forth by the Republican War Hawks. Federalists challenged Republican credibility, demanding President Madison to justify the march to war: "If there are any good causes of war in the possession of our administration, and they intend to have the united aid of the county in supporting the war, they must come out with them."[12] Some Federalists questioned the veracity of accounts of the impressment of American sailors aboard British ships, arguing that "the complaints on this subject were *impudent falsehoods*, fabricated for party purposes."[13] The majority of Federalists were willing to acknowledge the suffering of American sailors on British ships, but they argued that the Madison administration, rather than the British navy, bore direct responsibility for the troubling state of affairs. Federalist critics argued that Madison had incited the British to action as a consequence of his decisions and policies "favoring and befriending the eternal enemy of England."[14] By allowing French ships into American ports, the opponents of war complained, "we have certainly abandoned all appearance of a disposition to act as neutrals, and these impressments may be the first fruits of this anti-neutral conduct."[15] In addition, they contended that the impressment of American sailors was accidental and unintended, for British authorities were simply seeking English deserters from the Royal Navy. The impressment of American sailors was the result of an "evil that necessarily grows out of the resemblance that the English and Americans bear to each other in complexion, features, language, and character.—But under a treaty, the evil would find a regular remedy." Faced with these challenges, "the British made various successive efforts to adjust the difficulties which existed, but which by some fatality on our part always fell to the ground."[16]

As early as 1806, under the Monroe-Pinkney Treaty, Jefferson had been presented an opportunity to negotiate a settlement to the ongoing trade difficulties between England and the United States. Jefferson and his supporters, however, feared that the treaty would lead to a neocolonial existence for the United States, echoing many Republican criticisms of the earlier Jay Treaty. Fearful of potential Federalist maneuvering in Congress, Jefferson refrained from submitting the Monroe-Pinkney Treaty to the Senate for debate and approval.[17] Federalists were unwilling to let go of the "lost opportunity" that the agreement represented to them: "Had Monroe's treaty been ratified impressments would have ceased. For by an understanding accompanying that treaty, the British agreed to relinquish the practice of impressing seamen from on board our ships—even their own sailors."[18] To underscore their point, Federalists claimed that when news of the impressment of an American citizen reached British officials, all haste was made to secure the release of American seamen.[19] According to the Federalists, American sailors continued to suffer at the hands of the British because the American government was "not merely ineffectual but ridiculous. . . . It can indeed issue a *proclamation* and thus make known its own pitiful imbecility . . . and it can cry aloud against British outrage and caution the people not to vote for federalists; all that it can do, because it has often done it, but what can it do more?—Nothing."[20]

In addition to accusing the Republicans of exaggerating British actions and citing the failure of the Madison administration to negotiate with the English, the Federalists charged the Republicans with overlooking French violations of American rights and, worse still, with failing to fully recognize the danger posed by France. The *Portland Gazette* noted that the same people who were "harping on the subject of British aggression" were at the same time "justifying every act of the French government, and rejoicing at the usurpations and plundering acts of Bonaparte." Such abuse, they argued, would have long ago resulted in war if it had been committed by the English. "But party feelings cannot be excited," Federalists instructed, "by railing at French aggressions, as they can be by preaching about British impressments."[21] The French violations of American rights were far greater, according to the Federalists, than anything the English had done. "It is useless to multiply the instances in which [American sailors] are treated by the French worse than the Algerines treat the captives who[m] they reduce to slavery. Federalists take no pleasure in sickening the public mind by recitals of unavenged disgrace which the executive calmly pockets." But they felt obliged to highlight an incident in which French officers condemned and shot three American seamen "merely for being present though without taking a part in the recapture of their vessel by their messmates." This assault on American liberty had been "suffered to pass with scarcely any extraordinary notice." If the British had behaved in the same fashion, "all Washington would have been in a bustle. . . . The Tammany societies from one extremity of the continent to the other would have lifted up their hatchets and howled the most dismal yells for war; and poor Madison would have burst with impotent wrath."[22] By ignoring the repeated French assaults on American liberty and preparing for war against England, the United States seemed perilously close to political ruin and incorporation into the French empire. The *Connecticut Courant* lamented: "The country is fast asleep. Would to God it may not be the sleep of death! . . . We think we see our country to be already within the precincts of the French empire."[23]

To these Federalists, the Madison administration's hawkish position came not out of a sense of national pride but as a step toward tyranny and possible French control. In the face of such maneuverings and with a limited say in federal policies, a growing number of Federalists had backed away from some of their own bellicose rhetoric of the previous two decades. In defense of the nation, these Federalists called for restraint and limited federal action against British naval policies and operations, particularly impressment of American sailors.

Hawkish Republicans maintained their aggressive posture toward England and dismissed the political opposition as pampered Anglophiles. The Federalists, one Republican newspaper declared, were "the eternal apologists of Great Britain," who sought to conceal the fact "that thousands of American seamen are now held in bondage aboard the British navy."[24] Another proadministration publication charged that in concealing the true nature of the British attacks, the Federalists were in effect defending "the murder of our citizens—the impressment and captivity of freeborn Americans—the capture and confiscation of American property."[25] Writing as "Americanus," another Republican charged: "To read a federal newspaper, a stranger might imagine that [the] government had recently laid some odious tax upon the people. . . . Indeed scarcely any one would suspect that the persons who raised such a hedious outcry had any thing to eat or drink or wear." Yet, according to

Americanus, the Federalists who had raised the loudest cry against the Madison administration were better off than almost any other citizens in the entire world. These were men "who eat roast beef, plumb-puddings, fowls, and fish three or four times a day; who regale themselves with tea, coffee, cream butter, the finest bread, the choicest wines; whose vestments are silks and satins, the best linens and woolens, and the rarest of cloths; who in brief, enjoy all the comforts and all the delicacies of life in the greatest profusion." With so much wealth, comfort, and privilege, Americanus asked, what is it "that those noisy men want? Is it war? No! (they tell us) not that. Is it an embargo? O no! by no means! say they. Non-intercourse or non-importation? Not at all. What, then, is it *submission to the wrongs which Great Britain has inflicted on our lawful trade?* No! they cry as if indignant. Thus it is they clamor for everything; but press them to particulars and they want nothing." Republicans responded to the Federalist attacks by labeling those who opposed the Madison administration as spoiled whiners at best and outright traitors at worst.[26]

Republicans also campaigned to defend the Madison administration. Although the Federalists "have continually branded our rulers with the imputation of French influence," argued Jefferson's supporters, they "cannot produce a single evidence of the accusation."[27] Instead, Madison had worked tirelessly for the entire nation. The Embargo and Non-Intercourse Acts had been enacted "to save from the grasp of the belligerent powers the property of our merchants." The Madison administration, according to Republicans, "has invariably stood up for the merchants, and the merchants have invariably deserted the government." If they were unwilling to accept the help of the government, "let the brawlers at Boston and elsewhere manifest as much zeal against the wrongs of the English . . . as they do against the measures of their own [people]."[28] While the Federalists attacked Madison from their position of comfort and failed to come up with a plan of their own, "the American government will never lose sight of this business, till our seamen are released." Despite opposition claims, pro-war Republicans argued that an aggressive approach and likely war with England were the only way to secure American liberty.[29]

Reality, however, did not bear out the Republican claim. Even as the War Hawks in Congress built their case for war, British officials continued to soften in their position toward the United States. Two days before the declaration of war, the British foreign secretary rescinded the Orders in Council and shortly thereafter removed nearly all British limitations on American shipping. Despite British efforts, the United States declared war on England on June 18, 1812.³⁰

For many Federalists, the increasing Republican bellicosity represented a move toward tyranny—more an effort to destroy political opposition than a genuine attempt to protect American liberty. Violence against Federalist newspapers in the first year of the war seemed to confirm the minority party's worst fears. Baltimore's *Federal Republican* was one of the first targets of Republican animus. In the days leading up to the war, rumors circulated throughout Baltimore that the Federalist paper would be forcefully shut down if the editors did not moderate their anti-war stance. Despite the threats, the *Federal Republican* refused to yield, noting that if by giving in to Republican bullying, "a war would put the constitution and civil rights to sleep. Those who commenced it, would become dictators and despots, and the people their slaves."³¹ In June of 1812, the *Federal Republican* denounced the war as folly, "WAR AT HAND—As prelude to their approaching fall. God in his mercy has deprived our rulers of their senses."³² The paper published a series of editorials critical of the declaration of war, noting on numerous occasions not only the unjust nature of the conflict but the lack of preparation on the part of the federal government to fight a war. Baltimore Republicans promptly made good on their threats of violence. On June 22, 1812, a mob headed by a French apothecary named Philip Lewis destroyed the printing office of the *Federal Republican*.³³

Evoking the violence of the French Revolution, the Baltimore attack struck fear into the hearts of Federalists throughout the United States. Opposition papers throughout the country reprinted accounts of the attack and denounced the violence. One paper labeled the riots in Baltimore "almost equal in enormity to the barbarities exercised by the French blood drinkers."³⁴ Another noted that the Baltimore mob acted with the "characteristick cruelty and wickedness of Frenchmen."³⁵ Many Baltimore Federalists left town, while those who stayed in the city remained silent. "We were fearful of muttering our sentiments," remembered one Federalist, "lest we in turn might be attacked." Following the assaults in Baltimore, Republican mobs in Georgia and Pennsylvania attacked respectively the Savannah *American Patriot* and the Norristown *Herald*, destroying both papers. Other Federalist newspapers around the country received warnings to change their tone on the war or suffer attack.³⁶ The *Connecticut Courant* interpreted these attacks as revealing the Republicans' true intentions for going to war: "We now see, written in bloody characters, by what means disaffection must cease. The war, pretendedly for the freedom of the seas, is valiantly waged against the freedom of the press."[37] To the Federalists, the Baltimore riots and the attacks that followed around the country represented a real threat to the United States. The riots against Federalist newspapers were not simply an assault on Federalist opposition, they were strike against the basic freedoms of all Americans. The tumultuous rabble in Baltimore did not represent the extra-legal mobs of Anglo American tradition but rather the bloodthirsty murderers of the French Revolution. These attacks on the press seemed to validate every fear that many Federalists held concerning the growing Republican abuse of federal power.[38]

In the winter of 1813, when Congress authorized James Madison to pursue a policy of "retaliation" in the treatment of American prisoners, many Federalists saw this new policy as another step in the march toward tyranny. The policy declared that "the President of the United States is hereby authorized to cause full and ample retaliation to be done and executed on such British subjects, soldiers, seamen or marines or Indians, in alliance or connection with Great Britain, being prisoners of war."[39] Many Republicans offered their full support of the policy, arguing that such a policy would be the "Aegis—which shall protect all who fight under our banners."[40] Federalists, on the other hand, saw this measure as another horrifying sign that the United States was abandoning its founding principles and heading down the path to tyranny. One Federalist newspaper labeled Madison the "Emperour of America" and warned that the policy of retaliation would be most felt by American prisoners in the hands of the British.[41]

The motivation for the Madison administration's policy of retaliation was the fate of twenty-three naturalized American citizens captured during the Battle of Queenston Heights on the Niagara River along the border between New York and Ontario. In early October 1812, Major General Stephen Van Rensselaer led an American force of more than six thousand troops across the river into Canada. In fairly short order the Americans managed to seize control of the heights, drive the British forces from their position, and withstand a counterattack. The Americans then positioned six hundred U.S. troops, under the command of Lieutenant Colonel Winfield Scott, on Queenston

Heights. Van Rensselaer, hoping to strengthen his position, ordered the New York militia across the Niagara River to reinforce the American gains. The militiamen refused, countering that, as state militia, they were not required to cross an international border. Without reinforcement, Scott's unit was abandoned to a British counteroffensive and was soon forced to surrender. Known as the Battle of Queenston Heights, the engagement had initially appeared to be an American victory, but the final result was the capture of some 950 stranded and surrounded American soldiers.[42]

As prisoners of war, the Americans had little to fear in late 1812. Although there had been some reports of the mistreatment of sailors captured as prisoners of war and sent to England, soldiers captured in land battles could expect their exchange in relatively short order. Most of the officers were granted parole almost immediately after their capture and allowed to return to the United States, while the enlisted men were transferred to Quebec to await their exchange. Within a matter of weeks, British and American agents agreed to terms of exchange; the Americans at Quebec would be transported to Boston. Shortly before their departure, however, a group of British officers boarded the vessel bound for Boston and ordered the American prisoners to muster on deck. The officers proceeded to question each of the American prisoners, and those who spoke with an Irish accent were separated from the rest. If determined to be Irish, the men were to be sent to England, where they would stand trial for treason. The officers identified twenty-three Irishmen before General Scott emerged from below deck to inquire into the cause of the commotion. When learning the cause, he commanded the remaining Americans to be absolutely silent in order to prevent any further questioning by the British officers. Although Scott's men obeyed, his order came too late for the Irish-born Americans, who were herded aboard a frigate, clamped in irons, and taken to England.[43]

The fate of these twenty-three naturalized citizens, transported to England to stand trial for treason, sparked a national debate. Royal officials argued that despite these soldiers' claim of American citizenship, they had been born in the United Kingdom and were therefore liable to treatment as traitors to the crown. When news of the British action reached Washington, President Madison and congressional Republicans authorized a policy of retaliation against British prisoners of war in American detention.

Echoing Patriot efforts during the American Revolution, Republicans celebrated the new policy while simultaneously taking the opportunity to decry British brutality. Writing from New York, "Tit for Tat" noted that "the necessity of retaliation is ever to be regretted, and its practice to be avoided, if not absolutely necessary for the purposes of self-preservation. Retaliation, it must however be observed, is often beneficial: it prevents war, it mitigates war, it shortens war." Tit for Tat went as far as to argue that if a policy of retaliation had been put in place during the years leading to the war, the conflict itself might have been avoided. Anticipating opposition to the policy, Tit for Tat argued that "an ill-timed humanity . . . tends to embolden the enemy. Retaliation of every cruelty will render the instances of cruelty fewer."[44] Other supporters of retaliation contended that American soldiers were being held captive by "British savages, by men who have no sense of honor & who are callous to the feelings of humanity." Given the inhumanity of the British captors, a policy of retaliation seemed to be the only available course of action. "Hostages (naval commanders if possible) ought to be detained in close confinement. . . . Painful as retaliation is, it is a duty, and nothing else will teach Englishmen to treat their prisoners according to the usage of civilized nations."[45] The *Baltimore American* hoped that the American government would make full use of the policy:

> We trust that the government will rigidly pursue this system until the British officers and government may become sensible of the policy, if they are insensible to the benevolence of treating the American prisoners as human beings and equals. A similar proceeding for the future security of our seamen, who may fall into the enemy's hands, is loudly called for by justice and the public voice.[46]

To the Republicans, retaliation was a necessary tool to be employed to counterbalance British cruelty and to bring an end to the war. Such action, they insisted, was both just and popular. Beyond citing contemporary British cruelties and the demands of the "public voice," some Republicans cited historical precedent.

Republicans who supported the policy of retaliation saw this stand against the British threat to the Irish Americans as a natural outgrowth of George Washington's policies during the War of American Independence. The *Essex Register* declared, "This mode of retaliating upon the enemy has produced good effects on former occasions, and we trust that a speedy release of our unfortunate countrymen so cruelly and unjustly confined by the enemy, will be the immediate result of this spirited measure of our Government."[47] Other supporters of retaliation noted that "our government is called upon to act with resolution," to march forward with "an unyielding determination to retaliate!

Such a system had the happiest effects during the revolutionary war."⁴⁸ In Vermont, the *Green-Mountain Farmer* recalled, "In the time of our revolutionary struggle, the inflexibility of Washington obtained its object." As Washington demonstrated to all Americans, "the right of dealing a righteous retaliation has been vested in some measure with the President" and "in the present contest our government are exhibiting the inflexibility of Washington." The results of this decisiveness was that an "approving Heaven has smiled propitiously, and hitherto granted the same success."⁴⁹ Finally, the Newark *Centinel* reported:

> In the revolutionary war general WASHINGTON adopted the principles of *retaliation*. When gen. Lee was taken a prisoner and confined as a "*deserter* from their service," lieut. Col. Campbell, with *five* Hessian field officers, were selected and detained. And when capt. Huddy was hung by the *tories* in Monmouth county, Washington resolved on retaliation for this "deliberate murder," and "capt. Argile was designated by lot for this purpose." These spirited retaliations of the American nation had a salutary effect *then;*—we believe they will have the same happy effect *now!*⁵⁰

Citing British cruelty and historical precedent, Republicans supported the policy of retaliation as a necessary and justified course of action. This policy, the Republican newspaper explained, was as American as the Revolution itself.

Again, in the manner of the Revolution, Congress formed a special committee to report on "the spirit and manner in which war has been waged by the enemy." In a series of hearings, the committee "collected and arranged all the testimony on this subject that could at this time be procured." The testimony provided Congress with a litany of charges against the British, including the "Bad treatment of American prisoners" and the "Massacre and burning of American prisoners surrendered to officers of Great Britain by Indians in the British service." Based on this testimony, the committee concluded that "the British government has adopted a rigor of regulation" showing "instances of a departure from the customary rules of war by the selection and confinement in close prisons of particular persons." Sections of the committee's findings were reported and printed in newspapers around the country; a complete copy of the hearings was published in 1813. The full report went through two more printings by 1814.⁵¹

Republicans made their case for retaliation in both official and popular channels, arguing that reports of British "barbarities" and historical precedent offered justification for a policy that most agreed was a regrettable course of action. But Federalists still saw a nation edging toward tyranny.

Following Republican riots against opposition newspapers, many Federalists feared that the authorization of a policy of retaliation was just another step toward the complete destruction of America's constitutional values and the emergence of a Napoleon-style dictatorship in the United States, with James Madison at its head.

The core of the Federalists' argument was that President Madison had no right to retaliate against England for seizing twenty-three of its own citizens. They saw as a violation of international law Madison's efforts to interfere with the British right to try these soldiers. According to one Federalist, "the case is very simple. The British have taken 23 of their own subjects, fighting in the enemy ranks against their own country; and as this is a crime punishable with death by the laws of all civilized nations, these men have been sent home to be tried for the fact."[52] Madison's response to this simple case was seen by many Federalists, as well as by legal and military authorities in England, as a fundamental misinterpretation of international law. The *London Courier* asked: "Who is MR. MADISON, and WHAT IS AMERICA, that the public law of Europe should be changed at their fiat and for their convenience? By the chicanery of American naturalization the United States have endeavored to destroy at once the principle of natural law which has been recognized and acted upon in every other state." Citing Blackstone, the *London Courier* argued, "It is a principle of universal law . . . that the natural born subject of one prince, cannot, by any act of his own, no, not by swearing allegiance to another, put off, or discharge his natural allegiance to the former."[53]

Many Federalist critics argued that Madison's efforts were not made in defense of American values but in violation of international law. Rather than appearing as a defender of American liberty the policy of retaliation made Madison no better than the lawless Napoleon. The *Rhode Island American* charged Madison with acting "in imitation of the French Emporour," while in Boston, the *Repertory* labeled Madison "the Emperor of America."[54] If the president continued to act in this way—ignoring international law—he would only hurt U.S. standing in the larger Atlantic world. "The prisoners in possession of the enemy, if the facts alleged be true, are traitors, and have forfeited their lives by laws of nations," the *Evening Post* remarked. "If Mr. Madison proceeds in the course he has taken, he will find the whole civilized world united against him, with the solitary exception of even Bonaparte himself."[55] This was not nationalism, the president's critics contended, but a vain and ill-advised power grab, which was harming the entire nation.

In an essay printed in the Boston *Repertory*, the Federalists charged that Madison was trying to "make the world believe two things, and Bonaparte flatly contradicts him in both." The first of Madison's claims contended "that it is inconsistent in G. Britain to *naturalize* the subjects of other countries, and yet to forbid their own subjects from bearing arms against her when naturalized abroad. Bonaparte says there is nothing at all inconsistent in this. The grant of naturalization is confined to privileges within your own territory only." Madison's second claim charged that Britain "claims to hang all Englishmen found in arms against her. Bonaparte says, crime or no crime, it is what I will do to every scoundrel Frenchman whom I shall so take, let him be naturalized or not." The *Repertory* went on to cite French law stating that "Frenchmen *naturalized* abroad EVEN with our permission, can at no time carry arms against France under pain of being indicted in our courts and condemned to . . . death." Madison, the Federalists charged, had violated international law, under which even Napoleon operated his government and military. A repudiation of the law of nations, "Mr. Madison's new and cruel principle of retaliation . . . is to be the means of laying our cities to ashes."[56] Federalists saw the policy of retaliation as a threat not just to American prisoners, who might suffer at British hands, but to the entire nation, which would see all the world turned against it as a result of the president's despicable, inhumane policy.

The *Boston Daily Advertiser* advised, "Nothing can exceed the horror and barbarity of the system of *retaliation now going on*. In the nineteenth century, to find men adding willfully to all the complicated, unavoidable horrors of war, a system of refined cruelty which would have disgraced the most barbarous nation, is, indeed lamentable." Madison's pursuit of the policy of "retaliation without cause, is responsible for all the sufferings, all the bloodshed, all the desolated cities and other calamities which may ensue." There could be no debate about the twenty-three soldiers on trial in London, the *Boston Daily Advertiser* claimed. "Allegiance is perpetual" as evidenced by the case of Mr. D, "a merchant of London," who "was duly naturalized, was a free holder and voter in Boston," and "went back to his native country and without any *new* act, became a freeholder and burgess or freeman of London." Such evidence seemed to suggest "very logical[ly] and very clear[ly] we are aggressors, or rather Mr. Madison is, and must be responsible both to his country, and to God for all the blood which may be shed and all the misery which may be produced by this system."[57] In Providence, the *Rhode Island Gazette* claimed, "It is evidently the intention of Mr. Madison to make the war popular by sacrificing the lives of our fellow citizens." In response to the policy of retaliation, "the British threaten to retaliate *in extenso*, by hanging two for one." Madison planned "to save the lives of traitors. . . . Mr. M is to sacrifice the lives of honest native born Americans. His motives are evident. We say that these things are done for no other purpose than to widen the breach between the two countries—But we hope the people will turn their indignation upon those who are endeavoring to entail on them the miseries of a protracted war." Federalists feared that the policy of retaliation was little more than Madison's political ploy to prop up and expand the war against England.[58]

In addition to attacking the policy of retaliation on legal grounds, the Federalists also questioned what impact this policy might have on British-held prisoners who actually were American citizens. According to the *New York Evening Post*, Madison himself explained that the policy of retaliation "would be to return a specific injury, equivalent to the injury received." If equal treatment was the president's aim, the *Post* argued, "clearly then, what he could do in this case, and *all* he could do, would be to seize an equal number of American prisoners, who had been fighting in the enemy's ranks within the U. States, and who had been naturalized and become English *adopted citizens*." Instead, to "retaliate for this, the president has seized upon an equal number of men, against whom nothing can be alleged from any quarter." In acting in such a manner, the *Post* argued, Madison was placing the "crimes of the guilty on the heads of the innocent, and he shall press and execute the prisoners he has seized." Madison's conduct was "nothing short of MURDER."[59]

Such behavior, the Federalists apprehended, would open the way to mass cruelty on both sides of the conflict. The *Boston Gazette* charged, "This system, once begun, there will be no end to it. Great Britain has taken many more prisoners than we have—If we hang and shoot, they will hang and shoot." The outcome of retaliation would be "the natives of this country . . . butchered like cattle, merely for the sake of protecting British and Irish traitors."[60] The *Federal Republican*, publishing from Georgetown, reiterated its opposition: the policy of retaliation would trigger a "progressive series of Barbarities," in which "there will be but a momentary interval before the ordinary treatment of prisoners must be exchanged, as respects all, for the modes in which they are enslaved, immured, and deprived of life by nations over whom civilization has not dawned." These cruelties would be applied, according to the *Federal Republican*, "to the whole number of prisoners in

[British] possession, 1500, said to be." In addition to their promise to retaliate against all American prisoners, the *Federal Republican* reported, the British also threatened "destruction to all our exposed cities, towns, and villages," if the policy of retaliation continued. "We are now threatened with the destroying vengeance of [British] fleets, if our government persists in the course of retaliation."[61]

A letter in the *Boston Spectator* admonished Madison for placing the United States and Great Britain on a course to "exhibit a novel specimen of ferocity in their warfare" and that if "principles, held sacred for more than 300 years, are to be violated—if two nations, descended from common ancestors, breathing the same spirit of freedom, and professing the same religion are to be forced into a contest of unmeasured cruelty, there are men in this country who will deserve, and receive from the moderate, humane, and intelligent of both nations, a full share of censure, if not execration." According to the *Boston Spectator*, Madison's policy had destroyed centuries of legal and ethical principles, all for the sake of British traitors.[62]

The *Salem Gazette* offered direct evidence of the British perspective on the retaliation law republishing a column from the "London Sun, a ministerial paper generally distinguished for its moderation." The *Sun* reported that the American Congress had vested in "JAMES MADISON, a power to torture or murder British prisoners of war! Our indignation is so great, that we can scarcely find terms to reprobate this unparalleled instance of daring effrontery and atrocious injustice." The *Sun* declared that England, "proud of her rank among nations, vigorous, high in character, and clothed in strength," would tolerate no such actions or behavior. The American policy was more "desperately wicked" than any "entertained by any legal government in a civilized country. Under the authority thus granted, there is no cruelty that may not be committed, and when committed, justified." This legislation sanctioning retaliation made Madison little different from "BONAPARTE," putting "the lives of British subjects at his mercy, with no security but the caprice of the hostile head of a hostile faction." The policy of retaliation was utterly without civilized precedent. For "no law of nations—no principle consistent either with the original and indefeasible rights of man, or with the modified privileges which result from the social compact can sanction or even palliate them." If the Americans pursued the policy of retaliation, the *Sun* warned, there would be dire consequences:

> Be it at the peril of America if she dare for this to touch a hair of a British head—Her rulers have provoked and sought the combat, and she must submit to the evils they have thus brought upon her people. But if an Englishman is made to suffer one pain or penalty in consequence of this Act, we would raise our voice (if possible in thunder) to denounce the Government which did not instantly take tenfold vengeance in retaliating upon the guilty—for to hesitate a moment would be barbarity and not mercy.

The *London Sun*'s forceful denunciation of the American policy of retaliation and the threatened British response to it suggested that Federalist concern for the fate of American captives in British hands was well warranted.[63]

Another Federalist challenged the sincerity of Republicans' concern for American sailors. Writing in New York's *Evening Post*, this Federalist turned the calls for an end to impressment back on the Republicans who supported the policy of retaliation. If Republican "whining was anything but the grossest affectation, it would not be thus confined to the case of impressment; it would extend itself to the cases of real American prisoners in close confinement; cases, equally entitled to commiseration, at least." If Republican compassion for the plight of American citizens was real, the author argued, "these men would fill the ears of government with just reproaches for most inhumanly neglecting to provide relief for American prisoners in confinement, by sending off all the English prisoners in their possession in exchange." The brutal treatment of Americans could be prevented, according to this author, if only Republicans cared more about the safety of American citizens than they did about carrying on war with England.[64]

One of the most effective techniques in drawing attention to the danger of retaliation was employing the letters of American prisoners themselves. Those of two Americans held in Quebec were a key component of the Federalist critique of retaliation. The first letter, dated November 17, 1813, repudiated the "inhuman operation of the unchristian principle of RETALIATION." The author explained that he was "now in close confinement." As an American, the author stated, he would "willingly yield of his life" in the "service of his country." However, he felt the "deepest mortification and pain, mingled with the most poignant indignation," that he would lose his life for "transient" and "disaffected" foreigners. He now anticipated that his unnecessary confinement and potential execution marked "the beginning of the approaching catastrophe, by which the proud American will be disgraced."[65]

Another American prisoner in Quebec reported that he too was "now in close confinement in the Gaol of this City, as an hostage for some renegade Irishmen and Englishmen, deserters from the British army, and traitors to their country . . . for such villains I am now suffering the hardships and horrors of a Gaol, shut out from every comfort and blessing of society." The prisoner's only hope for his safe return was "if the question of retaliation be decided without further acts of violence . . . but if it is carried to the extremity of ferocity, I have no hopes ever to see my country or friends again— Remember sweet little Mercia [His only child]." In an editorial comment at the end of the letter, "MILITADES" remarked, "If there is any true-born American that can read this letter and not sincerely sympathize with the writer and his country, in the situation in which we are brought, of having real Americans imprisoned and exposed to be executed for British deserters, renegadoes, and traitors, I cannot but believe he has lost his *country's honor in foreign partialities.*" The employment of letters written by the captives one of the most powerful tools available to the Federalists. This approach drew on a long-standing American tradition that stretched as far back as the captivity narratives of early New England. Letters from—or the voices of—American prisoners suffering as a result of U.S. retaliation put on the divisive political debate a human face that no appeal to history or policy could equal.[66]

In both the House and Senate, Federalists tried to limit Madison's power of retaliation. In December 1813, the Federalist minority proposed legislation that would require the president to lay before Congress "all the evidence in his possession relative to the commencement, progress, and present state of the system of retaliation upon the prisoners of war to which the governments of the U. States and G. Britain have lately resorted."[67] In support of this legislation, Representative John Lovett of New York observed, "It is a fact, as notorious as lamentable, that the government of the United States has entered upon a broad system of retaliation upon prisoners of war—that rapid strides in that system have already been made towards a very serious, and possibly, fatal result." As a result of this policy, "many individuals are already deprived of their personal liberty, and in strong solicitude, are awaiting an uncertain fate. In every point of view, the subject of retaliation is important." Such an important issue could not be left to the president alone. Lovett stated: "It is the solemn duty of the house to examine with profound attention the ground we are advancing upon. . . . The voice of the nation and humanity . . . [implore Congress to] thoroughly investigate the business." Lovett and the other Federalist members of Congress saw themselves as one of the last bulwarks of

American liberty and principles against Madison's capricious tyranny. Federalist opposition to the Madison administration was an attempt to define the American president as the greatest threat to American liberty in the nation.[68]

The growing Federalist concerns over the issue of retaliation and expanded federal authority reached a boiling point in Worcester, Massachusetts, in December 1813. At the heart of the issue was the close confinement of ten previously paroled British officers to a "common gaol" in the Massachusetts town. These ten British officers had established themselves in the community and made friends with the its many Federalists. Most prominent of these friendships was that between British officer Charles Morris and local Federalist newspaperman Isaiah Thomas. In response to the confinement of these officers, Thomas and many of Worcester's most-distinguished citizens immediately denounced the draconian policy as further evidence of the Madison administration's abuse of federal power. The Worcester Federalists directed much of their ire toward James Prince, the U.S. marshal responsible for enforcing the policy in his federal district. Prince housed the British prisoners under close confinement in the Worcester jail. The conditions were a far cry from their earlier liberties. The ten officers shared only two cells, which were equipped with the most meager furnishings. When a group of local Federalists visited the jail, they found the prisoners

> suffering extremely from the dampness and impurity of the air, and the severity of the weather, it being one of the coldest nights of the present season. On examining the provisions which had been made for their lodging, we found that bags of dirty straw, with filthy and offensive rugs, had been taken from the common stock of the prison and thrown on the floor, without sheet or a blanket for their covering, and without a chair or any other furniture for their accommodation.

In addition to the poor conditions in the cells, the visitors claimed to have witnessed "a boisterous and declamatory harangue" from Marshal Prince "about the sufferings on board the Jersey prison ship and the barbarities inflicted upon American prisoners during the present war." Many of the Worcester Federalists believed that these outbursts were intended to convince the British prisoners that they would soon be hung in retaliation for all previous British abuse of American prisoners. Those sympathetic to the condition of the British officers were incensed by the mistreatment of men—educated, refined, and gallant—whom they had befriended. In their view, Madison's policy was a gross abuse of federal power.⁶⁹

News of events in Worcester soon spread beyond the town and incited the indignation of Federalists throughout the country. Running under the headline, "Retaliation with a Vengeance!" an article in the *Massachusetts Spy* reported that "the unfortunate gentlemen . . . are made subjects of . . . a retaliatory measure." Such policies employed by the Americans and the British, the *Spy* lamented, suggested a "time that both nations should cease to boast of their refinement and humanity; and acknowledge that the days of Gothick barbarity have returned."⁷⁰ The paper also included coverage of a gathering of the Worcester Federalists "to consider of something for the comfort of the British Officers, lately confined in gaol," and called into question "the right of the Marshal to make use of the gaol . . . without permission" from the town. The *Spy*'s coverage was quickly reprinted in Federalist newspapers all along the East Coast.⁷¹

As the criticism of the federal actions in Worcester spread through the country, Republicans rushed to challenge the Federalist interpretation of events, questioning their political rivals' patriotism in the process. The Republican *Baltimore Patriot* charged that the "*Worcester (Mass.) Gazette*" (also published as the *Massachusetts Spy*) was "the most infamous publication, which we have ever seen, out of the columns of the '*Common Sewer*.'" Furthermore, the editor of the *Patriot* charged, the Federalist editors who had cried foul at the close confinement of British officers had forgotten "the three thousand enslaved American seamen" and "the victims of the Indians. . . . This cold-blooded toryism is too contemptible to be tolerated." The *Patriot* also singled out the "virulent abuse of the government" that appeared in the *Massachusetts Spy* and that "was intended to please some eight or ten British prisoners." The Massachusetts Federalists "talk about '*conquest*,' '*butcheries*,' '*Alexander*,' '*Caesar*,' '*Napoleon*,' &c." and bark that the president had no clear goal for the war. Such attacks, replied the Republicans, contained "not one word of truth." Instead, "the President rests his reasons of the war on its *original, declared objects*." The Patriot doubted the Federalists' loyalty to their nation and wondered aloud to what "pitch of insolence have the tories risen in their strong-holds; and to what depth of infamy have their characters sunk?" The imprisonment of British officers in the Worcester jail gave both Federalists and Republicans fodder for their partisan attacks. Federalists indicted the Madison administration for cruelty and Republicans impugned the patriotism and loyalty of Federalist dissenters.[72]

To Federalists, however, the imprisonment of the British officers was far more than a wartime measure. Many in Worcester saw the U.S. marshal's usurpation of the town jail as yet another effort by the Madison administration to expand federal power at the expense of that states, counties, and municipalities. The *Massachusetts Spy* highlighted the Republican threat to local control when it compared the conduct of federal officials in Massachusetts and Kentucky as they dealt with prisoners of war. In "the *patriotic state of Kentucky*," federal authorities observed "nice and scrupulous regard to *her* rights, as a sovereign independent state ... in imprisonment of the [British] officers recently paroled at *Frankfort*. No secret order is issued to the marshal, commanding him to lock them up in the first gaol to be found, without asking permission of the sheriff." Running completely contrary to the highhanded legal process in Worcester, "a respectful letter is addressed by the secretary of state (under the direction of the president) to the chief magistrate of Kentucky, requesting that he would give facility to the execution of the order." Following this federal request, the governor of Kentucky, "not considering his power sufficient to authorize any such appropriation," turned to the commonwealth's legislature to secure its approval "by legislative act" the request of the president to house the prisoners. The *Spy* groused, "Such is the comity practiced by the president, towards the great and patriotick state of Kentucky—while the paltry reprobate state of Massachusetts is treated with as much contempt, as the little republic of St. Marino, was treated by his great prototype, Napoleon, in carving out kingdoms and empires for his royal brothers, sisters, and cousins!" By contrasting the proceedings of the federal government in Kentucky with those in Worcester, Massachusetts, Federalists sought to demonstrate that the Madison administration was expanding its authority at the expense of individual liberties and local control and that the president was becoming an emperor in the mode of Napoleon.[73]

The initial public outcry in Worcester managed to secure for the British prisoners jailed there improved conditions including limited freedom to leave their cells during the day. But their future was far from certain. The arrival of two military carriages in the second week of January raised concerns that the British prisoners were about to be transported out of Worcester and away from the protection of the local Federalists. Indeed, fearing a change of locale, the British officers planned their escape. On the night of January 12, when the jailkeeper arrived to lock the jail for the night, the officers seized him and grabbed his pistol, threatening to shoot him if he made the least noise. They then bound and gagged him, before making their escape into the night. Eventually the jailer escaped his bindings and raised the alarm. The town was thrown into great commotion "as if the whole British army had descended upon it." Isaiah Thomas later recalled: "Canon were fired in the night, and the bells rang an alarm—Barns, cellars and houses [were] searched for them, but none were found concealed therein. Mine among others." Five of the officers were recaptured the following night in Barre, twenty miles north of Worcester; the remaining officers managed to flee north and escape into Canada.[74]

Marshal Prince in Worcester immediately posted a "reward of FIVE HUNDRED DOLLARS to any person or persons who may apprehend, detain, and deliver over the nine British Prisoners to the Marshal or his Deputy of any District." Prince offered an additional five hundred dollars to anyone "having knowledge of . . . treacherous conduct" that "may lead to a conviction of the traitors." Prince believed that the officers had help and that he knew exactly who these traitors were. In a letter published by the *Boston Patriot*, he charged that "the unpleasantness" of the circumstances surrounding the imprisonment of the British officers in Worcester "was increased by the rude and inflamed conduct and language of the Hon. Francis Blake, who most singularly stated himself to be the *counsel for the prisoners of war.*" Prince accused Blake of interfering in federal business and explained that Blake "doubted the rights to confine them, outrageously abased the National Government in their bearing and openly declared [that] '*he was ready for rebellion when British field officers were arrested.*'" Blake's behavior was all the more outrageous, according to Prince, for he was "FORGETTING THAT OUR OWN COUNTRYMEN OF EQUAL RANK . . . WERE RUDELY AND UNFEELINGLY CONFINED WITH NOT HALF THE CONVENIENCES OR ACCOMODATIONS WHICH THESE PRISONERS WERE ABOUT TO RECEIVE." Prince saw Blake's behavior as a strong indication that he had aided the escape of the British prisoners. To Prince and many other Republicans, the Federalists were traitors, untrustworthy citizens who had turned against their own nation in the war with Britain.[75]

Prince went on to explain that the British officers would be confined under the best possible conditions that "the very friendly feelings of the Sheriff, his Deputy, the underkeeper and the HONORABLE MR BLAKE could suggest." Defending the humanity and ethics of the Madison administration, the marshal explained, "The prisoners were put into Debtors', and not Criminals' apartments. Three dollars and fifty cents for each per week was [*sic*] applied to their use by the government which sum supplied them with every luxury the country *affords*. Good feather beds, and blankets were procured for them." Prince's description of the prison conditions at Worcester was his attempt to undercut the criticism of the Madison administration and to demonstrate that the Federalist press had skewed the facts in its portrayal of conditions endured by British officers in American prisons.[76]

Francis Blake immediately fired back at Prince's charges. His letter, addressed "to the public," Blake stated that the "false and slanderous communication from the Marshal of this District published in the 'Boston Patriot' ... imperiously demands from me a reply." In recounting the events that transpired when Prince arrived with the captured British officers, Blake stated that he "civilly requested the Marshal (having then no cause of irritation against him) that he would be kind enough to communicate the authority by which the British officers were to be closely confined." According to Blake, Prince took an uncivil tone and "rudely and petulantly answered that the officers were prisoners of war, *that he was representing the President of the United States* and that he should exhibit no evidence of his authority, either to the prisoners or their friends." As for Prince's accusation that Blake supported rebellion, "it can scarcely be necessary to pronounce this A BASE AND MALICIOUS INFAMOUS FALSEHOOD!" Blake suggested that anyone who might be swayed to believe Prince because of the status of his office only need ask any of the other "respectable gentlemen who were present during our whole conversation," and they would verify that he had never uttered such sentiments.[77]

Blake also challenged "the vile and infamous libel upon some of the citizens of Worcester, contained in the 'inflated' and ridiculous 'PROCLOMATIONS' of President Prince." Blake categorized the Marshal as "a bloated pensioner upon the public sufferings, assuming the authority of the chief magistrate, and dealing out his Five Hundred Dollars to Spies and Informers, as bounty upon perjury, and encouragement to cut-throat scoundrels, to proscribe and persecute their fellow citizens." All this pomposity, according to Blake, was "a spectacle as hideous as was ever presented in the bloodiest period of the French revolution." On a personal level, Blake noted that he had "already had the horror of a domiciliary visit at midnight, and my house has been searched from the garret to the cellar, in pursuit of the prisoners I am accused of '*secreting.*'" It seemed to Blake that Prince must have been "in Paris when proscription and massacre were the daily amusements of the populace" and that the marshal must have been "an assiduous pupil in the school of Robespierre." The conflicting accounts sketched by Blake and Prince interwove national politics with personal honor and demonstrated the long reach of the retaliation policy into local affairs and personal lives—the most-basic ingredients of politics—during the war.[78]

In the *Massachusetts Spy,* "THOUSANDS" saw the dispute between Blake and Prince as symptomatic of the larger Republican effort to discredit all Federalists and paint them as traitors. He observed, "It was to be expected that the escape of the British officers confined in the gaol in this town, would be made use of, to excite the suspicion and indignation of the publick against the federalists." Despite the "false" and "unjust" nature of these charges, which "will readily be admitted . . . by men of either party, who from their personal knowledge, have had the means of judging," the scandalous charges of treason were "just what was to be expected from the unprincipled partiality of a democratick editor." In attacking Blake, Thousands charged, Prince and his Republican supporters had "unjustly aspersed the character of thousands of other men, equally 'friendly,' not to the escape, but to the human treatment of prisoners of war." In the face of Republican attacks which painted any opposition to the war as treason and Toryism, Federalists continued to fear for their rights and for the legacy of the American Revolution. As the power of the federal government continued to expand during the war, many Federalists feared the rise of tyranny.[79]

In the wake of the Worcester escape, the pseudonymous "HAMPDEN" published in the *Baltimore Patriot* an open address to James Madison: "SIR—I approach you with the respect which is due to the Chief Magistrate of a Republic and that frankness which becomes a faithful citizen." Hampden applauded Madison for his conduct during course of the war and the fulfillment of his duty in applying the policy of retaliation. That being said, Hampden asked whether the state of Massachusetts had a right to "interfere, and to measure and adjust the retaliation." He argued that "in the case in question, this was done. The Marshal was abused in the exercise of his proper duties. The Britons have escaped." The actions of Massachusetts represented the "*interference of a state authority in contravention of the authority of the United States.* To a mind rich in historical information, it is needless to suggest that tolerated encroachments are the stepping stones of usurpation. It is unnecessary, likewise to add, that a spark of disaffection, blown by insolence, and fed by passion, may spread into a flame of rebellion." With such insolence in Massachusetts, Hampden suggested, these events might "require the strong arm of government to control." Hampden's advice to the president confirmed many Federalist fears. Although Madison had refrained from reviving the Sedition Act of 1798, his administration made use of the Alien Enemies Act passed the same year and still in effect in 1812. Although enforcement was relatively lax during the first year of the conflict, during the next two these restrictions became increasingly stringent. To the Federalists, the threat of tyranny was omnipresent in American society.[80]

The five officers who were recaptured in Barre on the night of their escape were transferred to the reliably Republican town of Pittsfield on January 15 and moved again to the Philadelphia Penitentiary in March. After another failed escape attempt in April of 1814, the officers were finally released, when it was reported that the naturalized American soldiers were being treated as prisoners of war rather than traitors. Officers on both sides were again released on parole. Francis Blake, despite Prince's suspicions, was never officially charged with any crime. Three men in Barre were arrested in early February on suspicion of having aided the escaped prisoners but never brought to trial following a general exchange of prisoners of war that spring.[81]

While the furor over the Worcester escape eventually subsided and both the prisoners and those charged with aiding them were allowed to go free, the larger debate over federal power still churned in American politics. In February 1814, the Massachusetts General Court passed an act forbidding the use of state prisons by the federal government to house its detainees or convicts. In Taneytown, Maryland, Federalists gathered to celebrate "the late victories of the allied armies over Bonaparte," toasted "the Heroes of '76—Men who dared to be honest in the worst of times," "the Minority in Congress," "the Constitution of the United States—May the storms of party zeal never overleap its SACRED LIMITS," and called for "A speedy restoration, without retaliation, of the American captives."[82]

The Federalist response to the Madison administration's policy of impressment represented the evolution of the party's ideology, their understanding of the role of federal authority, and the fear that the United States was sliding toward tyranny. Beginning with the Jay Treaty in 1795, Federalists had begun to understand the importance of public sentiment or opinion. In the years that followed, especially following the election of 1800, Federalists continued to expand their commitment to the use of a "cultural politics" to make their voices heard on the national stage.[83] In challenging the policy of retaliation, Federalists employed all the skills that they had developed in the years since the ratification of the Jay Treaty to challenge the Madison administration's continued expansion of federal authority. Contrary to categorization of the Federalists as a subversive opposition, in working against the Madison administration and seeking to limit the policy of retaliation, the Federalists believed they were protecting the republican experiment rather than undermining it.[84] Federalists understood their opposition to retaliation as a means of preserving the United States from descending into the chaos of the French Revolution. Although the Federalists had once advanced an aggressively nationalist vision of federal authority, their time in the minority had softened that political program. The debate over the treatment of prisoners during the War of 1812 provides a clear example of this evolution in Federalist thought. By 1812, many Federalists' understanding of American nationalism had evolved to include a more nuanced view of federal power. After the attacks on Federalist newspapers on the East Coast, the policy of retaliation represented a clear example that the Madison administration sought to expand the power of the presidency well beyond its constitutional bounds. These events were made all the more critical by the fact that retaliation threatened the United States' tenuous position in the Atlantic world by violating international law and, at a more practical level, endangering the lives of all American prisoners in British hands.

Drawing on the lesson of the previous decade, even as Republicans boldly staked out an increasingly strident nationalist position, Federalists worked through the American press to influence public sentiment and call for limits to federal power. Although the Federalists sometimes employed extreme or caustic rhetoric, their actions during the course of this debate revealed a widespread effort to protect the American experiment rather than a chaotic campaign to destroy the Union and bring the United States under the control of England. In the national debate over the treatment of prisoners of war, the Federalists presented themselves as defenders of American values, not as traitorous Tories defending British interests. This defense of American values culminated with the Hartford Convention. Even when Republicans denounced the convention as a movement toward secession, many

Federalists saw the assembly as an effort to protect their liberties and, given the widespread frustration over the Republican conduct of the war, possibly to reestablish a Federalist presence in national politics. The Harford Convention was, however, ill-timed, and in the wake of the Treaty of Ghent and the American victory at the Battle of New Orleans, Federalist momentum was lost. This turn of events allowed the Republicans, who claimed victory in a "Second War of Independence," to label the Federalists as a party utterly out of step with the nation, even as the Federalists saw themselves as the last line of defense against Madisonian tyranny. Although the Federalists' political fortunes never recovered from the mistimed Hartford Convention, they would continue to develop their skills in shaping public sentiment. In the decades that followed the War of 1812, Federalists worked outside government, in the realm of publishing, printing, and association, to define the culture of the nation.[85]

CHAPTER 7

Mr. Madison's Other War

The Dartmoor Massacre, the End of the Barbary Wars, and American Self-Confidence, 1815–1816

Late in the winter of 1815, reports of Andrew Jackson's victory at New Orleans sparked widespread celebration throughout the United States. In Philadelphia, the *Weekly Aurora* commemorated the "CELEBRATION OF A GLORIOUS VICTORY AND GLORIOUS PEACE." The paper declared that such a victory was "unexampled in military history" and news of this event "could not but fill the heart of every American with exultation and joy."[1] The editor of the *American Advocate* in Hallowell, Maine, remarked that "in after times when the American historian shall detail the Victory of the 8th of January 1815, he will dwell upon it with enthusiasm . . . and involuntarily ejaculate 'O God! Thy arm was here! And not to us, but to thy arm alone, ascribe we all.'"[2] From Williamsburg, Ohio, came the hope that Jackson's victory had "redeemed" American shores "from the desolating visits of *His Majesty's* navy."[3]

On the floor of the U.S. House of Representatives, congressmen celebrated the American forces that had been "triumphantly victorious over the conquerors of the conquerors of Europe." Representative Charles Ingersoll of Pennsylvania rhapsodized: "Who does not rejoice that he is not an European! Who is not proud to feel himself an American—our wrongs revenged—our rights recognized."[4] As similar stories and celebrations reverberated throughout the United States, the unease over the near disastrous War of 1812 was displaced by the myth of a glorious American victory.[5]

The jubilation that followed the "miracle" at Ghent and Jackson's victory stood in stark contrast to the national mood only a few months earlier.[6] In the autumn of 1814, the American capital lay in ruins, the British controlled large sections of the New England coast, the nation's banking system lay on the edge of collapse, and the American military seemed to be on the verge of disintegration. The Madison administration was clearly caught up in a conflict that was well beyond its ability to fully comprehend, let alone control.[7] The surprising turn of events in the winter of 1815 fundamentally altered the mood of the nation and allowed Americans to begin mythologizing the war almost immediately after the fighting had concluded. Rather than lingering on the mismanagement and failures of the conflict, Americans remembered the War of 1812 as a defense of national honor and territorial sovereignty—a "Second War of Independence."[8] In celebrating the war as a heroic struggle for liberty, Americans worked to craft a unified national identity not out of some kind of a negative unfreedom but from a sense of self-confidence brought on by the "victory" in the War of 1812. A sense of positive nationalism helped to create a mood of solidarity that opened the way for a new era in American politics, an era free of partisan rancor and any serious foreign threats to American liberty. This mood or sensibility reached its zenith with James Monroe's tour of New England in the summer of 1817. As the newly inaugurated president traveled through what had once been the seat of Federalist power, newspapers throughout Boston remarked that a new "Era of Good Feelings" had begun in the United States and that the "demon of party" had departed, giving way to "a general burst of NATIONAL FEELING."[9]

Although a number of historians have viewed this period of national unity as evidence of a nearly seamless transition from the end of the War of 1812 to the Era of Good Feelings, the path connecting these two periods is not quite as direct and smooth as it seems.[10] The end of the war did indeed create an opportunity for Americans to define themselves as more than anti-British or anti-French—as more than Republican or Federalists. But this feeling of national unity and self-confidence did not completely erase a lingering uncertainty about the place of the United States in on world stage. Events in the Mediterranean and in England during 1815 conspired to bring this lingering unease to the surface, nearly ending the Era of Good Feelings before it could even begin. The renewed crisis with Algiers, which led to the final conflict with the Barbary States, and the Dartmoor Massacre in England presented a real challenge to the new sense of American unity and optimism emergent in the wake of the War of 1812. Although the Madison administration's decisive operation against Algiers helped to diffuse the Mediterranean threat and to preserve the post–New Orleans optimism and unity, the fallout over the death of British-held prisoners of war in Dartmoor prison was not so easily resolved. Instead, reports of the shooting marked a moment of resurgence for American anxiety that had been so common in the previous two decades. An examination of the public response to the Dartmoor Massacre and the final military engagement with the Barbary States reveals that although the end of the War of 1812 was a significant moment unto itself, only after Decatur's final victory in the Mediterranean did the young American republic truly enter a new era of self-confidence and political unity.[11]

The first great test of American postwar unity and national self-confidence was the renewal of hostilities with Algiers. The opening salvo of the latest Mediterranean conflict had actually occurred long before Jackson's victory at New Orleans, in fact just a few weeks after the American declaration of war against England in 1812. With the renewal of Anglo-American hostilities, the Algerian dey declared the existing level of American tribute unacceptable and issued orders to seize American vessels sailing through the Mediterranean. There is little evidence to suggest any direct British influence on the dey, but when news of the Algerian threat reached the United States, many Americans blamed the breakdown in relations with Algiers on English influence.[12] In the American press, pseudonymous author "Ghost of Montgomery" argued that the Algerian declaration of war was yet another British violation of American rights that could be added to the impressment of American sailors and the incitement of Native Americans against American settlers.[13] Regardless of the reasons behind the discord, Algiers claimed its first and only American casualty of the renewed conflict, the merchant ship *Edwin*, in August 1812, just off the southern coast of Spain. The crew was consigned to Algerian quarries, excavating rock by hand and forced to survive on meager rations.[14]

The ongoing war with England limited the Madison administration's options for securing the release of the American hostages, but the American crewmen were by no means forgotten by their government. Secretary of State James Monroe issued instructions to Mordecai M. Noah, the new U.S. consul to Tunis, to "devise a means for the liberation of our unfortunate countrymen at Algiers" and authorized him to "go as far as three thousand dollars a man." The success of the mission was doubly significant, Monroe continued, because the plight of the crew had "excited the warmest sympathy of their friends, and indeed the people generally of this country." Although Monroe's observation about the keen public interest in the crew of the *Edwin* may have been an exaggeration, his instructions to Noah were ameasure of the worry about the prospects for U.S. success in the ongoing war with England and in his nation's negotiations with Algiers.[15]

Monroe had good reason to fret about the chances of Noah's efforts securing the Americans' freedom. Negotiating from a position of relative weakness and relying on back channels, Noah had achieved little by the war's end. After more than a year of negotiations, he had secured the release of only two of the original crewmen and four French-speaking British-held captives who claimed to be American sailors from Louisiana—at a cost of nearly $25,000. Believing these results would provoke a public backlash in the United States and not wanting to lose the political momentum provided by Jackson's victory at New Orleans, the Madison administration acted quickly to minimize the damage of the failed negotiations. Before news of Noah's mission appeared in the press, Madison sent a war message to Congress, recommending that an act be passed "declaring the existence of a state of war between the United States and the Dey and Regency of Algiers."[16] Shortly after Madison delivered his message, supporters of his administration released a summary of a secret Congressional report making the full case for war. The *Daily National Intelligencer* published the initial report, which was quickly reprinted in newspapers across the nation. The truncated account revealed that American diplomats had tried to "procure the liberation of eleven or twelve of our citizens captive in Algiers," for "a ransom not exceeding 3000 dollars per man. To every attempt of this kind, the Dey replied 'that not for two millions of dollars would he SELL HIS AMERICAN SLAVES.'" Such demands left "no doubt" that peace with the Algiers could only be secured by American coercion or endurance of "the most base and humiliating conditions."[17]

Unlike his predecessor, Madison had no qualms about deploying the fullest extent of American naval power against a new Barbary threat. The administration's decisive action helped head off any partisan divisions that might emerge over the Algerian crisis. Just days before the president's war message, the Federalist *Portsmouth Oracle* had called for a "munificent private subscription" to redeem the "forlorn captives," who had been "languishing in slavery for nearly three years."[18] On the day Madison delivered his message to Congress, the *Boston Gazette*, in an unintentional ratification of the president's action, remarked that while "there is much humanity in this [the *Oracle*'s] proposal . . . the idea of paying tribute or succumbing to any power is abhorrent to our feelings." Instead, the editor of the *Gazette* hoped that "our gallant tars will be employed against [Algiers]."[19] Rather than challenging postwar unity, the ordeal of the *Edwin*'s crew, politicized by the Madison administration's rapid move to war, unified Americans of all political stripes as the nation began once again, to prepare for a naval conflict in the Mediterranean.

The sense of self-confidence that had been created as part of the mythologizing of the War of 1812 translated easily to the country's preparation for war with Algiers. In addition to playing off the most recent "victory" over England, the conflict with Algiers also allowed Americans to begin to reimagine military conflicts of the previous decade. Throughout the country, newspapers published accounts of America's earlier engagements with the Barbary States, reminding the people of the "depredations of the Barbary powers on our commerce" and of Jefferson's "victory" against Tripoli in 1805.[20] A local theater in Albany, New York, staged Susanna Rowson's play *Americans in Algiers, or a Struggle for Freedom*, with the coda of "an entire new song . . . called the SEIGE OF NEW ORLEANS."[21] In its weekly review of the news, *Niles' Weekly Register* went further than any other publication, declaring "the war against Algiers is among the most popular that one people ever declared against another. If we may judge the general feeling by what appears in the newspapers, it is almost universally approved." The Baltimore-based publication went on to celebrate American military victories in Tripoli, "that theatre of gallant deeds and *school for glory*," and in the War of 1812 and took note of "a series of well-fought battles on the *Niagara* frontier . . . [and] Orleans."[22]

Connecting American successes in the Mediterranean with the successful conclusion of the War of 1812 allowed Americans to create a national narrative that included a decade of military victories. This vision of the American past laid the foundation for expectations of future glories, beginning with an American victory over Algiers. Yet, for all of this hope and a seeming postpartisan cause to subdue the renewed Barbary threat, the scars of the past remained just below the surface. Even as Americans expressed their hope for the future, events in England provided one final opportunity for an upwelling of bitterly partisan and Anglophobic battles in the United States. The shootings at Dartmoor Prison in the spring of 1815 marked a brief but powerful resurgence of the political divisions that had wracked the nation during the War of 1812 and provided one final test for postwar unity and self-confidence.

The incident at Dartmoor occurred on April 6, 1815, when prison guards, under the command of Captain Thomas Shortland, shot and killed seven American prisoners of war and wounded nearly forty others. The shootings themselves were the result of a mismanaged series of negotiations, a restless prison population, and an increasingly frustrated and weary prison administration. Following the announcement of the "joyful tidings of peace" in late December 1814, the Americans held at Dartmoor immediately began to anticipate their return home. One of the prisoners, Charles Andrews, wrote, "Language is too feeble to describe the transports of joy, that so suddenly and unexpectedly filled every heart." These expressions of joy quickly took physical form as prisoners launched a massive celebration, obtaining "a quantity of powder of the soldiers" to construct fireworks and flying in the center of the prison a large white flag prominently displaying the slogan "FREE TRADE AND SAILOR'S RIGHTS." Feeling the need to limit the celebrations before they went too far, Shortland entered the yard and "politely requested that the white flag ... be taken down." The American prisoners agreed to Shortland's request only after he consented to "hoist an American ensign on one end of his own house, and a British one on the other end." While Shortland managed to avoid any sort of incident in this initial engagement, the celebration of peace was only the beginning of a pattern of collective action by the prisoners. A few weeks later, when Shortland implemented a new policy requiring all prisoners to stand in the cold, wet air of the prison yard to be counted each day, the Americans refused to comply. His attempt to force the Americans back to their barracks was met with a threat of violence. The English captain wisely withdrew his order, fearing that at that moment, his numbers were too thin to deal with an uprising. Despite Shortland's efforts to maintain order, as the days following the peace turned into months, tensions at the prison continued to mount, and the American prisoners became more obstinate.[23]

Reuben Beasley and Sir Anthony St. John Baker, the American and British agents responsible for negotiating the means and terms of the repatriation of prisoners, only made matters more difficult for the residents of Dartmoor. A series of disagreements and misunderstandings prolonged the negotiations. The Americans argued that each country should charter and pay for the return passage of prisoners under its watch, while the British contended that each nation should be responsible for its own countrymen. This difference of opinion resulted from the fact that the United States held about thirty-five hundred English prisoners at the end of the war and the British, about eight thousand Americans, most of them imprisoned in England.[24] Finally, on March 17, Shortland informed the American prisoners that they were to be released as soon as Beasley was ready to receive them. On that same day, however, an unwelcome letter from Beasley arrived at Dartmoor. He declared that none of the men would be returned to the United States until those Americans who had not been infected during the recent smallpox outbreak were inoculated. His instruction was one in a series of perceived slights by Beasley toward his countrymen. The prisoners, who had been collectively agitating against their guards, now turned their wrath on the U.S. agent for prisoners of war. The disgruntled American prisoners tried Beasley in absentia and hanged him in effigy from the top of prison number seven. As the prisoners' frustration mounted in the weeks that followed, tensions at Dartmoor began to reach new heights.[25]

Compounding the frustration of delay was a shortage of rations and supplies. Blame for this shortage lay partly with Beasley and with British suppliers at Dartmoor. During the final year of the war, Beasley had secured a small allowance for American prisoners to purchase soap, tobacco, sugar, and other sundries. This "tobacco money," as the prisoners called it, was issued every thirty-two days. Although it was a relatively small amount, these funds greatly improved the quality of life at the prison. Not only did the prisoners create markets among themselves, but local residents established stands around the edges of the prison, offering the inmates a wide variety of goods. The prisoners had come to rely on their "tobacco money" and these markets to supplement the rations and supplies provided them by their captors. Following the peace at Ghent, however, Beasley notified the prisoners that he would no longer be able to provide the monthly stipend; the payment had been a wartime measure and was thus no longer technically available.[26] At a practical level, the loss of these funds also resulted in the closure of many prison shops that local merchants had established and thus was a blow to the inmates' quality of life. Anger came to a head in the first days of April when the contractor who supplied the prison with bread decided to serve stale bread rather than the soft bread he was contracted to provide.[27]

The supplier waited to offload his leftovers until April 4, when Shortland was away from the prison at Plymouth. In protest, the Americans refused to eat the substandard rations and, by the day's end, had planned their response. Charles Andrews later recounted the prisoners' plan: "Thus desperate by starvation, we determined to force open the gates in front of the prison, disarm the soldiers, break open the store-house and supply ourselves; and provided the garrison should charge or fire upon us, to make a general attack, and take possession of the guard house and barracks." When the nightly order was given for the prisoners to return to their barracks, they instead gathered at the front gate of the prison, refusing to retire. Confronted with this revolt, the entire garrison was called to arms, and as news spread to the surrounding countryside, the local militia arrived to assist in restoring order.[28]

Its numbers reinforced, the prison guard, with bayonets fixed, advanced toward the unruly American mob, closing to within two yards of the prisoners. "The soldiers were then brought to a stand by the threats of the prisoners, who all declared, in the most determined tone, that if they [guards] attempted to fire or make a charge on them, they must abide by any consequences that would follow." In addition to threatening violence against the guard, the prisoners warned that they would level the store-house to the ground, "unless the bread was served out immediately. The contractor, clerks, &c. then immediately came forward and entered into this engagement, that if the prisoners would retire into the prison yards, that the bread should be immediately served to them." The promise of the standard rations brought an end to the confrontation. The prisoners returned to their barracks, taking with them one of the clerks as hostage until every prisoner had received his usual allowance of bread.[29]

The next morning, Shortland, having heard rumors that the prisoners had complete control of the garrison, returned with two hundred reinforcements. Expecting a fight to regain control of the prison, the captain instead "found all things quiet and tranquil; as the prisoners had obtained their usual allowance of bread, they were satisfied and sought nothing more. Capt. Shortland made an apology for the fault of the contractor, and things passed on tolerably well." Despite the peaceful resolution of the crisis, the tension of the near riot ultimately exploded into violence two days later.[30]

It is difficult to assemble a complete picture of the events at Dartmoor that led to the shooting on April 6. By almost all accounts, the commotion began at about 6:30 in the evening, when guards sounded the alarm in response to a group of prisoners trying to dig a hole in the wall between prisons six and seven, but agreement about the tragedy generally ends at that point. By some accounts the "unusually pleasant" day began lightheartedly with a number of prisoners playing ball in the yard. One prisoner recounted, in a memoir published twenty-five years later, that the Americans were "ready dogs and ripe for fun." According to this account, in the course of their play, the prisoners occasionally threw their ball "by accident over the wall, in the barrack yard." Initially, the prison guard was willing to return the ball but the "sulky sentinel" eventually grew tired of the prisoners' game and refused to play along, telling the prisoners to "come and take it." So the prisoners took the guard's retort as a challenge and began to dig a hole under the wall.[31]

The testimony of the guards varied even among themselves. Private James Groves, recounted that at "about five o'clock in the evening a ball was thrown over the wall," and he then "caught up the ball and threw it over the wall into the prison again," but that had been the only disturbance. Groves was relieved of duty at half past six o'clock, and "while on sentry he did not hear any attack upon the wall, and saw no breach whatever."[32] Lieutenant Samuel White, commanding the west guard of the prison on that evening, remarked that while he was in the barrack yard, "no person asked for a ball, or said a ball had been thrown over the wall."[33]

Regardless of what actually happened, by half past six o'clock the prisoners had dug a "hole in the wall which separated the barrack yard from the prison, large enough for a man of any size to come through." As the hole grew, so too did the crowd of prisoners, some men working with "iron bars in their hands removing stones from the wall."[34] Although one of the prisoners later claimed that the hole "had been made . . . out of mere play, without any design of escape," the prison guard was deeply concerned by the fracas.[35] British lieutenant Samuel White warned the prisoners that if they did not cease their digging "the whole of the military would be called out" to stop them. The prisoners responded to his demand by lobbing a volley of mortar and stones at the guards.[36]

What had likely begun as a game soon began to devolve toward violence. White and other members of the guard responded to the prisoners' volley of stones with a warning: the guard might be "obliged to commit violence to compel them to desist" if the Americans persisted. In response, according to one account, some of the prisoners refused to leave the spot and taunted the guards to "fire, fire!"[37] At that point, one of the soldiers sounded the alarm. Rather than scaring off the men at the wall, however, the bell only added to the confusion as "many of the prisoners ran up to the market square to learn of the cause of the alarm."[38]

Shortland, with the events of April 4 likely still fresh in his memory, was determined not to allow the incident to go any farther. The captain of Dartmoor moved quickly to restore order. Conflicting accounts of what happened next appear both in official testimony and prisoner narratives. One prisoner recalled that many of Shortland's officers "refused to take any part" in moving against the Americans based on the observation "that the terrified prisoners were retiring as fast as so great a crowd would permit, and hurrying and flying in terrible flight, in every direction to their respective prisons."[39] Another American witness claimed that when his officers refused to give the order to fire, "Shortland seized a musket out of the hands of a soldier which he fired."[40] In his narrative of events, Charles Andrews contended that, ignoring his officers' reticence, "Capt. Shortland was distinctly heard to give orders to the troops to fire upon the prisoners, although . . . [they] had offered no violence, nor attempted to resist, and the gates [were] all closed."[41] Prisoner James Taylor later claimed that Shortland ordered a charge only to amend his command with "it is no use to charge on the damn'd Yankee rascals—FIRE!"[42] Prisoner after prisoner claimed to have heard Shortland give the order to fire.

From the British side, a number of the guards, including Private James Groves, acknowledged that they "heard the word 'fire' given by some person" but did not know who had given the order.[43] Lieutenant Samuel White only heard gunshots but remarked, "The sentinels are ordered not to fire unless in case of absolute necessity, or where a prisoner or prisoners is or are in the act of escaping." White also pointed to the incident of April 4, when the prisoners had also been "very disorderly and refused to obey the commands," but no shots were fired.[44] Regardless of how the violence began, the initial shot was soon joined by repeated volleys with "prisoners falling, either dead or wounded, in all directions, while it was yet impossible for them to enter the prison."[45] By the time the soldiers had retreated from the prison, seven prisoners were dead and nearly forty wounded.[46]

Eager to avoid a renewal of hostilities with England, administration officials Henry Clay and Albert Gallatin worked with their British counterpart, Foreign Secretary Lord Castlereagh, to establish a special commission to investigate the shootings. After agreeing to the joint commission, Clay and Gallatin initially suggested that they would select Reuben Beasley, the American agent for prisoners of war, to represent the United States.[47] Despite this initial impulse, the American commissioners ultimately chose Charles King, son of prominent Federalist Rufus King, to represent the United States. Officially, Clay and Gallatin justified the choice by arguing that Beasley "might have too much occupation" with his efforts to secure passage for American prisoners out of Dartmoor. Unofficially, however, it is possible that Clay and Gallatin had read accounts in the London newspapers laying much of the blame for the "Disturbances at Dartmoor Prison" at the feet of Beasley, who, the paper reported, had "been burnt in effigy" by the prisoners just prior to their efforts to escape.[48] Regardless of the rationale behind their choice, the American commissioners simply wanted to move beyond the issue.

Once the delegates had been chosen, the joint British-American commission, led by American Charles King and Englishman Seymour Larpent, moved quickly toward a resolution. The commission undertook an examination of the "proceedings of the several courts of inquiry instituted immediately after the event," the "depositions taken at the coroner's inquest," at which "the jury found a verdict of justifiable homicide," and the testimony of both British and American witnesses. The inquiry "further proceeded to a minute examination of the prisons, for the purpose of clearing up some points which upon the evidence alone were scarcely intelligible." Based on their examination of the evidence, the officials were unable to determine "whether the firing first began in the square by order, or was a spontaneous act of the soldiers themselves." Whatever ignited the initial shooting, it clearly rolled forward and was "renewed both there and elsewhere without orders." Guards posted "on the platforms, and in several places about the prison," opened fire on prisoners "without any authority."[49]

The commissioners concluded that a number of soldiers had acted without orders, firing repeatedly into the crowd of prisoners. Further, although the initial shots may have been warranted to restore order, "under the circumstances it is very difficult to find any justification for the further continuance and renewal of the firing which certainly took place both in the prison yards and elsewhere." This second wave of firing "appears to have arisen from the state of individual irritation and exasperation on the part of the soldiers who followed the prisoners into their yards, and from the absence of nearly all the officers who might have restrained it." These ongoing attacks struck prisoners who were "endeavoring to enter in the few doors which the turnkeys... had left open." This round of musket fire seemed "to have been wholly without object or excuse, and to have been a wanton attack upon the lives of defenseless, at that time unoffending, individuals." Based on this conclusion, the commissioners "used every endeavor to ascertain if there was the least prospect of identifying any of the soldiers who had been guilty of the particular outrages here alluded to... but without success and all hopes of bringing the offenders to punishment should seem to be at an end."[50]

Although the findings of the inquiry admitted wrongdoing on the part of a number of the prison guards at Dartmoor, the inability to identify those responsible left the commission without any means to proceed. With such uncertainty, the commissioners issued their official conclusions on April 26, 1815, declaring that "whilst we lament, as we do most deeply, the unfortunate transaction which has been the subject of this inquiry, we find ourselves totally unable to suggest any steps to be taken as to those parts of it which seem most to call for redress and punishment." Authorities in both England and the United States accepted the commission's findings as the final word on the "unfortunate transaction," with English officials offering compensation to the families of the men who had been killed and American officials hoping to move on.[51]

Despite the speed with which the official inquiry had proceeded, the findings would not appear in the American press for nearly three months. In the intervening time, a wave of unofficial reports presented the American public with conflicting and incendiary versions of shootings at Dartmoor. The result was a political seesaw and a return to the partisan politics that had consumed the country in the decade leading to the War of 1812. Suddenly the goodwill and optimism that had brightened the months following Jackson's victory in New Orleans seemed to have dissipated. The initial accounts of the incident placed much of the blame on Reuben Beasley. Based on sources in the London press, American newspapers reported that the "unfortunate prisoners who amount to 5 or 6000 had recently become extremely impatient to be set at liberty," as the result of Beasley's delays in securing their departure. According to the English sources, the incident began when the prisoners burned Beasley "in effigy on Friday, & then proceeded to force their way out of the confines of the prison." In the face of this prison break, Shortland "went in among them alone and unarmed to endeavor to pacify them, but a pistol was snapped at him, and therefore the soldiers fired among the insurgents." Only "the prompt interference of the military... quelled the insurrection."[52]

The initial coverage of the incident in both Federalist and Republican newspapers, followed the British version of events, denouncing Reuben Beasley for his failures that ultimately led to the tragic events at Dartmoor. In the Republican-leaning press, Beasley was chided for his "disregard of the feelings and interests of the Prisoners in Dartmoor." The Republican papers charged that he had "maintained the most sullen and contemptuous silence and had refused them the least satisfaction upon those subjects in which it must be supposed their feelings were most deeply interested." Beasley's indifference must have only added to the "dissatisfaction occasioned by so long a detention after their countrymen were enjoying the blessings of peace." These circumstances must have given "rise to the attempt (noticed in the London papers) made by the prisoners on the 6th of April, to break through the gate of the prison, in which 6 to 12 of them were stated to have been killed."[53]

The Federalist press took things a bit farther, reviving partisan language of the previous decade, challenging the unity that had emerged after the war with Britain, and criticizing the administration's response to the renewed Algerian threat. Editors in Federalist newspapers around the country printed old-style partisan attacks. Washington's *Federal Republican* admonished, "If Mr. Beasley has neglected to provide for the speedy liberation of American prisoners as is here stated, he ought to be brought to account for it." The newspaper doubted, however, that the administration would punish one of their own, despite the "clear truth" of the matter, for fear of "impairing party influence" merely "for the sake of doing some hundred oppressed men justice."[54]

In Hudson, New York, the Federalist *Northern Whig* took a slightly different tack and portrayed the delayed redemption of the Americans at Dartmoor in a more nefarious light. The paper removed responsibility for the wrong-doing from Beasley, arguing that "we are inclined to attribute this unpleasant occurrence to another and very different cause. Mr. Beasley could not, in all probability act in this business without the orders of his own government." The delay in redeeming the American prisoners at Dartmoor was likely a ploy on the part of the Madison administration to induce these prisoners to serve in the U.S. Navy. The paper explained, "We have lately seen accounts that two American men of war are expected in England to make up their crews from the prisoners now in confinement there, for the Mediterranean service." The reason for this plot, according to the *Northern Whig*, was that as long as "shipping merchants offer greater inducements for seamen to enter their vessels than the government possibly can, our seamen will certainly prefer the merchant service." Under such circumstances, "we are inclined to think . . . that these 6,000 seamen have been kept in England by the orders of the government, in order to get them if possible by a kind of *ruse de guerre*, on board of the Mediterranean squadron."[55] Despite their differencing approaches, both Federalist newspapers returned to a line of political attack and applied a style of language that they had employ during the War of 1812, accusing the Madison administration of playing politics with the lives of American sailors.

Responding to the partisanship of the Federalist newspapers, the semi-official administration paper, the *Daily National Intelligencer*, defended Beasley by challenging the tone and accuracy of the British accounts of the "Disturbance at Dartmoor Prison."[56] Beasley's defender, writing under the penname "Nautilus," began by questioning the tone of the London-based accounts and reminding his readers of Madison's leadership in the conflict with Algiers. Nautilus challenged the London papers' use of the term "unfortunate" to describe the American prisoners. Such a label for the residents of Dartmoor was an understatement, "for what human being can be more unfortunate than the man, whom ill fortune has thrown a prisoner of war into the hands of Great Britain, and doomed to her Algerine tortures for months and years." Moving beyond the issue of tone, Nautilus challenged the accuracy of the account itself: "Will any man of common sense believe that a few (for all could not act) *unarmed* American prisoners could seriously attempt to force their way out of the confines of the prison, in the open face of day, and in full view of an armed soldiery?" Such behavior would be an act of madness, as the death of the seven prisoners demonstrated. Beyond the irrationality of the plan of escape described in the English account of events, Nautilus questioned the description of Shortland's response to the disturbance. "It would appear extremely imprudent on the part of Capt. Shortland," he contended, "to venture among them alone and unarmed, unless they were in a defenseless and perfectly quiet state." For under any other conditions, "we should imagine a *British* officer to be the last man on earth who ought to go in 'alone and unarmed' amongst some thousands of angry Americans, 'to endeavor to pacify them.'" Nautilus challenged nearly every aspect of the British accounts of the incident at Dartmoor and concluded that "taking the whole transaction then in its clearest and most reasonable point of view, there can no other legitimate inference be drawn from it than that of downright murder—and murder of the most ferocious cast."[57] Just as Federalist attacks on Beasley echoed wartime partisan attacks, Nautilus's assault on Shortland revived an older vision of American identity based not in American military success but in opposition to British brutality.

The June arrival of 260 American prisoners aboard the Swedish ship *Maria Christiana* in New York supported Nautilus's interpretation of events and only served to further the rhetorical backsliding. The *New York Weekly Museum* announced that "among the prisoners on board this ship, is Mr. Charles Andrews of this state, who has furnished the editor with a journal of particulars relative to the prisoners at Dartmoor prison, which he intends to publish in a pamphlet."[58] With the return of the prisoners to the United States, the tone of the coverage of the "incident at Dartmoor" took a distinct turn. No longer was the shooting of the American prisoners of war an "unfortunate incident"; rather, the events of April 6 came to be called the "HORRID MASSACRE!!!"[59] The prisoners accounts seemed to exonerate Beasley and instead placed the blame for the shootings squarely on "the blood thirsty SHORTLAND."[60] American papers began to report that the "affair of the 6th of April was owing to the unpardonable degree of wantonness on the part of the keeper of the prison." Nautilus's dissenting view of the tragedy published a week earlier soon became the norm. Opposition to British brutality reemerged as a central tenet of American identity.[61]

That summer, excerpts and summaries of Andrews's journal appeared in newspapers throughout the country. Running the pieces under the headline "HORRID MASSACRE!!!," these papers promised an account of the "bloody tragedy performed by the British soldiery."[62] The journal itself was published as a book, *The Prisoners' Memoirs, or, Dartmoor Prison,* in New York, with advertisements soon appearing up and down the Atlantic Coast. In addition to reporting the events of April 6, Andrews's 283-page journal offered a complete account of his time in Dartmoor, including everything from a detailed description of the buildings to a failed escape attempt in the summer of 1814. Along with Andrews's journal, a 16-page pamphlet titled *A Description of Dartmoor Prison with an Account of the Massacre of the Prisoners* was published by John Melish in Philadelphia. And in Boston, a broadside describing "the Horrid Massacre at Dartmoor Prison England" was sold to all those interested in the tragedy.[63] In all three accounts, the British captain Shortland was held accountable for the massacre. The broadside from Boston described a scene "where the unarmed American Prisoners of War were wantonly fired upon by the guard, under the command of the Prison Turn-key, the blood thirsty SHORTLAND; Seven were killed and about Fifty wounded, (several mortally,) without any provocation on the part of our unfortunate American Citizens!"[64] In Philadelphia, Melish's pamphlet containing "remarks and anecdotes, collected from some of the Prisoners," described Shortland as "universally execrated among the Prisoners for his inhumanity and cruelty before the late massacre; but they now abhor him as a murderer." The most-vituperative criticism of Shortland came from Andrews himself.[65]

Andrews's account of the Dartmoor Massacre centered on Shortland's role in the attack. The former Dartmoor captive described how Shortland gave the order to fire, even though the prisoners, retreating to their prisons, were "now completely in his power, and their lives at his disposal, and had offered no violence, nor attempted to resist, and the gates all closed." He described the prison guard advancing toward the men after the initial shots were fired. Once within killing range, the guards "instantly discharged another volley of musketry on the backs of those farthest out. . . . This barbarous act was repeated in the presence of this inhuman monster, Shortland—and the prisoners fell, either dead or severely wounded, in all directions before his savage sight." This first round of violence, as Andrews recounted, did not sate Shortland:

> His vengeance was not glutted by the cruel murder of the innocent men and boys, that lay weltering and bleeding in the groans and agonies of death along the prison-doors, but turned and traversed the yard and hunted a poor affrighted wretch, that had flew for safety close under the walls of prison No. 1 . . . these hell-hounds with this deamon at their head and with cool deliberate malice, drew up their muskets to their shoulders and dispatched the unhappy victim, while in the act of imploring mercy at their hands. His only crime was not being able to get into the prison without being shot before.

Andrews ended his account of the massacre with a final diatribe against the demonic captain: "Shortland! Thou foul monster and inhuman villain! Is thy soul glutted with the blood of the innocent victims, that fate had doomed to thy revengeful and blood-thirsty power? . . . Should the laws of your country not doom you to a death of the most severe nature, as a publick example for your well known crimes?"[66]

The hope of American and British officials that the Dartmoor affair might be quickly and quietly resolved was shattered by the return of the American prisoners. The inflamed rhetoric of their accounts intensified a resurgent partisan divide. Just as the initial reports implicating Beasley had sent the

Federalists press into a frenzy, the series of prisoners' accounts marked a return of vitriolic anti-British rhetoric in the Republican press. In a column first published in the *National Intelligencer* and later reprinted in newspapers throughout the United States, "AN AMERICAN" denounced the "massacre at Dartmoor" as an act of "cowardly and malignant barbarity" from the British. The most heinous aspect of the Dartmoor attack was that it came "in a time of peace, when the passions of war have had leisure to subside into forgiveness or oblivion," yet, even after the war had concluded, the British "entered like butchers into the fold of our unarmed and imprisoned countrymen." Even with all this evidence of British brutality, An American charged, the Federalist newspapers have "the intolerable insolence to charge us with the crime of hating the English!" What reason, the author questioned, have we "to love them, forsooth, because, two centuries ago their father persecuted our fathers out of their country?" Should Americans love the English "because they overwhelm us with eternal falsehoods; rob our churches; burn our towns; violate our women; break open our graves; and in a period of profound peace, murder our defenseless prisoners in cold blood?" The Federalists might hold a feast to honor the "commander of the assassins at Dartmoor," but the Republicans and all true American citizens would recognize the brutality of British actions at Dartmoor.[67]

Federalists responded by painting the Republican outrage over Dartmoor as a ruse designed to resurrect conflict with England. The *Federal Republican* reasoned that "every good man—we will not say in America only, but in the Christian world must abhor—must shudder" at the "Dartmoor business," but the tragedy was not an excuse to return to war. "The Dartmoor affair," according to the *Federal Republican,* had enlivened the hopes of "the faction who rule us" to resume the war. The paper warned, "Each war hawk felicitates himself with the assurances that the Union will be soon again plunged in all the comforts of cut-and-thrust work, or as Don Quixote says, 'up to the elbows in adventures.'" With this growing "military passion," the United States, "this once happy land—this chosen residence of peace and industry, is to be converted into A BARRACK OF SOLDIERS, in order that one set of miscreants may be elected into office, there to bestride the prostrate country—and another set fatten upon the public, and without possessing any other worth than the knavish arts of popular fraud and delusion." The Republicans, declared the *Federal Republican,* were using the "Dartmoor business" to play up military fears for their own ends, as they had done throughout the War of 1812. Furthermore, the Federalists argued, Republican goals were not to defend the principles of the United States but rather to "spunge up the means of their fellow citizens, and trample upon their rights." The motivations of those who railed against the tragic events at Dartmoor were "neither grief nor anger, nor pity, but party cunning actuates them, [and] each partisan assumes the character and brow of Jupiter . . . while tempests and wrath and lightning invelope [sic] the head—the heart is cheered by the prospect of party advantage." The consequence of all this political inflammation, the Republicans hoped, would be "another war, and then Mr. Monroe will be President, and General Aurora will again have his pay . . . and the federalists will be put down all together." The deeply partisan Federalist rhetoric accusing the Madison administration of cultivating anti-British sentiment to ensure the long-term Republican control of the presidency and the creation of a one-party state echoed the incendiary rhetoric of the previous decade as the nation prepared for war.[68]

The thrill of Jackson's victory and the anticipation of military success in Algiers, both of which had united the nation only weeks before, had been turned on its head. Rather than a sense of unified nationalism, the country seemed to fall back into a game of partisan one-upmanship as both Federalists and Republicans issued their own interpretations of the killings in Dartmoor. Reviving a line of attack that they had employed in the run up to and then throughout the War of 1812, the Federalists charged that the Republican vitriol directed toward Shortland and the British was a part of a larger plot to turn the United States into a garrison state centralized under one-party (Republican) rule dedicated to war with England. The Federalist revival of these shrill partisan attacks, however, ignored the party's own support for war against Algiers just weeks before.

The Republican response to deadly events in Dartmoor marked a return to a definition of nationalism that relied on American notions of the cruel and barbarous British "other." In a letter printed in newspapers in New York and Washington, "A Witness" claimed that "the savage and brutal mind of the brutal Shortland" had been inflamed by "the news of the British defeat at New Orleans," which he had received "but a few days before the butchery." Following this news, Witness sarcastically noted, the British captain of Dartmoor "*bravely* revenged upon the defenseless prisoners."[69] Other papers across the country called for Americans to "swear eternal hatred" against the English for the carnage at Dartmoor. One party loyalist harangued the

American people: "Read Americans, read over and over the extract from the journal of Mr. Andrews, and the report, on oath of the American prisoners. Read and weep for the injuries of your suffering countrymen." These injuries should be remembered for generations: "Swear to avenge them, let those feelings descend to your children, and to your children's children, until that nation shall be no more:—Instruct them to lisp the history of that horrible event, and as they gristle into manhood teach them to *hate* these English." Republicans called for "the anniversary of the 6th of April [to] be marked by humiliation and prayer for the souls of our fellow citizens thus hurried into eternity. Let us never forget it, and *never* forgive it."[70] Unlike the celebrations of the American victory at New Orleans, which defined Americans by their military and other accomplishments rather than contrasting them to the savage other—the British—the Republican response to Dartmoor revived a Revolutionary-era profile of the American based not on the success and glory of American arms but contrasted against British brutality, savagery, and inhumanity.

The weekly news summary provided in the June 17 issue of *Niles' Weekly Register* embodied this return. Prefacing the coverage of the Dartmoor Massacre, the *Weekly Register* remarked that accounts of the shootings "will doubtless interest the feelings of the American people; for the sufferings of the poor fellows confined in that depot (about to be as famous for the cruelties practiced in it as the *Jersey* prison ship) have, indeed, been extreme." The invocation of the prison ship *Jersey* from the American Revolution signaled the larger turn to the past. Just as had been the case in much of the American press, the news magazine looked to historical examples of British cruelty against American prisoners rather than to a bright future where Americans were a national power in their own right in the larger Atlantic world.[71]

In addition to its coverage of Dartmoor, which included selections from Andrews's journal, the *Weekly Register*'s coverage of other events from that week suggested just how far the revival of anti-British sentiment extended. Immediately following the several pages of Dartmoor stories were accounts of violence on the frontier. The headlines included news of "INDIAN MURDERS" in the Missouri Territory and "INDIAN HOSTILITY" in Alabama. In Missouri, the *Register* reported, Mr. Robert Ramsay and his family had been "horribly butchered" by "the *British allies.* . . . It is probable that, as in 1794, many *Englishmen* are among the savages exciting them to these horrid deeds." From the *Augusta Mirror,* the *Register* recounted renewed hostility with the

Creek Indians, which had been sparked by the promise of the British government to guarantee "all of their possessions as they existed in 1811." From an Ohio newspaper came the news that British-backed Native American forces refused to allow American possession of Fort Mackinaw on the Great Lakes. In both the Federalist and Republican press, the Dartmoor incident had resurrected old partisan habits and a fear-based approach to politics.[72]

An almost schizophrenic mood marked Independence Day celebrations in 1815 and persisted through much of the month of July. Commemorations of a glorious American past were mixed with Anglophobia and hope for success in the conflict with Algiers. Throughout the country, as Americans celebrated their independence and the memory of George Washington, speakers reminded their audiences of the bloodshed at Dartmoor. In an oration delivered in Alfred, Maine, John Holmes declared that "the cold blooded massacre at Dartmoor prison, is perhaps, without parallel in the history, even of *British* barbarities." In West Haven, Vermont, a toast demanded justice for those Americans murdered at Dartmoor. Declaring the shootings to be "in barbarity unequalled," the speaker stated that "the laws of God cry aloud for the punishment of the perpetrator" and asked that the American "government tear away the veil that shall attempt to conceal the crime." In New York, the revelers at the Tammany Society toasted the notion that "the massacre of our countrymen shall never be forgiven." In Maryland, the "Company of Independent Blues" called for "Shortland—the assassin of American prisoners," to be brought to justice. The toast was greeted with "hisses" and the "Rogue's March." In Salem, Massachusetts, "the officers of the Salem Regiment and a number of Citizens from this town" raised a glass to "the memory of our brave Countrymen who perished at Dartmoor Prison—May this deed of darkness sit heavy on the souls of their murderers." The residents of Newark, New Jersey, offered a "silent wave and Washington's Funeral March" to salute "the memory of our unfortunate countrymen who fell victims to the brutality of the infamous Shortland at Dartmoor prison."[73]

The promises never to forgive or forget and the melancholy tone surrounding the coverage of the events at Dartmoor on Independence Day were slightly offset by the initial reports of the U.S. fleet's arrival in the Mediterranean in June 1815. The news helped remind Americans of their celebratory mood that had enlivened the departure of the American squadron just months before. The first of these reports came from the imprisoned captain of the *Edwin*, George Smith. His letter, reprinted in newspapers as far west as Ohio and Kentucky, began to appear in newspapers throughout the Northeast in late June, just in time for Independence Day celebrations. Smith informed his readers that news of the imminent arrival of the American navy had sent Algiers into a state of "tumult and consternation." He entertained "no doubt" that the appearance of a strong fleet "would be the means of effecting an immediate peace."74

This news added to the conflicted nature of the Fourth of July celebrations around the country as toasts anticipating success of an American victory in the Mediterranean were offered alongside others commemorating the Dartmoor Massacre. The company of Independent Blues in Baltimore honored the "American Squadron commanded by our gallant Decatur—when they meet the Algerines may they teach those barbarians to respect our Stripes if they do not reverence our Stars." Independence Day revelers in Salem, Massachusetts, cheered "the Navy of the United States—first in deeds of glory—may it continue to be first in the affections of the American people." In West Haven, Vermont, a toast to "our Algerine squadron—victory exulting perches on their prows, while the rolling billows foaming, grant them passage to their ill advised enemies" was greeted with three cheers. The members of the Carlisle Guards in Pennsylvania toasted "those gallant spirits, our brave officers and their crews composing the present expedition against Algiers—may they return to their country victorious, crowned with laurels, glorious triumphant." The people of New Sharon, Maine, celebrated "our hardy Tars—in battle invincible, humane as brothers to the vanquished." Revelers in the town of Salisbury, New Jersey, hoped that "whilst the Legitimate and Illegitimate Sovereigns of Europe are engaged in their vocations of slaughter, may the sovereigns of America have the glory of subjugating the barbarians of Algiers." Braiding together the many issues facing the nation on that Fourth of July, the citizens of Delhi, New York, called for a remembrance of all "American captives—From Indians, British, and Algerines, good Lord deliver them."75

For all the conflicting messages delivered at these Fourth of July celebrations, Boston's Washingtonian Society preserved the earlier sense of optimism about the American experiment and its future. Like many other revelers, the Washingtonians celebrated the anticipated success of the American force in Algiers, and they did not stop there. While other toasts throughout the day called on Americans never to forget or forgive the shootings at Dartmoor, the toast given at this gathering of Bostonians declared the British terror in

April to be "the last efforts of Britain to retrieve the glory of her army."[76] In casting Dartmoor as the last gasp of a dying empire, this group of revelers stood above the newly revitalized partisan fray. If the naval campaign in the Mediterranean brought victory as Americans expected—as the Washington Society's revelers believed it would—the shootings at Dartmoor might be recast as an unfortunate and tragic detour on America's rise to glory, instead of a return to second-class status.

Complicating the divided mood that had marked the Fourth of July was the printing of official report of the joint Dartmoor commission. By late July, often appearing in the same issue as accounts of Independence Day toasts, the joint Anglo-American commission's findings challenged the prisoners' account of the shootings. Rather than settling the issue, the report further fractured public opinion and heightened partisan tension. A group of former prisoners immediately challenged the report's exoneration of Shortland, declaring that the official findings were a "misrepresentation" of the "inhuman transaction" at Dartmoor and that from the first, Shortland's conduct "had been cruel, oppressive, and overbearing." The report, the prisoners continued, was shot through with contradictions, and having been witness to the incident, they could not "conceive how Mr. King can possibly come forward, and say, on these grounds, it appeared to him that capt. Shortland was justified in giving the order for the alarm bell."[77]

Many Republican newspapers joined the prisoners' criticism of the investigation and questioning of King's motives and actions. Many proadministration newspapers raised doubt about "the conduct of Mr. King, in lending his name to Mr. Larpent's statement in the case of the Dartmoor Massacre." The *Baltimore Patriot* offered its opinion of "what *ought to have been* the conduct of an individual in his situation." King, the paper argued, ought "to have confined himself to a simple statement of the evidence." Additionally, the report "ought to have been free from everything like an inference or opinion," and "if Mr. King found that Mr. Larpent would not a sign [sic] a bare narrative of the testimony, nor put his name to any document that did not tend to exculpate the wretches who committed the murders, then Mr. King ought to have . . . made a full report of his own convictions touching the massacre." If Mr. King had acted in this manner, "he would have commanded the approbation of every rational man in America."[78] The leading anti-Federalist newspaper in New Hampshire, the *New Hampshire Patriot*, challenged the official findings, arguing that "the joint efforts of Mr. Larpent and Mr. King, do not, in any substantial points, contradict or weaken the statements we have before had from the unfortunate and gallant prisoners themselves who escaped the massacre." The *Patriot* also excoriated King, declaring "for shame upon any American citizen who put his name to such a report" and hoping that the "American public will form its unalterable opinion" on shootings by the "matter of fact" on which the prisoners' accounts were based rather than the "matter of art" that was the method of the Larpent-King report.[79]

Adding to this wave of Republican challenges to the official inquiry, Reuben Beasley tried to clear his name so recently pummeled in the press. He could not "forbear to notice the erroneous impression of the prisoners that their detention so long has been owing to me." A careful of the examination of the evidence, Beasley suggested, would "shew that the necessary steps were taken to provide for [the prisoners'] immediate transportation to their country" following the peace. "Therefore, whatever may have been their uneasiness under confinement," the former U.S. agent explained, "and whatever hostile feelings they may have towards me . . . I must say with confidence, that I could not prevent the one, nor have I deserved the other."[80] Unlike many of the attacks on the report by Republican newspapers, Beasley was simply hoping to clear himself of any culpability in the prisoners' violent fate. His letter was one of the final public acts of "a flawed character cast in a tragedy." Yet Beasley's defense was still another Republican challenge to the official hearings.[81]

Somewhat ironically, the Federalists offered a full-throated defense of the official report and called for an end to the inflamed rhetoric of the previous weeks. The editor of the Federalist *Newburyport Herald* argued that "on no occasion . . . have more unfair endeavours been used to inflate the publick mind than with regard to this unhappy event." It pained the editor that "on the late National festival" the anger over Dartmoor had diffused "acrimony" throughout "the Orations, the Songs, and the Toasts, which were spouted and sung and drunk by the party all over the country." These toasts decried "British cowardice, British barbarity, British murder," all for the sake of Republican politics. The toasts, the Federalists argued, were based on prisoners' accounts, "all of which concur in representing the conduct of the British as in the highest degree wanton and criminal." But these unofficial accounts should not be "taken in the case." Instead, the arrival of the "official report of Gentlemen" provided an account in which "we may reasonably place confidence." Relating the official findings, the editor hoped, would finally put an end to the partisan hyperbole and untruths. "We are glad that about these days no election was pending, which might be unduly influenced by the falsehoods that would have been predicated on this affair," for the such had been the practice of the Republicans, to trade on "anything that will excited hatred toward Britain, and lift their candidate to power!"[82] The seemingly upside-down nature of the discussion of the official findings was a first step in reviving the post–New Orleans nationalism and moving beyond the renewed partisanship. Additionally, news from the Mediterranean provided a means to redirect the passions swirling around the shootings at Dartmoor and revive the feelings of optimism and unity that had been so prevalent in the earliest days of 1815.

On March 2, 1815, the United States Senate voted 27–2 to go to war with Algiers. A day later, Madison signed the bill into law and ordered the dispatch of two squadrons to the Mediterranean to end the Barbary threat. The hero of Tripoli, Commodore Stephen Decatur, led the first squadron out of port on March 20, 1815. Comprising three frigates, a sloop, four brigs, and two schooners, this collection of ships was, to that point, the largest naval fleet ever assembled by the United States. In addition to the sizable fleet, Decatur's own experience in the earlier Barbary conflict and during the War of 1812 prepared him well for the expedition. The second squadron, under the command of Commodore William Bainbridge, left port two months later. Bainbridge, who had himself been held captive in Tripoli, commanded a squadron of seventeen warships, nearly double the size of Decatur's force.[83]

The American fleet was instructed to avoid rushed treaties. Secretary of State James Monroe suggested that negotiations should be conducted with the "dread or success" of American naval power. He advised, "If a just punishment should be inflicted on those people for the insult and injuries we have received from them . . . the peace might be more durable than if it should be concluded at the first approach of our squadron." Decatur took this advice to heart, seizing the Algerian flagship *Mashouda* and the Algerian brig *Estedio* before sailing to Algiers. The capture of these ships yielded nearly five hundred prisoners of war, who were taken to Cartagena, Spain, for detention until a peace settlement was reached.[84]

Following this initial success, Decatur led his squadron to Algiers to begin negotiations. On June 29, through the Swedish consul, he delivered Madison's message demanding peace of the Dey. The American seizure of the *Mashouda* and *Estedio* were critical points in the negotiations that followed. As Decatur later reported to Congress, "the impression made by these events was visible and deep." On confirming the American victories, the dey sent his captain of the port to negotiate with the Americans. The dey initially requested a ceasefire and the conduct of negotiations on Algerian soil, but Decatur refused both demands, insisting that hostilities would cease only after a treaty had been signed and that negotiations would take place onboard the American ships. When the Algerian delegation returned a day later, Decatur noticed that "their anxiety appeared extreme to conclude the peace immediately." He then presented the American demands, refusing to negotiate on any point, including a stipulation that Algiers pay reparations for damage to American property. The Algerian negotiator feared that the dey would reject the treaty; a demand for reparations "had never before been made upon Algiers." Despite this reservation, the Algerian negotiators "came back within three hours, with the treaty signed as we had concluded it, and the prisoners." Decatur's negotiations had finally secured peace with Algiers on American terms. Thirty years after the United States had first been exposed to the threat of Algerian corsairs, a lasting peace was established. Having concluded the negotiations, Decatur believed that this treaty "places the United States on higher ground than any other nation." In the wake of the success in Algiers, he sailed to Tunis and Tripoli, bringing a final end to the long-standing conflict with all the Barbary States. Although it would be months before news of the victory reached the United States, Decatur's belief in the significance of this treaty for the fledgling United States was well founded.[85]

In the wake of a tumultuous two months of public anger and frustration over the Dartmoor shootings, the initial reports of Decatur's success in the Mediterranean in the late summer of 1815 were welcome news throughout the United States. As Americans turned their attention to events in North Africa, the seeming resurgence of a partisan nationalism inspired by the shootings at Dartmoor were subsumed by a celebration of a final settlement with the Barbary States. Reports of peace with Algiers were lauded as "achieving more than all Europe has been able to do" and seen as clear evidence of a bright future for the United States.[86] The *Daily National Intelligencer* responded to the news of the American victory in the Mediterranean by offering a careful consideration of the "prospect before us," noting that the war in Algiers had served as a "new theater of glory for our tars." This victory was a clear demonstration of American power: the navy with "eagle rapidity" had "pounced upon the man stealing barbarian, and in a measure, already annihilated his marine . . . and threatened his capital!" The victory was made all the greater as it was this "youthful republic" that had "the high honor of reducing this nest of pirates, so long the pest of the christian world, to an observance of the rights of peace and war; and make the *civilized* nations of Europe blush for that vile jealousy, wicked policy, and dirty calculation of interest which induced them to permit or endure such depredations." Looking to the future, the *Intelligencer* saw the victory in Algiers as a defining moment for the youthful United States now striding boldly onto the world stage. The editor of the *Intelligencer* was careful not to miss the opportunity to remind his readers of that "strong monarchical party amongst us," whose aspirants to royalty and nobility had so often challenged administration policies and threatened the "cherish[ed] republican institutions" of the United States.[87]

The view from London was strikingly similar. An American in that city wrote that "the first operations of the American squadron have been followed by the recession of the Algerine pirates from their infamous, but, until hitherto, usual demand of tribute. The example of the United States government, we trust, will not be lost to the other maritime powers of Europe."[88] William Cobbett, the erstwhile "Peter Porcupine," having returned to London, wrote to congratulate the United States on its victory. Algiers was, Cobbett noted, "a sort of a cur," but now, "you have broken his jaws, and made him retire to his den." Such an action was "truly a noble use to make of naval power! It cannot fail to enhance your fame, to give pleasure to your friends, and to add to the mortification and vindictiveness of your enemies."[89]

The return of the U.S. squadron, a month after the initial reports of victory appeared in the American press, was marked with celebration. The American sailors found themselves "cheered by applause—hailed with welcome, and crowned with glory. In a few months Decatur, with a few vessels, has done more towards humbling the corsairs of Barbary, than Charles the Vth could effect by a fleet and army."[90] Some celebrated the return of the naval force by looking to antiquity for comparable success and an indication of future American glory. The *American Watchman* asked, "What was the Navy at the commencement of the late war? It increased more than double, not by the expense of building them, but by glorious capture!" The U.S. Navy was like that of "the infant Hercules." "Too mighty for the wily serpent," he "not only encounter[s] him with success; but WHEN THE DAY OF HIS MATURITY SHALL ARRIVE, WE HAVE THE MOST FLATTERING FORBODING THAT HE WILL BE ABLE TO VANQUISH THE MONSTER!"⁹¹

The *Baltimore Patriot,* the same paper that had continued to grumble in the aftermath of the Dartmoor massacre even after the arrival of the official report, now saw a great future for the country: "Knowing the gallant Decatur in times past, when outlines of his character were just unfolding, we saw in him that superior something—that genius, and chivalric cast of mind which distinguish the hero from the phlegmatic fighting officer." Based on these early indications, the paper continued, "the fortunes of Decatur have been with us a subject of peculiar interest." The negotiations in Algiers confirm that he had "commanded a peace upon terms more honorable than was ever before granted to an European nation, either by Algiers, Tunis, or Tripoli." To the operations of Decatur, "the language of Caesar could never have been more appropriately applied. The Barbarians of Africa humbled by a boldness truly characteristic of its author, and peculiarly situated to the occasion, in the language of that celebrated conqueror of antiquity, he might have said to his countrymen—'I came, I saw, I conquered.' Such . . . is the Illustrious Decatur." For the Baltimore paper, American victory and glory in the Mediterranean seemed to have finally erased the lingering fears and doubts raised by the Dartmoor Massacre.⁹²

Around the nation's capital, revelers held dinners to honor the victorious fleet. In December, "the citizens of Baltimore, always ready to testify their high sense of the merits of our naval and military heroes . . . gave to the Gallant DECATUR a public dinner." Held at the Fountain Inn, "a crowded company welcomed the entrance of Commodore Decatur; and the tables were honoured by the presence of all the officers of the navy now on this station." The toasts at the end of the evening highlighted "the valor we celebrate—It has illustrated the brightest page of our history; it deserves our deepest gratitude," along with noting that "Algiers and the other Barbary powers" had been "taught by Decatur's gallant squadron to respect the laws of nations." A month later in Washington, DC, "a number of the citizens of Pennsylvania now in this city and the greater part of the Pennsylvania delegation in Congress . . . gave a dinner at McKeowin's Hotel to commodore Decatur and captain [Charles] Stewart." There, they "sat down to dinner and spent the evening with the purest harmony and good humor." At the end of the dinner, of the congressmen from Pennsylvania presented a song entitled "Yankee Tars," which celebrated

> our *Yankee Tars,* to Afric's shore;
> Our Heroes, lastly led 'em—
> And Turkish banners bow before
> the starry flag of Freedom.

The refrain called on the revelers to

> toast the brave, for they will save
> Columbia's fame from sinking:
> The honor'd scars of Yankee Tars
> Are glorious themes for drinking.

Accounts of these dinners (along with the full text of "Yankee Tars") were published throughout the United States, granting all Americans the opportunity to appreciate and enjoy the celebration of the U.S. naval victories.[93]

Finally, the American victory also became the centerpiece of political speeches. Vermont governor Jonas Galusha, in his state of the state address, which was republished around the country, celebrated "the brave Decatur, and his gallant fellows," who "in the space of a few days, humbled the Dey of Algiers and compelled him to accept a peace dictated by the victor. This, several of the great naval powers of Europe have frequently attempted in vain."[94] In New York, the governor celebrated the victory of "DECATUR, with a few gallant tars," who had done "what Europe united had ever considered impossible. Algiers, as well as Britain, has bowed the neck to the Empire of the West."[95] Most significantly, Madison began his annual address to Congress in 1815 by noting that he had "the satisfaction, on our present meeting, of being able to communicate to you the successful termination of the war which had been commenced against the United States by the Regency of Algiers." He went on to celebrate Decatur's courage and enterprise in seizing two Algerian ships, and then "having prepared the way by his demonstration of skill and prowess, he hastened to the port of Algiers where peace was promptly yielded to his victorious force." In his address on the status of the United States, Madison's first priority was to extol the American victory over the Barbary corsairs in the Mediterranean. Although he highlighted the successful implementation of the Treaty of Ghent, Madison made no mention of the Dartmoor Massacre. In his assessment of the state of the Union in December 1815, the president envisioned and a wide cross-section of the American people saw an American future of freedom, progress, and glory reflected in the Decatur's remarkable naval victory at Algiers rather than the doom, helplessness, and pessimism suggested by the massacre at Dartmoor.[96]

At the time, Decatur's victory in Algiers seemed a seminal moment in American history. At least on par with the American "victory" over the British in the War of 1812, the defeat of the Barbary pirates demonstrated to the world and to its own citizens, the strength and energy of the United States. As the *Daily National Intelligencer* observed, "they who prostrated the bloody *cross* will bring down the pale *crescent*—the *eagle* on the ocean will not desert the pine tree's top that was his nesting place in the forest." The United States had defeated England and subjugated the Barbary States. The partisan jockeying for title of defender of the nation had been eclipsed. The Eagle stood proud.[97]

A year later, in the summer of 1816, American newspapers celebrated as a joint British and Dutch force prepared an attack on Algiers. The American papers reported that Decatur's victory and subsequent treaty "were so favourable, that it excited European envy." So successful, the American press argued, had the American forces been in achieving that which the European powers had failed to do on so many occasions that Decatur's victory "was a tacit reproach upon" the Europeans "and it stimulated their jealousy to exercise." There were, however, deeper meanings to this turn of events. The *Baltimore Federal Republican* argued that "there is a strong probability that all the Christian powers will unite for the extirpation of the barbary marauders. It is extremely astonishing to observe by what invisible chains the attention of the civilized world is now turning to Palestine." This combined effort, sparked by American success in Algiers, would serve "to recover that consecrated spot from the hands of the infidels" and lead to the "exclusion of the Turks from Palestine, and consequently the return of the Jews to Jerusalem." This event, the *Federal Republican* argued, was "near at hand," and the United States in bringing the other Christian nations to this moment had served as "instruments in an Almighty hand."[98]

The expansion of American self-confidence following the War of 1812 was as much a result of the final American victory over the Barbary States as it was a perceived second victory over Britain. The resurgence of partisan sentiment and Anglophobia during the Dartmoor crisis revealed how fragile the political unity and "national feelings" created by the myth of a glorious victory in the War of 1812 had been. The tone of the debate surrounding the Dartmoor Massacre echoed the American response to the plight of their fellow countrymen aboard British prison ships during the American Revolution. If only for a brief moment, Americans no longer focused on the "glorious exploits" of the immortal Jackson or even looked to future success in North Africa but instead were caught up in the "cold blooded massacre at Dartmoor." Just as the victory at Tripoli had been overshadowed by the news of the continued impressment of American sailors and the attack on the *Chesapeake* in 1807, the news of Dartmoor seemed to challenge the sense of optimism fueled by the final settlement of the War of 1812 and sparked a renewed wave of partisan posturing. It was only as news of the American expedition against Algiers began to filter back to the United States that the promise of a new, sustainable American self-confidence that had begun following the end of the War of 1812 was fully realized. In securing a final settlement with the Barbary States and achieving what no European nation had been willing or able to do in more than a century, the United States was able to overcome and largely silence the partisan bickering that had colored the American response to the events at Dartmoor. In forcing the a peace with the Barbary nations and with the British and Dutch following the American lead a year later, many in the United States now believed that their nation stood as one of the leading powers in the world. The end of the Barbary conflict allowed Americans to reimagine their place in the world. Now Americans could define themselves through a string of victories from the end of the Revolution, through the engagements with the Barbary States, and to the end of the War of 1812. American achievement rather than international insecurity defined who they were as a people and nation. Instead, Americans were able to establish their place in the world as a nation that had defeated the Barbary States of North Africa, outlasted the threat of European impressment (Spanish, British, and French), and withstood the might of the British military not once but twice. Americans had securely established themselves in the larger world and, by 1816, the Era of Free Security had begun.[99]

CONCLUSION

"To Promote Each Other's Welfare, and Mutual Feelings of Peace and Good Will"

The Insecurity Bookending an Era of Free Security

AMID A WAVE of patriotism that followed in the wake of the War of 1812 and the end of the Barbary Wars, Americans' opinions of Revolutionary War veterans were radically transformed. Once dismissed as the contemptible remnants of a "regular army," these men came to be seen, by the middle of the nineteenth century, as living links to a rapidly disappearing past. So commanding was the shift in perspective that by the late 1840s, public officials in Cambridge, Massachusetts, appointed a committee to solicit funds for the construction of a monument over the remains of twelve veterans "who fell martyrs to the cause of liberty and independence . . . in the battle of Bunker Hill." In New York, Walt Whitman led the charge for the creation of a "lofty monument" that might stand above the graves of those who had died aboard the city's prison ships. Far to the west, the people of booming Chicago were so desperate for a link to the Revolution that they seized on the dubious claims of David Kennison, who declared himself 112 years old and a veteran of every battle from Lexington to Yorktown. It was during the renewed interest in and veneration of the Revolutionary generation that former prisoner-of-war Charles Herbert's narrative first appeared in print in 1847.[1]

The publisher of the book described Herbert—through a "sketch of the author"—as "a true patriot' who would not be made, through "frowns" or "flatteries" to "abandon his country's interest . . . He can endure hunger, confinement or reproach—any thing but the extinguishing of his country's hope."[2] The portrayal of Herbert as a patriot who remained true to his country conformed to the well-established genre of American captivity narratives that stretched back to the seventeenth century. Like both Ethan Allen and John Dodge before him, Herbert took great care to highlight his undying support for the American cause. When laid low by the "itch" (most likely scabies) during his captivity, Herbert retitled an official list of "rebel prisoners" in the hospital, when he defiantly "scratched out the word rebel and wrote American."[3] Even as their time in captivity stretched from months to years, Herbert and his fellow prisoners, "resolved, although we are prisoners," to engage in a show of pride to mark the anniversary of the Declaration of Independence. Accordingly, on July 4, 1778, Herbert recorded that "when we were let out, we all hoisted the American flag upon our hats."[4] Herbert and his fellow captives saw their fidelity to the new nation and its government rewarded when, in 1779, they received their freedom as part of a prisoner exchange. The newly released Americans traveled to Paris where they met with Benjamin Franklin, John Adams, and Silas Dean before securing passage back to Massachusetts. The final entry in Herbert's journal recorded his arrival "home at Newbury, August 23d, 1780."[5]

In 1847, recognizing the renewed public interest in the Revolutionary generation, Herbert's publisher went on to promise that a "liberal share" of the proceeds from the sale of the volume would be donated to the widow of Charles Herbert, who had been unable to "obtain either the pension allowed by the law of our land to widows of Revolutionary soldiers and sailors" and was now "at the advanced age of eighty-four, lingering among us as a relic of a people precious in our memory."[6] Both the publication of the journal and the publisher's promise to support Herbert's widow reflected the popular interest in these narratives—in no small part due to the larger American effort to reconnect with the "precious" founding generation, the remnants of which were now passing away.[7]

The publication of Herbert's journal, for all its similarities to earlier captivity narratives, also marks a dramatic shift in tone from the accounts that had preceded it. In addition to the attention paid throughout the narrative to the sacrifice of the Revolutionary generation, the 1847 edition of Herbert's account included a striking comment on the Anglo-American relationship. The publisher declared his hope that the account of British charity toward the American prisoners might serve as "an everlasting monument to the benevolence of British Christians and may serve to soften our prejudices and lead to stronger sympathies for each other, and great efforts to promote each other's welfare, and mutual feelings of peace and good will." Although the narrative structure of much of Herbert's account would have been familiar to readers of Revolutionary War captivity narratives, the effort to highlight "the benevolence of British Christians" would have been a shock.[8]

It appears that by the middle of the nineteenth century, one of the key rationales for publishing a Revolutionary-era captivity narrative had been completely reversed. No longer was the story of a prisoner meant to evoke feelings of outrage toward a cruel British enemy. Instead, the story was meant to promote feelings of "good will" between the United States and Great Britain to highlight the deep connection between the two nations.[9] The redefinition of the goal of this Revolutionary captivity narrative, to demonstrate the kind treatment of American prisoners by "British Christians," marked a significant transition in the relationship between the United States and its former colonial master. While fear of an "other" had been a key part of building a distinct American identity in the decades immediately following Independence, by the middle of the nineteenth century, many Americans were confident enough to find the good and virtue in Great Britain. The "savage British other" had become "benevolent British Christians," who were not so different from the Americans themselves—the era of "free security" had begun. Free from serious external threat, Americans felt secure enough to turn their focus inward.

For much of the first half of the nineteenth century, before the "era of free security," accounts of American captivity at the hands of a foreign power, whether the British military or North African "pirates," had served as markers of the young United States' vulnerability in the Atlantic world. Prior to the ratification of the Constitution, the captivity of American sailors in North Africa and the national government's inability to secure their freedom were symptomatic of structural issues within the new American government, spurring the move to the Constitutional Convention. In the decades that followed ratification, accounts of American captivity by both the Barbary States and the British military generated a popular energy that played a significant role in shaping the emerging political culture of the early United States.

Faced with this American vulnerability on the international stage, both Federalists and Republicans quickly came to recognize the power of captivity narratives in motivating the public to act. As a consequence, both groups increasingly attempted to speak to the security concerns raised by the plight of captive Americans. Ultimately, in an attempt to curry electoral favor, both Federalists and Republicans used similar language to develop a nationalist rhetoric intended to serve as a core part of each parties' unique identity. Between 1790 and 1816. both parties endeavored to control the debate over American security and to depict their opponents' policies, although similar in many ways, as incapable of defending American liberty abroad.

Throughout the 1790s, during the Washington and Adams administrations, Federalist members of Congress worked to maintain control of the narrative surrounding the Barbary threat to American sailors. In one instance, the Federalist majority closed the congressional galleries during foreign-policy debates, allowing public access only after crafting a strong military response to the Barbary threat and passing legislation that provided for the creation of the U.S. Navy. By 1800, Republicans, who had criticized the Federalist use of naval force in response to the Barbary threat in the 1790s, were quick to embrace a military threat and wage a war of their own. While the shifting political landscape of both the United States and Atlantic world often resulted in a somewhat confused partisan response, both parties continually sought to claim the mantle of defender of American liberty and security—at times going so far as to contradict long-standing party principles in pursuit of this goal.

In wake of the American "victory" over the British in the War of 1812 and the termination of the Barbary threat, the partisan back and forth disappeared as Americans entered an era of political "good feelings" and international security. Subsequent to these successes, American geopolitical insecurity was replaced by a hard-won self-confidence made manifest in part in President James Monroe's annual message to Congress in December 1823. Confronted by Russian claims in the Pacific Northwest and by the threat of the intervention of the Holy Alliance in Central and South America, the president warned European powers that the American continents were "henceforth not to be considered as subjects for colonization by any European powers." The Monroe Doctrine, declaring the Western Hemisphere U.S. realm, simultaneously emerged from a growing sense of American self-confidence and a growing competition with Britain for influence in Latin America—all with tacit British approval.[10]

Following the Napoleonic Wars, the U.S. success in the Mediterranean, and the simultaneous creation of the Holy Alliance, Britain evolved from an existential threat to the United States to a potential ally. Britain remained the far superior power, but a shared interest in limiting the influence of the members of the Holy Alliance in both North and South America helped motivate a renewed special relationship between the United States and Great Britain. Moreover, the British Empire's global reach provided something of an umbrella under which the imperial ambitions of the United States could grow. As historian Jay Sexton has observed, British power in this era served "as a midwife to the rising American empire."[11] Thus, by the publication of Herbert's narrative in 1847, the effort to promote "mutual feelings of peace and good will" between the two nations was as much a reflection of the national mood in the nineteenth century as the older narratives had been of the eighteenth century.[12]

While the era of a free security would last for a century, it came to a crashing halt in the middle of the twentieth century. Following the Japanese attack on Pearl Harbor, Americans found themselves engaged in a second world war that was followed quickly by a cold war with the Soviet Union. Although the United States entered the Cold War in a geopolitical position fundamentally different than it had occupied at the beginning of the nineteenth century, the American perception of global Soviet threat produced a level of anxiety and insecurity that mirrored that of the Early American Republic. Insecurity abroad had informed and shaped U.S. domestic politics in the earliest years of the United States, and historians Campbell Craig and Fredrik Logevall argue that American politics during the Cold War were similarly international and domestic, or "intermestic," meaning "the two are dynamically intertwined." From this vantage point, "Republicans hit Democrats with being 'soft on communism,' with not doing enough to thwart either Soviet aggression abroad or subversive activity at home." Democrats countered by working hard to "demonstrate their anti-communist bona fides." Throughout the Cold War, "vociferous anti-communism became the default posture of virtually every serious candidate for national office."[13] Despite the distance of a century and the differences marking the geopolitical positions of the United States in these two temporally disparate eras, American politicians in both the early nineteenth and in the twentieth centuries well understood the "logic of the 'intermestic.'" Federalists and Democratic-Republicans of the nineteenth century and Republicans and Democrats of the twentieth came to understand the "sizeable political benefits that could be accrued by characterizing international incidents or trends, no matter how minor, as dangerous threats to the nation."[14]

While the era of free security is bookended by these periods of insecurity and "intermestic" politics, it is worth noting that a thin strand of insecurity remained very much entwined in American politics throughout the period and provided a thread of insecurity connecting the periods before and after the era of free security. Engaged in a controversial war with Mexico and struggling with the great debate over slavery and immigration, captivity narratives experienced a revival of popularity in the mid-nineteenth century, as stories of captivity in Catholic convents and slave narratives seized the imagination of the American public. These new captivity narratives refocused American anxiety away from the earlier external threats of British and North African captivity to growing internal dangers to American liberty from racial and religious "others."

A large immigration of Catholics to the United States in the mid-nineteenth century gave new life to anti-Catholicism in the country. The new movement was reminiscent of the anti-Catholicism dating back to the first British settlement in North America. Catholic captivity narratives, beginning with Maria Monk's *Awful Disclosures of the Hotel Dieu Nunnery* in 1836, helped to spark a series of anti-Catholic riots and attacks on Catholic priests, culminating with the populist Know Nothing movement of the 1850s.[15] Operating in parallel cultural tack, slave narratives such as the *Narrative of the Life of Frederick Douglass* (1845) and novels such as *Uncle Tom's Cabin* (1852) provided Americans with a view of the captivity and brutality practiced in southern slavery, helping to draw people to the abolitionist cause.

Catholic and slave narratives clearly demonstrated that the power of captivity to influence and shape American political debate was undiminished in the nineteenth century. The geopolitical position of the United States in world affairs had undergone a dramatic transformation by the 1850s, but the theme of captivity still spoke to American insecurities. Although the subject of these narratives had shifted from external to domestic captivity, this new generation of captivity narratives retained a hold on the American imagination and channeled American anxieties into political action. As they had since the colonial era, captivity narratives both reflected and shaped public opinion in the United States, ultimately influencing the direction of American politics.

Although the United States enjoyed a century of "free security," the uncertainly that had marked the earliest days of American Independence would remain a part of its political DNA. When properly exploited, the kernel of insecurity planted in American identity remained a viable means by which to motivate the American public to take action against internal and external enemies or threats. In the Revolutionary Era and the Early American Republic, this insecurity was a key component of both Federalist and Republican efforts to bring the American people around to their vision for the new nation, later delivering a key source of fuel for sparking the nativist, anti-Catholic Know Nothing movement of the 1850s. This insecurity also played a role in igniting the Civil War, with the abolitionist movement deploying slave narratives to build support for the cause of freedom. By the mid-twentieth century, the politics of fear and insecurity once again led to a fusion of international and domestic politics that helped to shape the contours of the Cold War with the Soviet Union.

Even in the wake of the Cold War and the collapse of the Soviet Union, the power of insecurity remains substantial and powerful in American society. In the early twenty-first century, Secretary of Defense Donald Rumsfeld instructed members of his department to "keep elevating the threat . . . [and] make the American people realize they are surrounded in the world by violent extremists."[16] Although framed differently two centuries later, the sentiment is one that would have been familiar to John Jay and many members of the founding generation.

Notes

Preface

1. Entry of October 13, 1785, *Journals of the Continental Congress, 1774–1789*, ed. Worthington C. Ford et al. (Washington, DC, 1904–1937), 29:833–34.

Introduction

1. Charles Herbert, *A Relic of the Revolution, Containing a Full and Particular Account of the Sufferings and Privations of All the American Prisoners Captured on the High Seas and Carried into Plymouth, England, during the Revolution of 1776* . . . (Boston: Charles H Peirce, 1847), 18–20; Francis Cogliano, *American Maritime Prisoners in the Revolutionary War: The Captivity of William Russell* (Annapolis, MD: Naval Institute Press, 2001), 42–47.
2. Herbert, *Relic of the Revolution*, 18–20; Cogliano, *American Maritime Prisoners in the Revolutionary War*, 45; Holger Hoock, *Scars of Independence: America's Violent Birth* (New York: Crown Books, 2017), 224–36; Wayne E. Lee, *Barbarians and Brothers: Anglo American Warfare, 1500–1865* (Oxford, UK: Oxford University Press, 2014), 145–46.
3. George Washington to Thomas Gage, August 11, 1775, in *The Papers of George Washington*, vol. 1, *16 June 1775–15 September 1775*, Revolutionary War Series, ed. Philander D. Chase (Charlottesville: University Press of Virginia, 1985), 289–91.
4. North's Act, as it came to be called, allowed for American prisoners to receive treatment similar to that of other prisoners of war. See Hoock, *Scars of Independence*, 226; Herbert, *Relic of the Revolution*, 18–20; Cogliano, *American Maritime Prisoners in the Revolutionary War*, 45.
5. Herbert, *Relic of the Revolution*, 19–20.
6. Richard L. Merritt, *Symbols of American Community, 1735–1775* (New Haven: Yale University Press, 1966), 58.
7. T. H. Breen, "Ideology and Nationalism on the Eve of the American Revolution: Revisions Once More in Need of Revising," *Journal of American History* 84, no. 1 (June 1997): 13–39; Linda Colley, *Britons: Forging the Nation, 1707–1837* (New Haven: Yale University Press, 2009), 134–41. Jon Butler has argued that the transformation of the British North American colonies began more than a century before the American Revolution *and* culminated in a "distinctly modern" and American society by 1770. See his *Becoming America: The Revolution before 1776* (Cambridge, MA: Harvard University Press, 2000), 2.
8. For an example of the mixed response to the war in England, see Colley, *Britons*, 139–41,

and Hoock, *Scars of Independence*, 63–67. On loyalist numbers, see Maya Jasanoff, *Liberty's Exiles: American Loyalists in the Revolutionary World* (New York: Vintage Books, 2012), 8.
9. Greg Sieminski, "The Puritan Captivity Narrative and the Politics of the American Revolution," *American Quarterly* 42, no. 1 (March 1990), 35–56.
10. On "democratic urges," see Seth Cotlar, *Tom Paine's America: The Rise and Fall of Transatlantic Radicalism in the Early Republic* (Charlottesville: University of Virginia Press, 2011), 4.
11. C. Vann Woodward, "The Age of Reinterpretation," *The American Historical Review* 66, no. 1 (October 1960): 1–19. He introduces the term *era of free security* on p. 3.
12. *Connecticut Journal* (New Haven), January 30, 1777; *Connecticut Gazette* (New London), February 28, 1777; *Continental Journal* (Boston), March 13, 1777; *Freeman's Journal* (Portsmouth, NH), March 22, 1777.
13. On the place of sailors in the popular imagination and public opinion in the early United States, see Brian Rouleau, *With Sails Whitening Every Sea: Mariners and the Making of the American Maritime Empire* (Ithaca, NY: Cornell University Press, 2014); Dane Morrison, *True Yankees: The South Seas and the Discovery of American Identity* (Baltimore, MD: Johns Hopkins University Press, 2014); and Nathan Perl-Rosenthal, *Citizen Sailors: Becoming American in the Age of Revolution* (Cambridge, MA: Belknap Press of Harvard University, 2015).
14. Todd Estes, *The Jay Treaty Debate, Public Opinion, and the Evolution of Early American Political Culture* (Amherst: University of Massachusetts Press, 2006), 9. Estes, while acknowledging the impact of the ratification debates surrounding the Constitution, argues that the period between 1794 and 1796 witnessed a revision of "the entire political system within which the nascent parties operated." This change occurred as the Federalists evolved their understanding of the public sphere by orchestrating a Jay Treaty petition drive with the direct intent to use the voice of the people to shape public policy. An examination of the debate over American captivity in North Africa reveals the likely roots of this shift. In responding to the crisis in Algiers through petitions, letters, newspapers, and the theater, many citizens in the American public demonstrated their involvement in national policy. It was recognition of the power of these active citizens that prepared the Federalists for the fight over the ratification of the Jay Treaty a year later. Based on the examination of the Algiers debate, the mobilization of public opinion around the Jay Treaty was part of an emerging public opinion that had begun as early as 1783. Mark Schmeller, "The Political Economy of Opinion: Public Credit and Concepts of Public Opinion in the Age of Federalism," *Journal of the Early Republic* 29, no. 1 (Spring 2009): 35–61; Christopher Young, "Connecting the President and the People: Washington's Neutrality, Genet's Challenge, and Hamilton's Fight for Public Support," *Journal of the Early Republic* 31, no. 3 (Fall 2011): 435–66.
15. *National Gazette* (Philadelphia, PA), December 19, 1791. Emphasis in the original.
16. Estes, *The Jay Treaty Debate*, 8–13; Colleen A. Sheehan, "The Politics of Public Opinion: James Madison's 'Notes of Government,'" *William and Mary Quarterly* 49, no. 4 (October 1992): 626.
17. Cotlar, *Tom Paine's America*, 4–6. See also Jeffrey Pasley, Andrew Robertson, and David Waldstreicher, eds., *Beyond the Founders: New Approaches to the Political History of the Early American Republic* (Chapel Hill: University of North Carolina Press, 2004).
18. Denver Brunsman, *The Evil Necessity: British Naval Impressment in the Eighteenth-Century Atlantic World* (Charlottesville: University of Virginia Press, 2013), 241–46. Christopher Magra in *Poseidon's Curse: British Naval Impressment and the Atlantic Origins of the American Revolution* (New York: Cambridge University Press, 2016) also ties anti-impressment sentiment to the coming of the Revolution, arguing that the roots of the issue extend as far back as 1746.

19. See Morrison, *True Yankees*, xii-xiii, and Lawrence Peskin, *Captives and Countrymen: Barbary Slavery and the American Public, 1785-1816* (Baltimore: Johns Hopkins University Press, 2009), 7-23.
20. Perl-Rosenthal, *Citizen Sailors*, explores the issue of the joint effort between sailors and the federal government in formally defining citizenship between 1796 and 1803. On the broader questions of American citizenship, see Douglas Bradburn, *The Citizenship Revolution: Politics and the Creation of the American Union, 1774-1804* (Charlottesville: University of Virginia Press, 2009).
21. Rouleau, *With Sails Whitening Every Sea*, 7.
22. The impact of American sailors' travels to China on American identity is discussed in Kariann Akemi Yokota, *Unbecoming British: How Revolutionary America Became a Postcolonial Nation* (New York: Oxford University Press, 2011), 115-44, and Morrison, *True Yankees*, 3-50.
23. Robbie J. Totten, "Security, Two Diplomacies, and the Formation of the U.S. Constitution: Review, Interpretation, and New Directions for the Study of the Early American Period," *Diplomatic History* 36, no. 1 (January 2012): 77-117; David Hendrickson, *Peace Pact: The Lost World of the American Founding* (Lawrence: University Press of Kansas, 2003). A number of works by Peter Onuf address this issue: Peter Onuf, *The Origins of the Federal Republic: Jurisdictional Controversies in the United States, 1775-1787* (Philadelphia: University of Pennsylvania Press, 1983); Peter Onuf and Cathy Matson, *A Union of Interests: Political and Economic Thought in Revolutionary America* (Lawrence: University Press of Kansas, 1990); and Peter Onuf and Nicholas Onuf, *Federal Union, Modern World: The Law of Nations in an Age of Revolutions, 1776-1814* (Madison, WI: Madison House, 1993).
24. On Nationalism, see Benedict Anderson, *Imagined Communities*, rev. edition (New York: Verso, 1991); Linda Colley, *Captives: The Story of Britain's Pursuit of Empire and How Its Soldiers and Civilians Were Held Captive by the Dream of Global Supremacy, 1600-1850* (New York: Pantheon Books, 2002), 219-27. For more on the evolving nature of "American Character," see Charles Royster, *A Revolutionary People at War: The Continental Army and American Character, 1775-1783* (Chapel Hill: The University of North Carolina Press, 1979); Michael Kammen, *A Season of Youth: The American Revolution and the Historical Imagination* (New York: Alfred Knopf, 1978); Alfred Young, *The Shoemaker and the Tea Party: Memory and the American Revolution* (Boston: Beacon Press, 1999); Sarah Purcell, *Sealed with Blood: War, Sacrifice, and Memory in Revolutionary America* (Philadelphia: University of Pennsylvania Press, 2002); David Waldstreicher, *In the Midst of Perpetual Fetes: The Making of American Nationalism, 1776-1820* (Chapel Hill: University of North Carolina Press, 1997). On public debate, see Christopher Grasso, *A Speaking Aristocracy: Transforming Public Discourse in Eighteenth-Century Connecticut* (Chapel Hill: University of North Carolina Press, 1999); Michael Warner, *Letters of the Republic: Publication and the Public Sphere in Eighteenth-Century America* (Cambridge, MA: Harvard University Press, 1990); David Copeland, "America 1750-1820," in *Press, Politics and the Public Sphere in Europe and North America, 1760-1820*, ed. Hannah Barker and Simon Burrows (New York: Cambridge University Press, 2002); Charles Clark, *The Public Prints: The Newspaper in Anglo-American Culture, 1665-1740* (Oxford, UK: Oxford University Press, 1994).
25. Paul Gilje, *Liberty on the Waterfront: American Maritime Culture in the Age of Revolution* (Philadelphia: University of Pennsylvania Press, 2004); Peskin, *Captives and Countrymen*; Rouleau, *With Sails Whitening Every Sea*; Morrison, *True Yankees*; Perl-Rosenthal, *Citizen Sailors*.
26. See James Brown Scott, *James Madison's Notes of Debates in the Federal Convention of 1787 and Their Relation to a More Perfect Society of Nations* (New York: Oxford University Press, 1918); Merle E. Curti, *Peace or War: The American Struggle, 1636-1936* (New York: W. W. Norton

and Company, 1936); Clarence Streit, *Freedom's Frontier: Atlantic Union Now* (New York: Harper, 1961). For further consideration of these authors, see Totten, "Security, Two Diplomacies," 81–83, and Hendrickson, *Peace Pact*, 285–88.

27. See Louis Hartz, *The Liberal Tradition in America: An Interpretation of American Political Thought Since the Revolution* (New York: Harcourt Brace, 1955); Bernard Bailyn, *The Ideological Origins of the American Revolution* (Cambridge, MA: Harvard University Press, 1967); Gordon Wood, *The Creation of the American Republic, 1776–1787* (Chapel Hill: University of North Carolina Press, 1969). For more on the concept of republicanism, see Daniel T. Rodgers, "Republicanism: The Career of a Concept," *Journal of American History* 79, no. 1 (June 1992): 11–38.

28. Marks, *Independence on Trial*; Hendrickson, *Peace Pact*; Onuf, *The Origins of the Federal Republic*; Onuf and Matson, *A Union of Interests*; and Onuf and Onuf, *Federal Union, Modern World*. For a more thorough review of the literature of this period, see Totten, "Security, Two Diplomacies."

29. Walter Hixson, *The Myth of American Diplomacy: National Identity and U.S. Foreign Policy* (New Haven: Yale University Press, 2008), 5–14.

30. Grasso, *A Speaking Aristocracy*, 4. A number of historians have placed the earliest moments of the public sphere in the American Colonies/United States at the beginning of the eighteenth century. See Warner, *Letters of the Republic*; Copeland, "America, 1750–1820"; Clark, *The Public Prints*. In addition to the growth of the American press, Richard John has demonstrated how the federal postal system encouraged the distribution of these newspapers to a national audience. Richard John, *Spreading the News: The American Postal System from Franklin to Morse* (Cambridge, MA: Harvard University Press, 1995). On parades and festivals see Waldstreicher, *In the Midst of Perpetual Fetes*. On theaters, see Heather S. Nathans, *Early American Theater from the Revolution to Thomas Jefferson: Into the Hands of the People* (Cambridge, UK: Cambridge University Press, 2003), 81.

31. Yokota, *Unbecoming British*, 9–12.

32. C. Vann Woodward, "The Age of Reinterpretation," 1–19. In his original definition of the term, Woodward sets the bounds of the era of "free security" between "the second war with England and the Second World War." I argue here for a slightly later start following the end of the conflict with the Barbary States.

33. Yokota, *Unbecoming British*; Haynes, *The Unfinished Revolution: The Early American Republic in a British World* (Charlottesville: University of Virginia Press, 2010); Rachel Hope Cleves, *The Reign of Terror in America: Visions of Violence from Anti-Jacobinism to Antislavery* (New York: Cambridge University Press, 2009). See especially Haynes, "Growing Up Anti-Jacobin," chap. 6 of *Unfinished Revolution*, 230–75.

34. On insecurity during the Cold War, see Campbell Craig and Fredrick Logevall, *America's Cold War: The Politics of Insecurity* (Cambridge, MA: Belknap Press of Harvard University, 2009), 2–11. I expand on this connection in the conclusion to this book.

35. See Colley, *Captives*, 219–27. For more on the evolving nature of "American character" during the Revolution, see Royster, *A Revolutionary People at War*; Kammen, *A Season of Youth*; Young, *The Shoemaker and the Tea Party*; Purcell, *Sealed with Blood*.

36. See Peskin, *Captives and Countrymen*, and Frederick Marks, *Independence on Trial: Foreign Affairs and the Making of the Constitution* (Baton Rouge: Louisiana State University Press, 1973).

37. See Onuf and Onuf, *Federal Union, Modern World*, 175–84.

38. Donald Hickey, *The War of 1812: The Forgotten Conflict* (Chicago: University of Illinois Press, 1989), 308–9; Roger H. Brown, *The Republic in Peril: 1812* (New York: Columbia University Press, 1964).

39. "The Prospect before Us," *Niles' Weekly Register* (Baltimore, MD), September 2, 1815, 1–3. See also C. Edward Skeen, *1816: America Rising* (Lexington: University of Kentucky Press, 2003), 23.

40. H. W. Brands, *American Dreams* (New York: Penguin Books, 2010), 218–19.

Chapter 1: "Obligations Arising from the Rights of Humanity"

1. Nathan Fiske, *An Historical Discourse Concerning the Settlement of Brookfield and Its Distresses during the Indian Wars* (Boston: Printed by Thomas and John Fleet, 1776), 25–29. See also Joseph Foot, *An Historical Discourse Delivered at West Brookfield, Massachusetts, November 27, 1828, on the Day of the Annual Thanksgiving* (West Brookfield: Merriam and Cooke, 1843).
2. Fiske, *Remarkable Providences*, 28–29.
3. For more on the contest to set the tone of public debate during the Revolution, see Philip Davidson, *Propaganda and the American Revolution, 1763–1783* (Chapel Hill: University of North Carolina Press, 1941); Bernard Bailyn and John Hench, eds., *The Press and the American Revolution* (Boston: Northeastern University Press, 1981); and Jeffrey Pasley, *"The Tyranny of Printers": Newspaper Politics in the Early American Republic* (Charlottesville: University of Virginia Press, 2001), 33–38.
4. Rowlandson's narrative was advertised in the *Massachusetts Spy* (Worcester, MA), September 12, 1771, September 26, 1771, and October 3, 1771; *New London Gazette* (CT), December 3, 1773; and *Newport Mercury* (RI) March 7, 1774, and March 14, 1774. Williams's narrative was noted in the *New London Gazette* (CT), April 9, 1773, March 23, 1776, and May 3, 1776. See also Jill Lepore, *The Name of War: King Philip's War and the Origins of American Identity* (New York: Vintage Books, 1998), 186–90; Greg Sieminski, "The Puritan Captivity Narrative and the Politics of the American Revolution," *American Quarterly* 42, no. 1 (March 1990): 35–56.
5. For the meaning of the Revolution to a Boston shoemaker, see Alfred Young, *The Shoemaker and the Tea Party: Memory and the American Revolution* (Boston: Beacon Press, 1999). On sailors and the Revolution, see Paul Gilje, *Liberty on the Waterfront: American Maritime Culture in the Age of Revolution* (Philadelphia: University of Pennsylvania Press, 2004). On the place of soldiers in the development of American citizenship, see Ricardo Herrera, *For Liberty and the Republic: The American Citizen as Soldier, 1775–1861* (New York: New York University Press, 2015).
6. George Washington to Thomas Gage, August 11, 1775, and Thomas Gage to George Washington, August 13, 1775, in *The Writings of George Washington from the Original Manuscript Sources, 1745–1799*, ed. John C. Fitzpatrick (Washington, DC: Government Printing Office, 1936).
7. *Pennsylvania Evening Post* (Philadelphia), September 28, 1775; *Story and Humphrey's Pennsylvania Mercury* (Philadelphia), September 29, 1775; *Pennsylvania Ledger* (Philadelphia), September 30, 1775. See also *Journals of the Continental Congress 1774–1779*, ed. Worthington C. Ford et al. (Washington, DC, 1904–1937); 4:370.
8. Linda Colley, *Captives: The Story of Britain's Pursuit of Empire and How Its Soldiers and Civilians Were Held Captive by the Dream of Global Supremacy, 1600–1850* (New York: Pantheon Books, 2002), 221–22. For more on the importance of the press in the years leading up to and during the American Revolution, see Bailyn and Hench, eds., *The Press and the American Revolution* (Worcester, MA: American Antiquarian Society, 1980), and David Copeland, "America 1750–1820," in *Press, Politics and the Public Sphere in Europe and North America, 1760–1820*, ed. Hannah Barker and Simon Burrows (Cambridge, UK: Cambridge University Press, 2002), 140–58. On American efforts to seize and retain the moral high ground, see Holger Hoock, *Scars of Independence: America's Violent Birth* (New York: Crown Books, 2017).
9. See Frederick Mackenzie, *Diary of Frederick Mackenzie* (Cambridge: Harvard University Press, 1930), 1:44; Larry Bowman, *Captive Americans: Prisoners of War during the American Revolution* (Athens, OH: Ohio University Press, 1976); Edwin Burrows, *Forgotten Patriots: The Untold Story of American Prisoners during the Revolutionary War* (New York: Basic Books, 2008); Charles Metzger, *The Prisoner in the American Revolution* (Chicago: Loyola University Press, 1971). In several instances, members of the British military took it upon

themselves to punish treason with death. See David Hackett Fischer, *Washington's Crossing* (Oxford, UK: Oxford University Press, 2004), 375–79.
10. Colley, *Captives*, 216–20.
11. Ibid., 218–24. American prisoners were finally granted prisoner-of-war status in 1782. For more on the issue of citizenship see Douglas Bradburn, *The Citizenship Revolution: Politics and the Creation of the American Union 1774–1804* (Charlottesville: University of Virginia Press, 2009); Rogers M. Smith, *Civic Ideals: Conflicting Visions of Citizenship in U.S. History* (New Haven: Yale University Press, 1997); and James H. Kettner, *The Development of American Citizenship* (Chapel Hill: University of North Carolina Press, 1978).
12. Bowman, *Captive Americans*, 1–31.
13. Burrows, *Forgotten Patriots*, 53–54.
14. The appeal by Humanitus was reprinted in *Pennsylvania Evening Post* (Philadelphia), November 7, 1776.
15. Burrows, *Forgotten Patriots*, 80.
16. Cogliano, *American Maritime Prisoners in the Revolutionary War: The Captivity of William Russell* (Annapolis, MD: Naval Institute Press, 2001), 60–62.
17. Gilje, *Liberty on the Waterfront*, 118–20; Bowman, *Captive Americans*, 51–58.
18. Bowman, *Captive Americans*, 9–16.
19. Ibid., 43.
20. *Pennsylvania Evening Post* (Philadelphia), November 7, 1776, and January 9, 1777. Data on morality rates can be found in Cogliano, *American Maritime Prisoners in the Revolutionary War*, 149–50; Howard Peckham, *The Toll of Independence: Engagements and Battle Casualties of the American Revolution* (Chicago: University of Chicago Press, 1974), 131–33; and Burrows, *Forgotten Patriots*, 195–204. See also Hoock, *Scars of Independence*, 215–44.
21. See *Pennsylvania Evening Post* (Philadelphia), November 7, 1776; *Norwich* (Connecticut) *Packet*, December 2, 1776; *Massachusetts Spy* (Worcester), January 2, 1777; *Freeman's Journal* (Portsmouth, NH), January 7, 1777.
22. *Pennsylvania Evening Post* (Philadelphia), January 9, 1777.
23. Ibid.
24. *Connecticut Gazette* (New London), January 17, 1777; *New England Chronicle* (Boston), January 23, 1777; *Pennsylvania Evening Post* (Philadelphia), January 9, 1777.
25. See *Connecticut Journal* (New Haven), January 30, 1777; *Connecticut Gazette* (New London), February 28, 1777; *Continental Journal* (Boston, MA), March 13, 1777; and *Freeman's Journal* (Portsmouth, NH), March 22, 1777. Burrows, *Forgotten Patriots*, 75–77.
26. *Pennsylvania Evening Post* (Philadelphia), January 30, 1777
27. *Journals of the Continental Congress* 7 (1777): 277–79. Burrows, *Forgotten Patriots*, 81–83.
28. *Journals of the Continental Congress* 7 (1777): 277–79; John Adams to Abigail Adams, April 27, 1777, and John Adams to Abigail Adams, April 28, 1777, in *Letters of Delegates to Congress*, vol. 6, ed. Paul H. Smith et al. (Washington, DC: Library of Congress, 1976), 661–62, 667–68.
29. *Independent Chronicle* (Boston, MA), August 29, 1777; *Pennsylvania Packet or the General Advertiser* (Philadelphia), January 28, 1778; *Wochentliche Philadelphische Staatsbote* (Philadelphia, PA), May 28, 1777.
30. *Independent Ledger* (Boston, MA), February 1, 1779; *Exeter Journal* (NH), February 9, 1779; *Connecticut Courant* (Hartford), February 9, 1779; Burrows, *Forgotten Patriots*, 143–44.
31. Thomas Dring, *Recollections of the Jersey Prison Ship*, ed. Albert Greene, The American Experience Series (New York: Corinth Books, 1961).
32. *Pennsylvania Packet* (Philadelphia), January 16, 1781. See also *American Journal and General Advertiser* (Providence, RI), February 7, 1781; *Independent Chronicle and Universal Advertiser* (Boston, MA), February 8, 1781; *New York Gazette and Weekly Mercury* (NY), February 12, 1781. The full Congressional response can be found in *Massachusetts Spy* (Worcester), February 15, 1781.

33. Burrows, *Forgotten Patriots*, 148–54; *Independent Ledger* (Boston, MA), August 12, 1782; *Salem Gazette* (MA), August 22, 1782; *Pennsylvania Packet* (Philadelphia), August 29, 1782.
34. *New York Gazette and the Weekly Mercury* (NY), February 12, 1781.
35. Ibid.; Cogliano, *American Maritime Prisoners in the Revolutionary War*, 160.
36. *New York Gazette and Weekly Mercury* (NY), February 12, 1781.
37. *American Journal* (Providence, RI), February 17, 1781. The account is also in *Norwich Packet and the Weekly Advertiser* (CT), February 20, 1781, and *New Jersey Gazette* (Elizabethtown), February 21, 1781.
38. Bowman, *Captive Americans*, 93–96.
39. Ibid.
40. Gilje, *Liberty on the Waterfront*, 119.
41. Bowman, *Captive Americans*, 93–96.
42. Gilje, *Liberty on the Waterfront*, 118–29.
43. Ethan Allen, *A Narrative of Colonel Ethan Allen's Captivity* (Philadelphia, PA: Printed for and sold by William Mentz, 1779); John Dodge, *An Entertaining Narrative of the Cruel and Barbarous Treatment and Extreme Suffering of Mr. John Dodge during His Captivity of Many Months among the British* (Danvers, MA: Printed and sold by E. Russell, 1780). Other prisoner narratives published as books following the Revolution include John Blatchford, *Narrative of the Life and Captivity of John Blatchford* (New London: T. Green, 1788); Israel Potter, *Life and Remarkable Adventures of Israel R. Potter, (a native of Cranston, Rhode-Island) Who Was a Soldier in the American Revolution, after Which He Was Taken Prisoner by the British, Conveyed to England, Where for 30 Years He Obtained a Livelihood, by Crying "Old Chairs to Mend"* (Providence, RI: Printed by H. Trumbull, 1824); and Charles Herbert, *A Relic of the Revolution, Containing a Full and Particular Account of the Sufferings and Privations of All the American Prisoners Captured on the High Seas and Carried into Plymouth, England, during the Revolution of 1776* (Boston: Charles H. Peirce, 1847).
44. For more on the issue of fact versus fiction in autobiographies, see Myra Glenn, *Jack Tar's Story: The Autobiographies and Memoirs of Sailors in Antebellum America* (New York: Cambridge University Press, 2010), 8–12.
45. John Pell, *Ethan Allen* (New York: Houghton Mifflin, 1929). See Michael Bellesiles, *Revolutionary Outlaws: Ethan Allen and the Struggle for Independence on the Early American Frontier* (Charlottesville: University Press of Virginia, 1993); and Charles A. Jellison, *Ethan Allen: Frontier Rebel* (Syracuse, NY: Syracuse University Press, 1969).
46. Allen, *Narrative of Colonel Ethan Allen's Captivity*, 32–33.
47. Ibid., 40–44. For a more detailed examination of the similarities between colonial captivity narratives and those of the American Revolution, see Greg Sieminski, "The Puritan Captivity Narrative," 36-38.
48. For a slightly different interpretation of Dodge's narrative, see Daniel Williams, ed., introduction to *Liberty's Captives: Narratives of Confinement in the Print Culture of the Early Republic* (Athens: University of Georgia, 2006), 17–18.
49. For more on Barbary captivity, see Lawrence Peskin, *Captives and Countrymen: Barbary Slavery and the American Public, 1785–1816* (Baltimore: Johns Hopkins University Press, 2009).
50. Richard Slotkin, *Regeneration through Violence: The Mythology of the American Frontier, 1600–1860* (Middletown, CT: Wesleyan University Press, 1973), 23.
51. See ibid., 95–96, 247, 278–94, and Sieminski, "The Puritan Captivity Narrative," 35–36.
52. Dodge, *An Entertaining Narrative*, 29.
53. Ibid., 34–36.
54. Ibid., 36–37.
55. Ibid., 50.
56. Philip Freneau, *The British Prison Ship*, in *Poems Relating to the American Revolution* (New

York: W. J. Widdleton, 1865), 78–101. See Burrows, *Forgotten Patriots*, 168-75, for an extended examination of Freneau's wartime experience.

Chapter 2: "The More We Are Treated Ill Abroad"

1. *Connecticut Gazette* (New London), May 13, 1785. See also *State Gazette of South Carolina* (Charleston), May 26, 1785; *Connecticut Courant* (Hartford), May 16, 1785; *Essex Journal* (Newburyport, MA), May 25, 1785; *Vermont Journal* (Windsor, VT), May 31, 1785. There is some question as to the authenticity of the letter, but regardless of the authorship, the unsettling contents of the letter and its widespread re-publication suggest the significance of its impact.
2. Nathan Perl-Rosenthal, *Citizen Sailors: Becoming American in the Age of Revolution* (Cambridge: Belknap Press of Harvard University, 2015), 49–51; Lawrence Peskin, *Captives and Countrymen: Barbary Slavery and the American Public, 1785–1816* (Baltimore: Johns Hopkins University Press, 2009), 7–10, 99–102.
3. Robbie J. Totten, "Security, Two Diplomacies, and the Formation of the U.S. Constitution: Review, Interpretation, and New Directions for the Study of the Early American Period," *Diplomatic History* 36 (January 2012): 77–117; David Hendrickson, *Peace Pact: The Lost World of the American Founding* (Lawrence: University Press of Kansas, 2003); Peter Onuf, *The Origins of the Federal Republic: Jurisdictional Controversies in the United States, 1775–1787* (Philadelphia: University of Pennsylvania Press, 1983); Peter Onuf and Cathy Matson, *A Union of Interests: Political and Economic Thought in Revolutionary America* (Lawrence: University Press of Kansas, 1990); and Peter Onuf and Nicholas Onuf, *Federal Union, Modern World: The Law of Nations in an Age of Revolutions, 1776–1814* (Madison, WI: Madison House, 1993).
4. Totten, "Security, Two Diplomacies," 79.
5. Entry for October 13, 1785, *Journals of the Continental Congress, 1774–1789*, ed. Worthington C. Ford et al. (Washington, DC, 1904–37), 29:833–34.
6. Perl-Rosenthal, *Citizen Sailors*, 5–7; Peskin, *Captive and Countrymen*, 7–11. See also Ronald P. Formisano, *For the People: American Populist Movements from the Revolution to the 1850s* (Chapel Hill: University of North Carolina Press, 2008), 28–32. Although Formisano does not address international affairs, his examination of the populist impulse of the era is illustrative of the power of an engaged citizenry.
7. Jack N. Rakove, *The Beginnings of National Politics: An Interpretive History of the Continental Congress* (New York: Alfred A. Knopf, 1979).
8. United States, "The Articles of Confederation and Perpetual Union, 1781," in *American State Papers* (Chicago: Encyclopedia Britannica, 1952), 6–9; Rakove, *The Beginnings of National Politics*; Onuf and Onuf, *Federal Union, Modern World*, 115, 113; Hendrickson, *Peace Pact*.
9. Frederick Marks, *Independence on Trial: Foreign Affairs and the Making of the Constitution* (Baton Rouge: Louisiana State University Press, 1973); Peskin, *Captives and Countrymen*; Totten, "Security, Two Diplomacies."
10. Lawrence Peskin in *Captives and Countrymen* has found a similar level of uncertainty in the American public during this period, arguing that "the initial impact of Algerian captures was enormous," but he goes on to argue that during the 1780s, there was a general "lack of interest" in Algiers and that "the press in the 1780s did little to vilify Algerians," for domestic newspapers were more concerned with internal weakness. See pp. 90–101. I argue here that the Algerian threat during the 1780s had a much deeper impact on the American public that Peskin suggests and fueled a surge of public participation in the debate about how best to redeem the captive sailors.
11. Morocco was the one exception. The Moroccan people maintained their independence from the Ottoman Empire throughout the period under consideration.

12. Richard B. Parker, *Uncle Sam in Barbary: A Diplomatic History*, ADST DACOR Diplomats and Diplomacy Series (Gainesville: University of Florida Press, 2004); Frank Lambert, *The Barbary Wars: American Independence in the Atlantic World* (New York: Hill and Wang, 2005); Michael Kitzen, *Tripoli and the United States at War* (London: McFarland and Company, 1993); Linda Colley, *Captives: The Story of Britain's Pursuit of Empire and How Its Soldiers and Civilians Were Held Captive by the Dream of Global Supremacy, 1600–1850* (New York: Pantheon Books, 2002), 43–72; and Robert C. Davis, *Christian Slaves, Muslim Masters: White Slavery in the Mediterranean, the Barbary Coast, and Italy, 1500–1800* (New York: Palgrave, 2003).
13. Parker, *Uncle Sam in Barbary*, 6.
14. Lambert, *The Barbary Wars*, 34.
15. Parker, *Uncle Sam in Barbary*, 40.
16. James Cathcart cited in Lawrence Peskin, "The Lessons of Independence: How the Algerian Crisis Shaped Early American Identity," *Diplomatic History* 28 no. 3 (Summer 2004): 298.
17. Ray W. Irwin, *The Diplomatic Relations of the United States with the Barbary Powers, 1776–1816* (Chapel Hill: University of North Carolina Press, 1931), 34–37.
18. Thomas Jefferson to James Monroe, May 10, 1786, in *The Papers of Thomas Jefferson*, ed. Julian P. Boyd et al., vol. 9 (Princeton, NJ: Princeton University Press, 1954), 499–503; Peskin, *Captives and Countrymen*, 94–96.
19. Jefferson to Adams, July 11, 1786, in *The Adams-Jefferson Letters: The Complete Correspondence between Thomas Jefferson and Abigail and John Adams*, ed. Lester Cappon (1959; Chapel Hill: University of North Carolina Press, [1988]), 142.
20. Adams to Jefferson, July 31, 1786, in ibid., 146–47.
21. Entry for October 13, 1785, *Journals of the Continental Congress*, 29 (1785): 833–34; Peskin, *Captives and Countrymen*, 99–101.
22. *Connecticut Journal* (New Haven), July 27, 1785; Irwin, *The Diplomatic Relations of the United States*, 37.
23. *Falmouth Gazette* (ME), October 25, 1785; *Continental Journal* (Boston, MA), October 27, 1785; *Providence Gazette* (RI), October 29, 1785; *Connecticut Courant* (Hartford), October 31, 1785; *Connecticut Journal* (New Haven), November 2, 1785; *State Gazette of South Carolina* (Charleston), November 3, 1785; *Connecticut Courant* (Hartford), November 28, 1785; *Connecticut Journal* (New Haven), November 23, 1785; *Middlesex Gazette* (Middletown, CT), November 29, 1785; *Essex Journal* (Newburyport, MA), December 30, 1785; *Massachusetts Spy or Worcester Gazette*, December 6, 1785. For an analysis of the tone and style of these letters, see Peskin, *Captives and Countrymen*, 24–34.
24. Thomas Jefferson, "Report on American Trade in the Mediterranean, December 28, 1790," in *The Papers of Thomas Jefferson*, vol. 18, 423–30. Merill Peterson, *Thomas Jefferson and the New Nation: A Biography* (New York: Oxford University Press, 1970), 310; Marks, *Independence on Trial*, 37.
25. John McCusker and Russell Menard, *The Economy of British America, 1607–1789* (Chapel Hill: University of North Carolina Press, 1985), 36; Marks, *Independence on Trial*, 52–55; Max Edling, *A Revolution in Favor of Government: Origins of the U.S. Constitution and the Making of the American State* (Oxford, UK: Oxford University Press, 2003), 83–86.
26. *Boston Gazette* (MA), January 9, 1786.
27. Roger H. Brown, *Redeeming the Republic: Federalists, Taxation, and the Origins of the Constitution* (Baltimore: Johns Hopkins University Press, 1993), 144.
28. Entry for October 20, 1785, *Journals of the Continental Congress* 29 (1785): 843.
29. Rufus King to John Adams, May 5, 1786, in Charles King, *The Life and Correspondence of Rufus King*, vol. 1 (New York: G.P. Putnam's Sons, 1894), 173; Marks, *Independence on Trial*, 39.
30. Rufus King to John Adams, May 5, 1786, in King, *Life and Correspondence of Rufus King*, vol. 1, 173.

31. McCusker and Menard, *The Economy of British America*, 366–77.
32. *Pennsylvania Packet* (Philadelphia), November 19, 1785; *Loudon's New York Packet* (NY), November, 21, 1785; *Connecticut Journal* (New Haven), November 23, 1785: *Virginia Journal* (Alexandria), December 1, 1785; Parker, *Uncle Sam in Barbary*, 60–63.
33. Petition of 20 December 1785 from the Public Record Office at Kew, England (FO 3/6, 172–173), cited in Parker, *Uncle Sam in Barbary*, 220–21.
34. Three of these eleven captives were eventually redeemed by friends (who were later reimbursed by the U.S. government), four died in captivity, and the other four were ultimately redeemed through American efforts. See Parker, *Uncle Sam in Barbary*, 222.
35. *New York Packet* (NY), April 3, 1786; *Pennsylvania Packet* (Philadelphia), April 10, 1786; *Carlisle Gazette* (PA), April 19, 1786; *Maryland Chronicle or the Universal Advertiser* (Fredericktown), May 10, 1786.
36. *New York Journal* (NY), February 9, 1786; *Independent Gazetteer* (New York, NY), February 18, 1786; *Massachusetts Gazette* (Boston), February 27, 1786; *Essex Journal* (Newburyport, MA), March 1, 1786; *Charleston Evening Gazette* (SC), March 28, 1786; Kitzen, *Tripoli and the United States at War*.
37. Samuel Huntington to John Jay, January 10, 1785, in *Letters of Members of the Continental Congress*, ed. Edmund C. Burnett, vol. 8 (Washington, DC: Carnegie Institution of Washington, 1936), 73.
38. Thomas Jefferson to John Lamb, May 11, 1786, in *Journals of the Continental Congress* 30 (1786): 259–62; Irwin, *The Diplomatic Relations of the United States*, 37–38.
39. American Peace Commissioners (Thomas Jefferson and John Adams) to John Jay, March 28, 1786, in *The Papers of Thomas Jefferson*, vol. 9, 357–59.
40. Ibid.
41. John Lamb to the American Peace Commissioners, May 20, 1786, Manuscript/Mixed Material, General Correspondence, 1651–1827, Series 1, The Thomas Jefferson Papers, 1606–1827, Manuscript Division, Library of Congress, Washington, DC, http://hdl.loc.gov/loc.mss/mtj.mtjbib001936; Parker, *Uncle Sam in Barbary*, 49–50: Irwin, *The Diplomatic Relations of the United States*, 37–40.
42. *New York Journal or the Weekly Register* (NY), August 17, 1786; *Middlesex Gazette* (Middletown, CT), August 21, 1786.
43. *Independent Gazetteer* (New York, NY), February 5, 1787; *New York Packet* (NY), February 13, 1787; *New Jersey Journal* (Elizabethtown), February 14, 1787; *Massachusetts Gazette* (Boston), February 20, 1787.
44. *Massachusetts Gazette* (Boston), February 23, 1787.
45. Adams to Jefferson, July 31, 1786, in *The Adams-Jefferson Letters*, 146. Rufus King to John Adams, May 5, 1786, *The Life and Correspondence of Rufus King*, vol. 1, 173.
46. *Pennsylvania Evening Herald* (Philadelphia), October 18, 1786; *Massachusetts Centinel* (Boston), October 28, 1786; *Newport Mercury* (RI), October 30, 1786; *American Recorder and the Charlestown Advertiser* (MA), November 3, 1786; *Cumberland Gazette* (MD), November 9, 1786.
47. *Daily Advertiser* (New York, NY), February 6, 1786; *Columbian Herald or the Patriotic Courier of North America* (Charleston, SC), March 6, 1786.
48. *Daily Advertiser* (New York, NY), February 7, 1786.
49. *Independent Gazetteer* (New York, NY), May 27, 1786; *Columbian Herald or the Patriotic Courier of North America* (Charleston, SC), June 15, 1786; *Charleston Evening Gazette* (SC), June 16, 1786.
50. *Daily Advertiser* (New York, NY), February 7, 1786. Italics added.
51. Les hostilites des corsaires Barbariques on fait une grande sensation en Amerique. Louis Guillaume Otto to Thomas Jefferson, January 15, 1786, Manuscript/Mixed Material, General

Correspondence, 1651–1827, Series 1, The Thomas Jefferson Papers, 1606–1827, Manuscript Division, Library of Congress, Washington, DC, https://www.loc.gov/item/mtjbib001736/.
52. Peskin, "The Lessons of Independence," 298–99.
53. *Columbian Herald or the Patriotic Courier of North America* (Charleston, SC), January 2, 1786; *Pennsylvania Evening Herald* (Philadelphia, PA), February 1, 1786.
54. *Pennsylvania Packet and Daily Advertiser* (Philadelphia, PA), July 4, 1786; *New Jersey Journal* (Elizabethtown), July 5, 1786; *Pennsylvania Herald and General Advertiser* (Easton, PA), July 8, 1786; *Middlesex Gazette* (Middletown, CT), July 10, 1786.
55. *Pennsylvania Packet* (Philadelphia), August 7, 1786; *The New York Journal or the Weekly Register* (New York City), August 24, 1786. For more on the challenge to "opulent" Americans, see Robert Allison, *The Crescent Obscured: The United State and the Muslim World 1776–1815* (New York: Oxford University Press, 1995), 127–51.
56. Petition of Hannah Stephen February 22, 1787, item no. 42, 287–88, roll 56, microfilm, (Washington, DC: National Archives and Records Service, 1971) *Papers of the Continental Congress, 1774-1789*, Microcopy No. 47, National Archives Microfilm Publications, Records of the Continental and Confederation Congresses and the Constitutional Convention, Record Group 360, National Archives, Washington, DC. See also Entry for April 23, 1787, *Journals of the Continental Congress* 32 (1787): 229–30. Stephens petition, despite gaining the attention of Congress, was unsuccessful, and she petitioned President George Washington in 1791. See her petition in *The Papers of George Washington*, Presidential Series, vol. 9, 23 September 1791–29 February 1792, ed. Mark A. Mastromarino (Charlottesville: University Press of Virginia, 2000), 268–69.
57. Entry for May 2, 1787, *Journals of the Continental Congress* 32 (1787): 250.
58. Kitzen, *Tripoli and the United States at War*, 12–13.
59. Entry for July 31, 1787, *Journals of the Continental Congress* 33 (1787): 441–44.
60. Entry for October 8, 1787, ibid., 617–36.
61. Entry for July 31, 1787, ibid., 441–44.
62. Entry for August 2, 1787, ibid., 451–53.
63. Humanitas's letter was published in *Independent Gazetteer* (New York, NY), April 2, 1787; *American Recorder* (Charlestown, MA), April 20, 1787; and *Essex Journal* (Newburyport, MA), May 2, 1787.
64. *Independent Gazetteer* (New York, NY), June 23, 1787, and June 25, 1787; *Pennsylvania Packet and Daily Advertiser* (Philadelphia, PA), June 23, 1787.
65. *Columbian Herald or the Patriotic Courier of North America* (Charleston, SC), October 11, 1787.
66. Entry for May 11, 1786, *Journals of the Continental Congress* 30 (1786): 259–62; Irwin, *Diplomatic Relations of the United States*, 37–38.
67. *Connecticut Courant* (Hartford), June 11, 1787; *Independent Journal* (New York, NY), June 2, 1787.

Chapter 3: "A Speedy Release to Our Suffering Captive Brethren in Algiers"

1. Algerine Captives to George Washington, September 22, 1788, Manuscript/Mixed Material, General Correspondence, 1597–1799, Series 4, George Washington Papers, Manuscript Division, Library of Congress, Washington, DC, https://www.loc.gov/item/mgw436243/.
2. George Washington to Matthew Irwin, July 20, 1789, *The Papers of George Washington*, Presidential Series, vol. 3, 15 June 1789–5 September 1789, ed. Dorothy Twohig (Charlottesville: University Press of Virginia, 1989), 155–58. The efforts to draw attention to the plight of the captive sailors (which included appeals by the sailors themselves) and the subsequent response of the American public are best understood in the context of Jurgen

Habermas's description of the "public sphere." See Jürgen Habermas, *The Structural Transformation of the Public Sphere: An Inquiry into a Category of Bourgeois Society*, trans. Thomas Burger (Cambridge, MA: MIT Press, 1989). Recent works by Todd Estes, *The Jay Treaty Debate, Public Opinion, and the Evolution of Early American Political Culture* (Amherst, MA: University of Massachusetts Press, 2006) and Lawrence Peskin, *Captives and Countrymen: Barbary Slavery and the American Public, 1785–1816* (Baltimore: Johns Hopkins University Press, 2009) have demonstrated that by the 1790s, all the pieces were in place for an expansive public sphere in the United States. Issues of foreign policy helped shape the dynamic that was emerging between the newly created federal government and the American people.

3. See Richard Hofstadter, *The Idea of a Party System: The Rise of Legitimate Opposition in the United States, 1780–1840* (Berkeley: University of California Press, 1969); Richard Buel, *Securing the Revolution: Ideology in American Politics, 1789–1815* (Ithaca: Cornell University Press, 1972), especially chaps. 6–7; and James Roger Sharp, *American Politics in the Early Republic: The New Nation in Crisis* (New Haven: Yale University Press, 1993). Peskin, *Captives and Countrymen*, 103–9, connects the growing interest in the American captives in Algiers as part of a "grandiose theory of British conspiracy against America." Peskin also argues that "foreign affairs, beginning with Algiers, taught Americans . . . what it meant to be an independent nation." See pp. 105–9.
4. Jefferson to Adams, July 11, 1786, in *The Adams-Jefferson Letters: The Complete Correspondence between Thomas Jefferson and Abigail and John Adams*, ed. Lester Cappon (1959; reprint, Chapel Hill: University of North Carolina Press, [1988]), 142; Robert Allison, *The Crescent Obscured: The United States and the Muslim World, 1776–1815* (New York: Oxford University Press, 1995), 16–20; Peskin, *Captives and Countrymen*, 50–57. Jefferson continued to hope for a military solution and even as he pushed for negotiations, he still believed that a military response was preferable to payment of any tribute.
5. Ralph Ketcham, *Presidents above Party: The First American Presidency, 1789–1829* (Chapel Hill: University of North Carolina Press, 1984), 90.
6. Hofstadter, *The Idea of a Party System*, 91; Buel, *Securing the Revolution*, 70, 106–7.
7. Charles Hitchcock Sherrill, *French Memories of Eighteenth-Century America* (New York, 1915), 249, 254.
8. Buel, *Securing the Revolution*, 93–112; Sean Wilentz, *The Rise of American Democracy: Jefferson to Lincoln* (New York, 2005), 53–60; Doron Ben-Atar and Barbara B. Oberg, eds., "Introduction: The Paradoxical Legacy of the Federalists," in *Federalists Reconsidered*, (Charlottesville: University of Virginia Press, 1998), 1–18.
9. James Madison to Thomas Jefferson, 24 October 1787, *The Papers of James Madison Digital Edition*, ed. J. C. A. Stagg (Charlottesville: University of Virginia Press, Rotunda, 2010), http://rotunda.upress.virginia.edu/founders/JSMN-01-10-02-0151.
10. James Madison, "For the *National Gazette*," ibid., http://rotunda.upress.virginia.edu/founders/JSMN-01-14-02-0145. See also Colleen Sheehan, "The Politics of Public Opinion: James Madison's 'Notes on Government,'" *William and Mary Quarterly* 49, no. 4 (October 1992): 609–27, and Peskin, *Captives and Countrymen*, 55–58.
11. *New York Daily Gazette* (NY), March 8, 1794.
12. Gary Wilson, "American Hostages in Moslem Nations, 1784–1796: The Public Response," *Journal of the Early Republic* 2, no. 2 (Summer 1982): 123–41.
13. *Columbian Gazetteer* (New York), December 19, 1793; *Independent Gazetteer* (Philadelphia), December 21, 1793; *New Hampshire Gazette* (Portsmouth), December 28, 1793; *Western Star* (Stockbridge, MA), December 30, 1793; *Vermont Gazette* (Bennington), January 3, 1794; *South Carolina State Gazette* (Charlestown), January 3, 1794; *The Mirrour* (Concord, NH), January 6, 1794; *The Massachusetts Magazine; or, Monthly Museum. Containing the Literature, History, Politics, Arts, Manners & Amusements of the Age*, March 1794, 189. For more on

the changing dynamic of the letters from the prisoners themselves, see Peskin, *Captive and Countrymen*, 38–42.
14. The closing of the galleries seemed to be a common occurrence and a source of frustration to both Republican members of Congress and printers who had hoped to deliver news to their readers. See particularly *Gazette of the United States* (Philadelphia), December 30, 1793, and the *New York Daily Gazette*, January 3, 1794. Todd Estes "Shaping the Politics of Public Opinion: Federalist and the Jay Treaty Debate," *Journal of the Early Republic* 20, no. 3 (Autumn, 2000): 395–96; Noble E. Cunningham Jr., introduction to *Circular Letters of Congressmen to Their Constituents, 1789–1829* (Chapel Hill: University of North Carolina Press, 1978), 1:xl–xlii.
15. I have only been able to find the text from a few of these petitions, although references to the many "humane petitions" that had been presented to Congress appear in a number of sources, including *Dunlap's American Daily Advertiser* (Philadelphia), February 19, 1793. Wilson, "American Hostages in Moslem Nations," 137; *Annals of Congress*, 3rd Cong., 1st sess., 531.
16. *House Journal*, 3rd Cong., 1st sess., March 5, 1794, 169.
17. *House Journal*, 3rd Cong., 1st sess., March 27, 1794, 221.
18. *Providence Gazette* (RI), May 24, 1794.
19. Wilson, "American Hostages in Moslem Nations," 135; *House Journal*, 3rd Cong., 1st sess., April 4, 1794, 235.
20. Benevolence to the President of the United States, April 4, 1794, cited in Allison, *The Crescent Obscured*, 127–29.
21. *Daily Advertiser* (New York) December 26, 1793.
22. *Aurora General Advertiser* (Philadelphia), March 6, 1794.
23. *Dunlap's American Daily Advertiser* (Philadelphia), March 29, 1794.
24. *Columbian Centinel* (Boston), April 2, 1794.
25. *Providence Gazette* (RI), December 3, 1794.
26. *Dunlap's American Daily Advertiser* (Philadelphia), August 22, 1794.
27. Wilson, "American Hostages in Moslem Nations, 1784–1796," 133.
28. *Independent Gazetteer* (Worcester, MA), July 26, 1794.
29. *The New York Magazine, or Literary Repository*, August 1794, 516–18.
30. Heather S. Nathans, *Early American Theater from the Revolution to Thomas Jefferson: Into the Hands of the People* (New York: Cambridge University Press, 2003), 81.
31. *New York Daily Gazette* (NY), January 3, 1794; *Massachusetts Mercury* (Boston), February 18, 1794; *Gazette of the United States* (Philadelphia), October 23, 1794; *General Advertiser* (Philadelphia), January 27, 1794.
32. Susanna Rowson, *Slaves in Algiers; or a Struggle for Freedom*, in *Plays by American Women*, ed. Amelia Howe Kritzer (Ann Arbor: University of Michigan Press, 1995), 60–61. Rowson's play was originally published in 1794.
33. *Gazette of the United States* (Philadelphia), March 24, 1794.
34. *New York Daily Gazette* (NY), March 29, 1794.
35. *Gazette of the United States* (Philadelphia), April 19, 1794.
36. *American Minerva* (New York), May 23, 1794.
37. *Weekly Museum* (New York), June 28, 1794.
38. *Gazette of the United States* (Philadelphia), July 24, 1794; *The Diary or Loudon's Register* (New York), March 11, 1794.
39. *Columbian Centinel* (Boston), March 19, 1794.
40. *South Carolina State Gazette and Timothy's Daily Adviser* (Charleston), July 7, 1794.
41. *Dunlap's American Daily Advertiser* (Philadelphia), July 28, 1794.
42. David Waldstreicher, *In the Midst of Perpetual Fetes: The Making of American Nationalism, 1776–1820* (Chapel Hill: University of North Carolina Press, 1990), 222–23, 180.

43. *Gazette of the United States* (Philadelphia), December 30, 1793; *New York Daily Gazette* (NY), January 3, 1794; *Spooner's Vermont Journal* (Windsor), January 20, 1794.
44. Anthony New to William Latane, in *Circular Letters of Congressmen to Their Constituents*, ed. Cunningham Jr., 1:15.
45. *Connecticut Journal* (New Haven), February 20, 1794.
46. Jefferson to Adams, 11 July 1786, in *The Adams-Jefferson Letters*, 142.
47. *Greenleaf's New York Journal and Patriotic Register*, February 12, 1794; *The Debates and Proceedings in the Congress of the United States*, vol. 4, Third Congress, December 2, 1793. to March 3, 1795 (Washington: Gales and Seaton, 1849), 250, 486–98, 1426–28; Allison, *The Crescent Obscured*, 20–24.
48. *Independent Gazetteer* (Worcester), March 15, 1794. For a breakdown of the votes on this legislation, see *Gazette of the United States* (Philadelphia), February 21, 1794, and *Dunlap's Daily American Advertiser* (Philadelphia), March 15, 1794.
49. *Western Star* (Stockbridge, MA), June 3, 1794.
50. *American Minerva* (New York), May 28, 1794, and *Gazette of the United States* (Philadelphia), June 4, 1794. Italics are in the original.
51. *City Gazette and Daily Advertiser* (Charleston, SC), June 11, 1794.
52. *Gazette and Country Journal* (Boston, MA), December 8, 1794. Pintard's proposal was greeted with a public acknowledgment and order when James Farquhar announced his intention to purchase six pipes of wine in a letter that was published in the *Boston Gazette* (MA), December 8, 1794.
53. Reprinted around the country in the *American Minerva* (New York), October 28, 1794; *Gazette of the United States* (Philadelphia), October 31, 1794; *Dunlap's American Daily Advertiser* (Philadelphia), November 4, 1794; *American Apollo* (Boston), November 6, 1794; *Catskill Packet* (Catskill, NY), November 8, 1794; *Western Star* (Stockbridge, MA), November 11, 1794; *City Gazette* (Charleston, SC), November 19, 1794. For more on Humphrey's involvement and literary efforts on behalf of the captives see Peskin, *Captives and Countrymen*, 61–67.
54. *American Minerva* (New York), October 28, 1794. Reprinted in the *Gazette of the United States* (Philadelphia), October 31, 1794; *Dunlap's American Daily Advertiser* (Philadelphia), November 4, 1794; *American Apollo* (Boston), November 6, 1794; *Catskill Packet* (NY), November 8, 1794; *Western Star* (Stockbridge, MA) November 11, 1794; *City Gazette* (Charleston, SC), November 19, 1794.
55. Allison, *The Crescent Obscured*, 132.
56. *Salem Gazette* (MA), November 25, 1794.
57. *Impartial Herald* (Newburyport, MA), January 23, 1795. Reprinted in *Federal Orrery* (Boston, MA), January 29, 1795; *Providence Gazette* (RI), January 31, 1795; *Courier of New Hampshire* (Concord, NH), January 31, 1795; *Newport Mercury* (RI), February 3, 1795; *Massachusetts Spy or Worcester Gazette* (MA), February 4, 1795; *Norwich Packet* (CT), February 12, 1795; *Connecticut Gazette* (New London), February 19, 1795; *Vermont Gazette* (Burlington), February 20, 1795.
58. *New Hampshire Gazette* (Portsmouth), February 3, 1795. Reprinted in *Boston Gazette* (MA), February 16, 1795; *Dunlap's American Daily Advertiser* (Philadelphia), February 23, 1795; *City Gazette* (Charleston, SC), February 27, 1795.
59. *Columbian Centinel* (Boston), February 7, 1795.
60. Richard Parker, *Uncle Sam in Barbary: A Diplomatic History*, ADST-DACOR Diplomats and Diplomacy Series (Gainesville, FL: University of Florida Press, 2004), 91–95.
61. *American Minerva* (New York), February 27, 1795; *Federal Intelligencer* (Baltimore, MD), February 24, 1795; *Columbian Centinel* (Boston), February 28, 1795. See also Allison, *The Crescent Obscured*, 143–44.
62. *New Hampshire Gazette* (Portsmouth), February 17, 1795.

63. *Greenleaf's New York Journal* (New York), February 7, 1795; *Salem Gazette* (MA), February 17, 1795; *New Hampshire Gazette* (Portsmouth), February 17, 1795.

64. *A Discourse Delivered February 15, 1795 . . . for the Benefit of Our American Brethren at Algiers* (Salem, 1795).

65. *Philadelphia Gazette* (PA), February 28, 1795; *Providence Gazette* (RI), February 28, 1795. Seabury's motives for supporting the cause were likely more complex than they initially appear. He had been a loyalist during the Revolution and as one of the first Episcopal bishops in the United States following Independence, some Americans questioned his loyalty to the young nation See especially the attack on Seabury's call for contributions in the *American Mercury* (Hartford, CT), April 20, 1795.

66. *Dunlap's American Daily Advertiser* (Philadelphia), March 3, 1795.

67. *New Hampshire Gazette* (Portsmouth), March 10, 1795; *Spooner's Vermont Journal* (Windsor), March 16, 1795. See also Allison, *The Crescent Obscured*. My interpretation of the success of the collection efforts differs from that of Allison, who contends that "the thanksgiving day was a failure as a charity." In the face of the Congressional act to end the crisis through military means, the widespread collections were a strong indication that many citizens had little faith in a naval solution to the crisis.

68. George Washington to Alexander Hamilton, May 29, 1794, Washington Papers (Library of Congress). See also Michael Kitzen, *Tripoli and the United States at War* (London: McFarland and Co., 1993), 17–19. The money was acquired with the assistance of British bankers in Lisbon and Jewish bankers in Algiers, and supplemented, ironically, with four warships as payment to the dey. Of the American ships that had been commissioned during the crisis, three were eventually completed and the other contracts were withdrawn in March 1796 after the treaty had been negotiated with Algiers (see Parker, *Uncle Sam in Barbary*, 116–23; Lambert, *Barbary Wars*, 86–88).

69. Todd Estes, *The Jay Treaty Debate*, 212–13.

Chapter 4: "Millions for Defence, but Not a Cent for Tribute"

1. *Impartial Register* (Salem, MA), May 4, 1801; *Centinel of Freedom* (Newark, NJ), May 12, 1801; and *Carolina Gazette* (Charleston, SC), May 14, 1801.

2. *Boston Gazette* (MA), May 11, 1801, reprinted in *Newburyport Herald* (MA), May 12, 1801; *Kennebec Gazette* (Augusta, ME), May 22, 1801; *Western Star* (Stockbridge, MA), May 25, 1801.

3. On the Jay Treaty debates, see Todd Estes, *The Jay Treaty Debate, Public Opinion, and the Evolution of Early American Political Culture* (Amherst: University of Massachusetts Press, 2006). While the Federalists were able to channel public support behind the treaty's ratification, as the full details of the treaty became public, port cities experienced massive protests in the streets. See Paul Gilje, *Liberty on the Waterfront: American Maritime Culture in the Age of Revolution* (Philadelphia: University of Pennsylvania Press, 2004), 142. On the XYZ Affair and the subsequent Quasi War, see David Waldstreicher, "Federalism, the Styles of Politics, and the Politics of Style," in *Federalists Reconsidered*, ed. Doron Ben-Atar and Barbara B. Oberg (Charlottesville: University Press of Virginia, 1998), 99–117, and Gilje, *Liberty on the Waterfront*, 143–44.

4. See Todd Estes, "Shaping the Politics of Public Opinion: Federalists and the Jay Treaty Debate," *Journal of the Early Republic* 20, no. 3 (Autumn 2000): 393–422.

5. David Waldstreicher, "Federalism, the Styles of Politics," 112. For more on support for the Adams administration during the Quasi War, see Gilje, *Liberty on the Waterfront*, 143–44.

6. Jeffrey Pasley, *'The Tyranny of the Printers': Newspaper Politics in the Early American Republic* (Charlottesville: University of Virginia Press, 2001), 105–6.

7. David Hackett Fischer, *The Revolution of American Conservatism: The Federalist Party in the Era of Jeffersonian Democracy* (New York: Harper and Row, 1965), 150–81.
8. See Secretary of State James Madison's instructions to James Cathcart, April 18, 1802, in *Naval Documents Related to the United States Wars with the Barbary Powers*, vol. 2 (Washington, DC: Government Printing Office, 1940), 126. See also Allison, *The Crescent Obscured*, 25–34.
9. Robert Allison has argued that Jefferson's greatest victory in the conflict with Tripoli was his ability to demonstrate that a war could be won while military power remained subservient to civil power and that cost of the war ought to be shouldered by those who benefitted most directly from its conduct. See his *Crescent Obscured*, 30–32.
10. *Journal of the Executive Proceedings of the Senate of the United States*, 5th Cong., 1st sess., May 29, 1797, 241. For a more complete assessment of relations with the Barbary States during the Adams administration, see Allison, *The Crescent Obscured*, 153–85, and Frank Lambert, *The Barbary Wars: American Independence in the Atlantic World* (New York: Hill and Wang, 2005), 91–103.
11. John Quincy Adams to Timothy Pickering, January 14, 1800, in *The Writings of John Quincy Adams*, ed. Worthington Chauncey Ford, vol. 2 (New York: MacMillan Company, 1913), 447–48.
12. *Connecticut Courant* (Hartford), May 4, 1801, *National Intelligencer* (Washington, DC), May 4, 1801, *Massachusetts Spy* (Worcester), May 6, 1801. Italics in original.
13. William Eaton to Secretary of State Timothy Pickering, November 10, 1800, in *Naval Documents*, vol. 1, 397–98.
14. *Alexandria Times* (VA), October 28, 1800.
15. Cited in Lambert, *The Barbary Wars*, 123.
16. See *Impartial Register* (Salem, MA), May 4, 1801.
17. *National Intelligencer* (Washington, DC), May 29, 1801; *Philadelphia Gazette* (PA), June 1, 1801.
18. See Ray Irwin, *The Diplomatic Relations of the United States with the Barbary Powers, 1776–1816* (Chapel Hill: University of North Carolina Press, 1931), 122–23.
19. *Newburyport Herald* (MA), August 4, 1801, reprinted in *Washington Federalist* (DC), August 12, 1801; *Kennebec Gazette* (Augusta, ME), August 14, 1801.
20. *Newburyport Herald* (MA), August 4, 1801, reprinted in *Washington Federalist* (DC), August 12, 1801; *Kennebec Gazette* (Augusta, ME), August 14, 1801.
21. "Notes on a Cabinet Meeting," *The Works of Thomas Jefferson*, ed. Paul Leicester Ford, vol. 1 (New York: G. P. Putnam's Sons, 1904), 365–66. In addition to Attorney General Levi Lincoln, Jefferson's cabinet included Secretary of the Treasury Albert Gallatin, Secretary of State James Madison, Secretary of War Henry Dearborn, and Secretary of the Navy Robert Smith.
22. Jefferson to the Bashaw, May 21, 1801, *Naval Documents*, vol. 1, 470.
23. *Newburyport Herald* (MA), June 9, 1801; *New Hampshire Gazette* (Portsmouth), June 9, 1801; Lambert, *The Barbary Wars*, 125–27.
24. *New York Gazette* (NY), November 11, 1801; *Massachusetts Spy* (Worcester), November 18, 1801.
25. *Gazette of the United States* (Philadelphia, PA), October 1, 1801; *Commercial Advertiser* (New York, NY), October 2, 1801; *Columbian Centinel* (Boston, MA), October 7, 1801; *American Mercury* (Hartford, CT), October 8, 1801; *City Gazette* (Charleston, SC), October 10, 1801; *Portland Gazette* (ME), October 12, 1801; *Columbian Minerva* (Baltimore, MD), October 13, 1801.
26. Report of Lieutenant Sterrett, August 6, 1801, *Naval Documents*, vol. 1, 537; Lambert, *The Barbary Wars*, 129–30.
27. *American Citizen* (New York, NY), November 3, 1801, reprinted in *Poulson's American Advertiser* (Philadelphia, PA), November 4, 1801; *Washington Federalist* (DC), November 6, 1801;

New Jersey Journal (Elizabethtown), November 11, 1801; *Connecticut Gazette* (New London), November 11, 1801; *Alexandria Advertiser* (VA), November 14, 1801; *New York Evening Post* (NY), November 23, 1801; *Oracle of Dauphin* (Harrisburg, PA), November 30, 1801; *Rhode Island Republican* (Newport), December 5, 1801.

28. *New York Evening Post* (NY), November 23, 1801; *Oracle of Dauphin* (Harrisburg, PA), November 30, 1801; *Rhode Island Republican* (Newport), December 5, 1801.
29. *Telescope* (Leominster, MA), November 12, 1801; *Patriot* (Stonington, CT), November 13, 1801.
30. Reprinted in *New York Daily Advertiser* (NY), December 10, 1801; *Alexandria Advertiser* (VA), December 15, 1801; *Washington Federalist* (DC), December 15, 1801; and *Massachusetts Mercury* (Boston), December 18, 1801.
31. Jefferson to James Madison, August 28, 1801, *The Republic of Letters: The Correspondence between Thomas Jefferson and James Madison, 1776–1826*, ed James Morton Smith, (New York: W.W. Norton & Co, 1995), 2:1194. When the United States was first faced with demand for tribute from the North African states in 1785, Jefferson argued that the Americans would be best served by standing up to the Barbary States and refusing to pay any tribute. "I was very unwilling," he reported "that we should acquiesce in the European humiliation of paying tribute to those lawless pirates, and endeavored to form an association of the powers subject to the habitual depredation from them." Jefferson to Adams, July 11, 1786, in *The Adams-Jefferson Letters: The Complete Correspondence between Thomas Jefferson and Abigail and John Adams*, ed. Lester Cappon (1959; reprint, Chapel Hill: University of North Carolina Press, [1988]), 142.
32. *House Journal*, 7th Cong., 1st session., December 8, 1801.
33. "An Act for the Protection of the Commerce and Seamen of the United States," February 6, 1802, in *Naval Documents*, vol. 2, 51; Lambert, *Barbary Wars*, 132–33.
34. *New York Evening Post* (NY), December 17, 1801.
35. James Madison to James Cathcart, April 18, 1802, *Naval Documents*, vol. 2, 126–27.
36. Captain Andrew Morris to James Cathcart, June 17, 1802, *Naval Documents*, vol. 2, 176–77; Lawrence Peskin, *Captives and Countrymen: Barbary Slavery and the American Public, 1785–1816* (Baltimore: Johns Hopkins University Press, 2009), 144–45.
37. *New York Gazette* (NY), September 30, 1802, reprinted in *Alexandria Advertiser* (VA), October 4, 1802; *Newport Mercury* (RI), October 5, 1805; *American Telegraphe* (Bridgeport, CT), October 6, 1802; *Otsego Herald* (Cooperstown, NY), October 14, 1802; *Oracle of Dauphin* (Harrisburg, VA), October 13, 1802.
38. *Philadelphia Gazette* (PA), October 18, 1802, reprinted in *Alexandria Advertiser* (VA), October 21, 1802; *American Citizen* (New York, NY), October 21, 1802; *Columbian Courier* (New Bedford, MA), October 22, 1802; *Centinel of Freedom* (Newark, NJ), October 26, 1802; *American Mercury* (Hartford, CT), October 28, 1802; *Kennebec Gazette* (Augusta, ME), October 28, 1802; *Weekly Wanderer* (Randolph, VT), November 6, 1802.
39. See Peskin, *Captives and Countrymen*, 137–53.
40. *Gazette of the United States* (Philadelphia, PA), October 4, 1802.
41. *New York Gazette* (NY), November 3, 1802.
42. *Philadelphia Gazette* (PA), November 20, 1802, reprinted in *Mercantile Advertiser* (New York, NY), November 24, 1802; *Alexandria Advertiser* (VA), November 29, 1802; *Republican* (Baltimore, MD), November 29, 1802; *Albany Centinel* (NY), November 30, 1802; *Kennebec Gazette* (Augusta, ME), December 9, 1802; *Windham Herald* (CT), December 9, 1802.
43. *House Journal*, 7th Cong., 2nd sess., December 15, 1802.
44. *Chronicle Express* (New York, NY), December 27, 1802; *Telescope* (Leominster, MA), November 12, 1801.
45. The speech and the consuls' letters appeared in the American press in throughout late December 1802 and early January 1803. See *Olio* (Washington, DC), December 16, 1802;

National Intelligencer (Washington, DC), December 22, 1802; *Daily Advertiser* (New York, NY), December 23, 1802; *Commercial Register* (Norfolk, VA), December 24, 1802; *Philadelphia Gazette* (PA), December 28, 1802.

46. *National Intelligencer* (Washington, DC), December 22, 1802, reprinted in *Commercial Register* (Norfolk, VA), January 1, 1803; *American Citizen* (New York, NY), January 4, 1803; Peskin, *Captives and Countrymen*, 145. William Eaton greatly disapproved of the manner in which O'Brien had worked to secure the release of the captives, believing that his actions would only lead to greater American dependence on Algiers. See Peskin, *Captives and Countrymen*, 145–46.
47. *National Intelligencer* (Washington, DC), December 22, 1802, reprinted in *Daily Advertiser* (New York, NY), December 30, 1802; *Republican Watch-Tower* (New York, NY), January 5, 1803; *Chronicle Express* (New York, NY), January 10, 1803.
48. In 1786, discussing the use of military force against the Barbary States, Adams had cautioned Jefferson, that engaging them in war would mire the United States in an interminable conflict. Adams to Jefferson, July 31, 1786, in *The Adams-Jefferson Letters*, 146.
49. Richard Dale to "Rear Admiral Soderstrom, Commander-in-chief of His Swedish Majesty's Ships in the Mediterranean," February 2, 1802, *Naval Documents*, vol. 2, 45–46.
50. "1803—Apr. 8," *The Works of Thomas Jefferson*, ed. Ford, vol. 1, 298.
51. "Concerning Commodore Morris' squadron in the Mediterranean," August 31, 1803, *Naval Documents*, vol. 2, 531; Lambert, *The Barbary Wars*, 137–39.
52. Lambert, *The Barbary Wars*, 139.
53. Edward Preble to Robert Smith, December 10, 1803, *Naval Documents*, vol. 3, 256.
54. Italics in original. *Newburyport Herald* (MA), April 6, 1804.
55. *National Intelligencer* (Washington, DC), March 23, 1804.
56. *National Intelligencer* (Washington, DC), March 23, 1804; *Political Calendar* (Newburyport, MA), April 9, 1804.
57. *Aurora General Advertiser* (Philadelphia, PA), March 31, 1804, May 19, 1804, and May 23 1804; *Boston Gazette* (MA), April 26, 1804, and October 15, 1804. See Peskin, *Captives and Countrymen*, 158–59. Peskin's examination of the use of the term *slave* is part of a larger examination of "masculinity and servility" in the debate surrounding the capture of the *Philadelphia*.
58. William Bainbridge to Edward Preble, December 5, 1803, *Naval Documents*, vol. 3, 253–54; Edward Preble to Stephen Decatur, January 31, 1804, ibid., 376; Stephen Decatur to Edward Preble, February 16, 1804, ibid., 414–15.
59. *Columbian Courier* (New Bedford, MA), May 18, 1804; *Aurora General Advertiser* (Philadelphia, PA), May 23, 1804.
60. *National Intelligencer* (Washington, DC), May 28, 1804.
61. Edward Preble to Robert Livingston, March 18, 1804, *Naval Documents*, vol. 3, 498–99.
62. Richard Farquhar to Thomas Jefferson, November 15, 1803, *Naval Documents*, vol. 3, 222.
63. Lambert, *The Barbary Wars*, 146.
64. *New York Evening Post* (NY), January 12, 1805; *Aurora General Advertiser* (Philadelphia, PA), January 16, 1805; *Pennsylvania Correspondent* (Doylestown), January 29, 1805.
65. *Aurora General Advertiser* (Philadelphia, PA), October 17, 1805; Allison, *The Crescent Obscured*, 31–34.
66. *Aurora General Advertiser* (Philadelphia, PA), October 4, 1805, and October 19, 1805.
67. *United States Gazette* (Philadelphia, PA), January 9, 1806. Italics added.
68. *Evening Post* (New York, NY), February 28, 1806; Lambert, *The Barbary Wars*, 157–60.
69. *Commercial Advertiser* (New York, NY), August 3, 1805; *Otsego Herald* (Cooperstown, NY), October 24, 1805.

Chapter 5: "We Shall Ever Be Prey of the Jealous and Monopolizing Spirit of the English"

1. *Salem Register* (MA), July 22, 1805; *Independent Chronicle* (Boston, MA), July 25, 1805; *Providence Phoenix* (RI), July 27, 1805; *New Hampshire Gazette* (Portsmouth), July 30, 1805; *Connecticut Gazette* (New London), July 31, 1805; *Kennebec Gazette* (Augusta, ME), August 1, 1805; *Centinel of Freedom* (Newark, NJ), August 6, 1805; *City Gazette* (Charleston, SC), August 8, 1805; *Hornet* (Fredericktown, MD), August 13, 1805.
2. For more charges of Republican exaggeration, see Denver Brunsman, "Subjects vs. Citizens: Impressment and Identity in the Anglo-American Atlantic," *Journal of the Early Republic* 30, no. 4 (Winter 2010): 560, and Richard Buel, *America on the Brink: How the Political Struggle over the War of 1812 Almost Destroyed the Young Republic* (New York: Palgrave Macmillan, 2005).
3. *Columbian Centinel* (Boston, MA), July 24, 1805, reprinted in *Boston Gazette* (MA), July 25, 1805; *The Post Boy* (Windsor, VT), July 30, 1805; *Alexandria Advertiser* (VA), August 1, 1805; *Balance* (Hudson, NY), August 6, 1805.
4. Denver Brunsman, *The Evil Necessity: British Naval Impressment in the Eighteenth-Century Atlantic World* (Charlottesville: University of Virginia Press, 2013), 241–43. Brunsman has labeled these efforts to limit British impressment as "the first significant victory of the American Revolution." See also Christopher Magra, *Poseidon's Curse: British Naval Impressment and the Atlantic Origins of the American Revolution* (New York: Cambridge University Press, 2016).
5. James Zimmerman, *Impressment of American Seamen* (New York: Columbia University Press, 1925), 20–26.
6. Paul Gilje, "'Free Trade and Sailors' Rights': The Rhetoric of the War of 1812," *Journal of the Early Republic* 30, no. 1 (Spring 2010): 9–11; Brunsman, "Subjects vs. Citizens," 573–77.
7. Zimmerman, *Impressment of American Seamen*, 53–63; Gilje, "Free Trade and Sailors' Rights," 11–12.
8. Second draft of Seventh Annual Message to Congress, October 27, 1807, *The Works of Thomas Jefferson*, ed. Paul Leicester Fort, vol. 10 (New York: G. P. Putnam's Sons, 1905), 516. Frank Lambert, *The Barbary Wars: American Independence in the Atlantic World* (New York: Hill and Wang, 2005), 170–78.
9. Brunsman, "Subjects vs. Citizens," 581–82; Douglas Bradburn, *The Citizenship Revolution: Politics and the Creation of the American Union, 1774–1804* (Charlottesville: University of Virginia Press, 2009), 105.
10. *Democrat* (Boston, MA), June 30, 1804; *Carolina Gazette* (Charleston, SC), August 31, 1804; *Maryland Herald* (Elizabethtown), September 26, 1804.
11. *Evening Post* (New York, NY), June 27, 1804.
12. *Carolina Gazette* (Charleston, SC), August 31, 1804.
13. *Balance* (Hudson, NY), August 20, 1805; *United States Gazette* (Philadelphia, PA), September 9, 1805; Zimmerman, *Impressment of American Seamen*, 16–17.
14. *Balance* (Hudson, NY), September 11, 1804; *Connecticut Gazette* (September 19, 1804). See also *Boston Gazette* (MA), December 17, 1804. See Paul Gilje, *Liberty on the Waterfront: American Maritime Culture in the Age of Revolution* (Philadelphia: University of Pennsylvania Press, 2004) for more on the politics and voting patterns of port cities.
15. *Aurora General Advertiser* (Philadelphia, PA), February 27, 1805; *The Enquirer* (Richmond, VA), March 8, 1805; and *Vermont Gazette* (Bennington), March 25, 1805.
16. *Aurora General Advertiser* (Philadelphia, PA), February 4, 1805.
17. *Aurora General Advertiser* (Philadelphia, PA), February 27, 1805; *The Enquirer* (Richmond, VA), March 8, 1805; *Vermont Gazette* (Bennington), March 25, 1805.
18. *Salem Register* (MA), July 22, 1805; *Centinel of Freedom* (Newark, NJ), August 6, 1805; *City Gazette* (Charleston, SC), August 8, 1805.

19. *Columbian Centinel* (Boston, MA), July 24, 1805; *Boston Gazette* (MA), July 25, 1805; *The Post Boy* (Windsor, VT), July 30, 1805; *Alexandria Advertiser* (VA), August 1, 1805; *National Intelligencer* (Washington, DC), August 2, 1805; *Balance* (Hudson, NY), August 6, 1805.
20. *Boston Gazette* (MA), October 21, 1805; *Newport Mercury* (RI), October 26, 1805; *Washington Federalist* (DC), November 6, 1805.
21. *True American* (Trenton, NJ) article reprinted in *The Sun* (Pittsfield, MA), September 7, 1805; *Political Observatory* (Walpole, NH), September 14, 1805; *New Hampshire Gazette* (Portsmouth), September 24, 1805; and *Suffolk Gazette* (Sag Harbor, NY), September 30, 1805.
22. *True American* (Trenton, NJ) article reprinted in *Spirit of the Press* (Philadelphia, PA), October 12, 1805; *American Mercury* (Hartford, CT), November 7, 1805; *Weekly Wander* (Randolph, VT), November 11, 1805.
23. *Salem Register* (MA), October 14, 1805; *Aurora General Advertiser* (Philadelphia, PA), October 23, 1805.
24. *Newark Centinel* (NJ) article reprinted in the *Aurora General Advertiser* (Philadelphia, PA), November 27, 1805.
25. James Madison to James Monroe, April 23, 1806, Additional General Correspondence, 1780 to 1837, Series 2, James Madison Papers, 1723 to 1859, Manuscript Division, Library of Congress, Washington, DC, https://www.loc.gov/item/mjm022193/.
26. Zimmerman, *Impressment of American Seamen*, 116–22.
27. Ibid., 120.
28. Monroe and Pinkney to Madison, November 11, 1806, *American State Papers*, 1, Foreign Relations, 3:137–40.
29. Zimmerman, *Impressment of American Seamen*, 122–23; Donald Hickey, "The Monroe-Pinkney Treaty of 1806: A Reappraisal," *William and Mary Quarterly* 44, no. 1 (January 1987): 65–88.
30. Hickey, "The Monroe-Pinkney Treaty," 65.
31. Madison to Monroe, March 20, 1806, quoted in Zimmerman, *Impressment of American Seamen*, 128.
32. Zimmerman, *Impressment of American Seamen*, 135–41; Robert Cray, "Remembering the USS *Chesapeake*: The Politics of Maritime Death and Impressment," *Journal of the Early Republic* 25, no. 3 (Fall 2005): 445–74; Spencer Tucker and Frank Reuter, *Injured Honor: The Chesapeake-Leopard Affair, June 22, 1807* (Annapolis, MD: Naval Institute Press, 1996).
33. *Mercantile Advertiser* (New York, NY), June 29, 1807; Zimmerman, *Impressment of American Seamen*, 135–41; Cray, "Remembering the USS *Chesapeake*," 454.
34. *Commercial Advertiser* (New York, NY), June 29, 1807; *The Public Advertiser* (New York, NY), June 30, 1807; *Litchfield Monitor* (CT), July 1, 1807.
35. Gilje, *Liberty on the Waterfront*, 146; Cray, "Remembering the USS *Chesapeake*," 454–55.
36. *Alexandria Daily Advertiser* (VA), June 30, 1807.
37. *People's Friend* (New York, NY), July 3, 1807.
38. *Democratic Press* (Philadelphia, PA), July 9, 1807.
39. *Commercial Advertiser* (New York, NY), June 30, 1807, also in *Democratic Press* (Philadelphia, PA), June 30, 1807.
40. *The Public Advertiser* (New York, NY), June 30, 1807; *Aurora General Advertiser* (Philadelphia, PA), July 3, 1807; *Republican Star* (Easton, MD), July 14, 1807; *True Republican* (New London, CT), July 15, 1807; *City Gazette* (Charleston, SC), July 22, 1807; *Sun* (Pittsfield, MA), July 25, 1807. The use of the pseudonym "Franklin" was likely an acknowledgment of Benjamin Franklin's well-established opposition to the practice of impressment. See Brunsman, *The Evil Necessity*, 241–42.
41. *Norfolk Ledger* (VA) article reprinted in *New York Evening Post* (NY), July 1, 1807; *Poulson's American Daily Advertiser* (Philadelphia, PA), July 1, 1807.

42. *Boston Gazette* (MA), July 9, 1807.
43. *Commercial Advertiser* (New York, NY), June 30, 1807.
44. *The Public Advertiser* (New York, NY), June 30, 1807; *Aurora General Advertiser* (Philadelphia, PA), July 3, 1807; *Republican Star* (Easton, MD), July 14 1807; *True Republican* (New London, CT), July 15, 1807; *City Gazette* (Charleston, SC), July 22, 1807; *Sun* (Pittsfield, MA), July 25, 1807.
45. *People's Friend* (New York, NY), July 3, 1807.
46. *Aurora General Advertiser* (Philadelphia, PA), October 4, 1805, and October 19, 1805.
47. Thomas Jefferson to William Cabell, July 24, 1807, in *The Writings of Thomas Jefferson*, ed. Albert Bergh, vol. 11 (Washington, DC: The Thomas Jefferson Memorial Association, 1904), 294–96.
48. *The Public Advertiser* (New York, NY), June 30, 1807; *Aurora General Advertiser* (Philadelphia, PA), July 3, 1807; *Republican Star* (Easton, MD), July 14, 1807; *True Republican* (New London, CT), July 15, 1807; *City Gazette* (Charleston, SC), July 22, 1807; *Sun* (Pittsfield, MA), July 25, 1807.
49. Dumas Malone, *Jefferson the President: Second Term, 1805–1809*, vol. 5 of *Jefferson and His Time* (Boston: Little, Brown and Company, 1974), 469–506; Zimmerman, *Impressment of American Seamen*, 156–57; Gilje, *Liberty on the Waterfront*, 146; Cray, "Remembering the USS *Chesapeake*," 467.
50. Malone, *Jefferson the President*, 561–65; Alan Taylor, *The Civil War of 1812: American Citizens, British Subjects, Irish Rebels, and Indian Allies* (New York: Alfred A. Knopf, 2010), 115–19.
51. *American Citizen* (New York NY), January 11, 1808.
52. *Balance* (Hudson, NY), January 19, 1808, and *Spectator* (New York, NY), January 13, 1808, reprinted in *Commercial Advertiser* (New York, NY), January 11, 1808; *Alexandria Advertiser* (VA), January 22, 1808; *Newburyport Herald* (MA), February 2, 1808.
53. *New York Herald* (NY), February 27, 1808; *Trenton Federalist* (NJ), February 29, 1808; *Hampshire Federalist* (Springfield, MA), March 3, 1808; *Alexandria Advertiser* (VA), March 12, 1808.
54. *Columbian Centinel* (Boston, MA), May 21, 1808, reprinted in *Portland Gazette* (ME), May 23, 1808; *Hampshire Federalist* (Springfield, MA), May 26, 1808. For more on the impact of the Embargo on sailors, see Gilje, *Liberty on the Waterfront*, 146–51.
55. Gilje, *Liberty on the Waterfront*, 146–47; Taylor, *The Civil War of 1812*, 118–19.
56. Thomas Jefferson to James Madison, September 1, 1807, in *The Republic of Letters: Correspondence between Thomas Jefferson and James Madison, 1776–1826*, ed. James Morton Smith (New York: W. W. Norton and Company, 1995), 3:1495.
57. *National Aegis* (Worcester, MA), February 10, 1808; Lambert, *The Barbary Wars*, 176–78.
58. *National Aegis* (Worcester, MA), February 10, 1808; *Newport Mercury* (RI), February 6, 1808; *Pittsfield Sun* (MA), February 6, 1808.
59. Thomas Jefferson to James Madison, August 28, 1801, and Thomas Jefferson to James Madison, September 1, 1807, in *The Republic of Letters*, ed. Smith, 2:1194, 1495.

Chapter 6: "Floating Hells of Old England"

1. *Repertory* (Boston, MA), June 30, 1812; *Orange County Patriot* (Goshen, NY), June 9, 1812.
2. *Boston Daily Advertiser* (MA), October 11, 1813; Entry for 25 November 1813, *The Diary of Isaiah Thomas*, ed. Benjamin Thomas Hill (Worcester, MA: American Antiquarian Society, 1909), 205.
3. The War of 1812 is often discussed in terms of sectional differences. New England shipping interests opposed the conflict, while southern and western interests sought to protect American sailors and western settlers from British and Native American attacks

respectively. An examination of the historiography, however, suggests that a political interpretation structured along party lines is more accurate and productive. Roger H. Brown, *The Republic in Peril: 1812* (New York: Columbia University Press, 1964) presents the coming of war as a continuation of the partisan differences of the 1790s. J. C. A. Stagg, *Mr. Madison's War: Politics, Diplomacy, and Warfare in the Early American Republic, 1783–1830* (Princeton, NJ: Princeton University Press, 1983) attempts to shift the focus away from Congress and the War Hawks to President Madison, who came to see Canada as a central front in the battle to force England into respecting neutral rights. Donald Hickey, *The War of 1812: The Forgotten Conflict* (Urbana: University of Illinois Press, 1989) contends that although the Republican Party had come to dominate national politics after the election of 1800, a resurgent Federalist Party offered a more-rational and better-reasoned approach to international relations as the Republicans rushed to war with England. Jeffrey Pasley, *"The Tyranny of the Printers": Newspaper Politics in the Early American Republic* (Charlottesville: University of Virginia Press, 2001) offers some insight into the nature of the partisan divide as it played out in the press during this period. Richard Buel Jr., *America on the Brink: How the Political Struggle over the War of 1812 Almost Destroyed the Young Republic* (New York: Palgrave, 2005) places much of the blame for the conflict on the Federalists, arguing that their attempts to subvert the national government forced the United States into war. Alan Taylor, *The Civil War of 1812: American Citizens, British Subjects, Irish Rebels, and Indian Allies* (New York: Alfred A. Knopf, 2010) demonstrates the factional border politics of the first decade of the nineteenth century giving way to hardened international boundaries and to both American and, what Taylor labels, a "Canadian" nationality in the wake of the War of 1812.

4. William Plumer to John Quincy Adams, August 18, 1812, reel 3, microfilm, William Plumer Papers, 1774–1845, Manuscript Division, Library of Congress, Washington, DC; Hickey, *The War of 1812*, 19–27.
5. *Eastern Argus* (Portland, ME), January 3, 1811.
6. *Alexandria Daily Gazette* (VA), January 8, 1811. See also *Republican Farmer* (Bridgeport, CT), January 9, 1811; *The Bee* (Hudson, NY), January 18, 1811; and the *Essex Register* (Salem, MA), January 19, 1811.
7. *New Hampshire Patriot* (Concord), January 8, 1811.
8. *Essex Register* (Salem, MA), February 23, 1811. The letter was also published in *The Bee* (Hudson, NY), March 8, 1811, and *Carolina Gazette* (Charleston, SC), March 29, 1811.
9. *Essex Register* (Salem, MA), January 16, 1811, reprinted in *The Farmer's Repository* (Charlestown, VA), February 1, 1811, and *Carolina Gazette* (Charleston, SC), February 22, 1811.
10. *A Narrative of Joshua Davis, an American Citizen, Who Was Pressed and Served on Board Six Ships of the British Navy* (Baltimore, MD: B. Edes, Printer, 1811), 63–72. Davis's narrative followed a series of narratives that emerged following the end of the conflict with Tripoli and that recounted Barbary captivity. The parallels between the British and Barbary treatment of American sailors were readily comprehended by the American audience. See William Ray, *Horrors of Slavery: or the American Tars in Tripoli* (Troy, NY: Printed by Oliver Lyon for the author, 1808); Jonathan Cowdry, *American Captives in Tripoli* (Boston: Printed and sold by Belcher and Armstrong, 1806); Paul Gilje, *Liberty on the Waterfront: American Maritime Culture in the Age of Revolution* (Philadelphia: University of Pennsylvania Press, 2004), 153–55; Paul Michel Baepler, ed., *White Slaves, African Masters: An Anthology of American Barbary Captivity Narratives* (Chicago: University of Chicago Press, 1999); Jacob Rama Berman, "The Barbarous Voice of Democracy: American Captivity in Barbary and the Multicultural Specter," *American Literature* 79, no. 1 (March 2007): 1–27.
11. *A Narrative of Joshua Davis*, 72–74.
12. *Commercial Advertiser* (New York, NY) September 6, 1811, reprinted in *Connecticut Journal* (New Haven), September 26, 1811.

13. *American Mercury* (Hartford, CT), January 3, 1811.
14. *Columbian Centinel* (Boston, MA), May 8, 1811, reprinted in *New Bedford Mercury* (MA), May 10, 1811; *Portland Gazette* (ME), May 13, 1811.
15. *Trenton Federalist* (NJ), May 13, 1811.
16. *Commercial Advertiser* (New York, NY), September 6, 1811, reprinted in *Connecticut Journal* (New Haven), September 26, 1811.
17. For more on the treaty, see Anthony Steel, "Impressment in the Monroe-Pinkney Negotiations, 1806–1807," *American Historical Review* 57, no. 2 (January 1952): 352–69, and Donald Hickey, "The Monroe-Pinkney Treaty of 1806: A Reappraisal," *William and Mary Quarterly* 44, no. 1 (January 1987): 65–88. Hickey argues that while the treaty did not bring an end to all impressment, the treaty itself was favorable to the United States and would have greatly limited the practice of impressment. Contemporary Federalists, however, were quick to overstate the lost opportunity to stop the practice and made additional sweeping claims for the terms of the treaty.
18. *Washingtonian* (Windsor, VT), May 27, 1811.
19. See *Portland Gazette* (ME), May 13, 1811; *New Bedford Mercury* (MA), May 10, 1811, and May 31, 1811; *Trenton Federalist* (NJ), May 13, 1811.
20. *Balance* (Hudson, NY), May 7, 1811, reprinted in *Washingtonian* (Windsor, VT), May 27, 1811.
21. *Portland Gazette* (ME), January 7, 1811.
22. *Northern Whig* (Hudson, NY), May 31, 1811, reprinted in *Portsmouth Oracle* (NH), June 8, 1811.
23. *Connecticut Courant* (Hartford), July 17, 1811, reprinted in *Alexandria Gazette* (VA), August 12, 1811.
24. *American Mercury* (Hartford, CT), January 3, 1811.
25. *New Hampshire Patriot* (Concord), February 19, 1811.
26. *National Intelligencer* (Washington, DC), May 25, 1811, reprinted in *American Watchman* (Wilmington, DE), May 29, 1811; *Farmer's Repository* (Charlestown, VA), May 31, 1811.
27. *New Hampshire Patriot* (Concord), February 19, 1811.
28. *National Intelligencer* (Washington, DC), May 25, 1811.
29. *American Mercury* (Hartford, CT), January 3, 1811.
30. Hickey, *The War of 1812*, 41–44.
31. *Federal Republican* (Washington, DC), June 1, 1812.
32. Cited in *Franklin Herald* (Greenfield, MA), June 23, 1812.
33. The *Federal Republican* critiques of the war were reprinted throughout the country in papers including the *Alexandria Gazette* (VA), June 20, 1812; *New-York Spectator* (NY), June 20, 1812; *New York Herald* (NY), June 20, 1812; *Poulson's American Daily Advertiser* (Philadelphia, PA), June 22, 1812; *Franklin Herald* (Greenfield, MA), June 23, 1812. For specifics of this incident, see Hickey, *The War of 1812*, 59–61, and Paul Gilje, "The Baltimore Riots of 1812 and the Breakdown of the Anglo-American Mob Tradition," *Journal of Social History* 13, no. 4 (Summer 1980): 547–64.
34. *Newport Mercury* (RI), August 8, 1812.
35. *Repertory*, (Boston, MA), August 7, 1812.
36. Hickey, *The War of 1812*, 68–69.
37. *Connecticut Courant* (Hartford), August 25, 1812. See also *The Courier* (Charleston, SC), August 8, 1812, and *The Federalist* (Trenton, NJ), August 3, 1812, cited in Hickey, *The War of 1812*, 350.
38. My take on the Baltimore riots differs from that earlier historians. Paul Gilje reads the Baltimore riots as a precursor to the urban unrest of the Jacksonian Era, while Donald Hickey sees the Federalist reaction to the Baltimore riots as a defense of individual rights, see Hickey, *The War of 1812*, 59–61, and Paul Gilje, "The Baltimore Riots of 1812 and the Breakdown of the Anglo-American Mob Tradition."

39. *Connecticut Herald* (New Haven), March 30, 1813.
40. *New York Shamrock* (NY), March 20, 1813.
41. *Rhode Island American* (Providence), October 15, 1813; *The Repertory* (Boston, MA), December 21, 1813.
42. Donald Hickey, *The War of 1812*, 86–87.
43. Winfield Scott, *Memoirs of Lieut.-General Scott* (New York: Sheldon and Company Publishers, 1864), 54–68; Benson Lossing, *Pictorial Field-Book of the War of 1812* (New York: Harper and Brothers, 1868), 408–9; Ralph Robinson, "Retaliation for the Treatment of Prisoners of War in the War of 1812," *American Historical Review* 49, no. 1 (October, 1943): 65–70.
44. *Military Monitor* (New York), April 19, 1813.
45. *Salem Gazette* (Salem, MA), June 5, 1813.
46. *Baltimore American* (MD) article reprinted in *Albany Argus* (NY), June 18, 1813; *New York Statesman* (Albany), June 23, 1813; *Essex Register* (Salem, MA), June 26, 1813; *Ohio Register* (Clinton), June 26, 1813; and *Otsego Herald* (Cooperstown, NY), July 3, 1813.
47. *Essex Register* (Salem, MA), October 9, 1813, reprinted in *Alexandria Gazette* (VA), October 21, 1813; *Farmer's Repository* (Charlestown, VA), October 21, 1813; *Rhode Island Republican* (Newport), October 21, 1813; *True American* (Bedford, PA), October 27, 1813.
48. *City Gazette* (Charleston, SC), November 23, 1813; *Carolina Gazette* (Charleston, SC), November 27 1813.
49. *Green-Mountain Farmer* (Bennington, VT), May 25, 1813.
50. Newark *Centinel* (NJ) article reprinted in the *American Watchman* (Wilmington, DE), December 15, 1813.
51. United States House of Representatives, *Barbarities of the Enemy: Report of the Committee . . . as Relates to the Spirit and Manner in Which the War Has Been Waged by the Enemy* (Washington: A & G Way Printers, 1813). See *Baltimore Patriot* (MD), August 13, 1813; *New York Spectator* (NY), August 18, 1813; *Rhode Island Republican* (Newport), August 19, 1813; *Charleston City Gazette* (SC), August 20, 1813; *American Mercury* (Hartford, CT), August 24, 1813; *Boston Yankee* (MA), August 20, 1813.
52. *Evening Post* (New York), November 22, 1813.
53. *London Courier* article reprinted in *City Gazette* (Charleston, SC), October 16, 1813.
54. *Rhode Island American* (Providence), October 15, 1813; *Repertory* (Boston, MA), December 21, 1813.
55. *Evening Post* (New York), November 22, 1813, reprinted in *Connecticut Journal* (New Haven), November 29, 1813, and the *Northern Whig* (Hudson, NY), November 30, 1813.
56. *Repertory* (Boston, MA), December 21, 1813.
57. *Boston Daily Advertiser* (MA), December 16, 1813.
58. *Rhode Island American* (Providence), November 19, 1813.
59. *New York Evening Post* (NY), December 30, 1813.
60. *Boston Gazette* (MA), November 25, 1813.
61. *Federal Republican* (Washington, DC), November 19, 1813.
62. *Boston Spectator* (MA), January 8, 1814.
63. *London Sun* article reprinted in *Salem Gazette* (MA), July 27, 1813.
64. *Evening Post* (New York), December 10, 1813.
65. *Evening Post* (New York), December 21, 1813, reprinted in *New York Herald* (NY), December 22, 1813; *Connecticut Herald* (New Haven), December 28, 1813; *Alexandria Gazette* (VA), January 1, 1814.
66. *New York Evening Post* (NY), December 21, 1813, reprinted in *Boston Gazette* (MA), December 23, 1813; *Portland Gazette* (ME), December 27, 1813; *Federal Republican* (Washington, DC), December 27, 1813; *Alexandria Gazette* (VA), January 11, 1814.
67. *New York Commercial Advertiser* (NY), December 24, 1813. See also *House Journal*, 13th

Cong., 2nd sess., December 21, 1813, and *Senate Journal*, 13th Cong., 2nd sess., February 2, 1814, and March 9, 1814.
68. *Federal Republican* (Washington, DC), December 24, 1813.
69. Entries for November 25, December 3-5, 1813, *The Diary of Isaiah Thomas*, 205-9; *Columbian Centinel* (Boston, MA), January 19, 1814.
70. *Massachusetts Spy or Worcester Gazette* (MA), December 8, 1813, reprinted in *Rhode Island American* (Providence), December 10 1813; *Boston Repertory* (MA), December 11, 1813; *Connecticut Journal* (New Haven), December 13, 1813; *Poulson's American Daily Advertiser* (Philadelphia, PA), December 14, 1813; *New York Evening Post* (NY), December 17, 1813; *Federal Republican* (Washington, DC), December 24, 1813.
71. Thomas, *The Diary of Isaiah Thomas*, 208-9. *Massachusetts Spy or Worcester Gazette* (MA), December 8, 1813, reprinted in *Rhode Island American* (Providence), December, 10 1813; *Boston Repertory* (MA), December 11, 1813; *Connecticut Journal* (New Haven), December 13, 1813; *Poulson's American Daily Advertiser* (Philadelphia, PA) December 14, 1813; *New York Evening Post* (NY), December 17, 1813; *Federal Republican* (Washington, DC), December 24, 1813.
72. *Baltimore Patriot* (MD), December 14 and 21, 1813.
73. *Massachusetts Spy* (Worcester), January 5, 1814, reprinted in *Boston Daily Advertiser* (MA), January 13, 1814, and *Repertory* (Boston, MA), January 13, 1814.
74. Thomas, *The Diary of Isaiah Thomas*, 213-16.
75. *Boston Patriot* (MA), January 15, 1814.
76. Ibid.
77. Ibid.
78. *Columbian Centinel* (Boston, MA), January 19, 1814. The personalization of politics is more fully described in Joanne Freeman's *Affairs of Honor: National Politics in the New Republic* (New Haven: Yale University Press, 2001). Freeman's work only goes to the election of 1800. But this incident bears numerous similarities to the political battles described by Freeman. While she argues that personal politics was critical in a period before the establishment of political parties, this debate suggests a fusion of the personal and national politics even as the parties emerged as legitimate players at the national level
79. *Massachusetts Spy* (Worcester), January 19, 1814.
80. *Baltimore Patriot* (MD), January 25, 1814; Hickey, *The War of 1812*, 70, 176-77.
81. Entries for January 12 and 15, 1814, *The Diary of Isaiah Thomas*, 214-17.
82. Hickey, *The War of 1812*, 180. *Boston Daily Advertiser* (MA), February 4, 1814.
83. See John Brooke, "Cultures of Nationalism, Movements of Reform, and the Composite-Federal Polity from Revolutionary Settlement to Antebellum Crisis," *Journal of the Early Republic* 29, no. 1 (Spring 2009): 12.
84. Richard Buel, *America on the Brink*, focusing primarily on the Massachusetts Federalists, argues that the Federalists worked "to subvert that national government after 1800" and goes as far as to declare, "Federalist behavior, rather than British actions, was the critical factor propelling the Republicans to declare war in 1812." See ibid., 2. Buel's account fails to fully engage the Federalist rationale for opposing the war, instead portraying Federalists from a distinctly Republican perspective.
85. See Brooke, "Cultures of Nationalism," 16, and Pasley, *The Tyranny of the Printers*, 351-52.

Chapter 7: Mr. Madison's Other War

1. *Weekly Aurora* (Philadelphia, PA), February 28, 1815.
2. *American Advocate* (Hallowell, ME), February 25, 1815.
3. *Western American* (Williamsburg, OH), February 18, 1815.

4. *Annals of Congress*, 13th Cong., 3rd sess., 1156, 1161.
5. For more on the myth of the glorious war, see Donald Hickey, *The War of 1812: A Forgotten Conflict* (Urbana: University of Illinois Press, 1989), 308–9, and Alan Taylor, *The Civil War of 1812: American Citizens, British Subjects, Irish Rebels, and Indians Allies* (New York: Alfred Knopf, 2010), 420–21.
6. Taylor, *The Civil War of 1812*, 415–17.
7. J. C. A. Stagg, *Mr. Madison's War: Politics, Diplomacy, and Warfare in the Early American Republic, 1783–1830* (Princeton, NJ: Princeton University Press, 1983), 379.
8. Myra Glenn, *Jack Tar's Story: The Autobiographies and Memoirs of Sailors in Antebellum America* (New York: Cambridge University Press, 2010), 55–57.
9. *Columbian Centinel* (Boston, MA), July 12, 1817; *New Haven Herald* (CT), July 7, 1817; Andrew Robertson, "'Look on this Picture . . . And on This!' Nationalism, Localism, and Partisan Images of Otherness in the United States, 1787–1820," *American Historical Review* 106, no. 4 (October 2001): 1263–80.
10. C. Edward Skeen argues, "There is considerable evidence that indeed an 'Era of Good Feelings' arose after the war and lasted at least into 1817." Andrew Robertson observes, "In the aftermath of the War of 1812, a sense of 'national feeling' reemerged, and the definitions of national identity held by Republicans and Federalists once again converged." See C. Edward Skeen, *1816: America Rising* (Lexington: University of Kentucky Press, 2003), 24, and Robertson, "'Look on This Picture,'" 1279.
11. It is important to note that fear of a general English threat or the administration's mishandling of the situation became the center the national debate rather than any real outrage over the murder of the American sailors. Sam Haynes has recently argued that this undercurrent of Anglophobia lingered until the middle of the nineteenth century as Americans attempted to reconcile "two fundamentally opposing impulses—the desire to repudiate and emulate the ancient regime." See his *The Unfinished Revolution: The Early American Republic in a British World* (Charlottesville: University of Virginia Press, 2010), 2.
12. Lawrence Peskin, *Captives and Countrymen: Barbary Slavery and the American Public, 1785–1816* (Baltimore: Johns Hopkins University Press, 2009), 194–97.
13. *Daily National Intelligencer* (Washington, DC), January 6, 1813.
14. Frederick Leiner, *The End of the Barbary Terror: America's 1815 War against the Pirates of North Africa* (Oxford, UK: Oxford University Press, 2006), 6–8.
15. Mordecai M. Noah, *Correspondence and Documents Relative to the Attempt to Negotiate for the Release of American Captives at Algiers* (Washington, DC, 1816), 5–8. See also Peskin, *Captives and Countrymen*, 196–98, and Leiner, *The End of the Barbary Terror*, 30–31.
16. Message of the President to Congress, *American State Papers*, 1, Foreign Relations 13:3, 748.
17. *Daily National Intelligencer* (Washington, DC), March 7, 1815, reprinted in *Poulson's American Daily Advertiser* (Philadelphia, PA), March 9, 1815; *Commercial Advertiser* (New York, NY), March 10, 1815; *Alexandria Gazette* (VA), March 11, 1815; *Boston Gazette* (MA), March 16, 1815; *City Gazette* (Charleston, SC), March 16, 1815; *Western American* (Williamsburg, OH), March 18, 1815; *Columbian Patriot* (Middlebury, VT), March 22, 1815.
18. *Portsmouth Oracle* (NH), February 18, 1815.
19. *Boston Gazette* (MA), February 23, 1815.
20. *Boston Daily Advertiser* (MA), March 16, 1815; *Daily National Intelligencer* (Washington, DC), March 23, 1815; *Mechanics Gazette* (Baltimore, MD), March 29, 1815; *Weekly Recorder* (Chillicothe, OH), April 12, 1815.
21. *Albany Argus* (NY), March 31, 1815.
22. *Niles' Weekly Register* (Baltimore, MD), April 15, 1815.
23. [Charles Andrews], *The Prisoners' Memoirs, or, Dartmoor Prison* (New York: Printed for the Author, 1815), 135–38; Paul Gilje, *Liberty on the Waterfront: American Maritime Culture in the Age of Revolution* (Philadelphia: University of Pennsylvania Press, 2004), 184–85.

24. Ira Dye, "American Maritime Prisoners of War, 1812–1815," *Ships, Seafaring and Society: Essays in Maritime History*, ed. Timothy Runyan (Detroit, MI: Wayne State University Press, 1987), 306–7.
25. Gilje, *Liberty on the Waterfront*, 185–86.
26. Dye, "American Maritime Prisoners of War," 305–8.
27. Gilje, *Liberty on the Waterfront*, 186.
28. Andrews, *The Prisoners' Memoirs*, 167–68.
29. Andrews, *The Prisoners' Memoirs*, 169–70; John Melish, *A Description of Dartmoor Prison, with an Account of the Massacre of the Prisoners* (Philadelphia: J. Bioren, Printer, 1815), 167–72.
30. Andrews, *The Prisoners' Memoirs*, 169–70.
31. Josiah Cobb, *A Green Hand's First Cruise* (Boston: Otis, Broaders, and Company, 1854 [1841]), 2:213–14. This is also the account most closely followed in Gilje, *Liberty on the Waterfront*, 187.
32. *Annals of Congress*, 14th Cong., 1st sess., 1537.
33. Ibid., 1524.
34. Ibid., 1522.
35. Andrews, *The Prisoners' Memoirs*, 173.
36. *Annals of Congress*, 14th Cong., 1st sess., 1522.
37. Ibid., 1521–24.
38. Melish, *A Description of Dartmoor Prison*, 6.
39. Andrews, *The Prisoner's Memoirs*, 175.
40. Melish, *A Description of Dartmoor Prison*, 6.
41. Andrews, *The Prisoner's Memoirs*, 175–76.
42. Benjamin Waterhouse, *A Journal of a Young Man of Massachusetts . . . at Dartmoor Prison* (Boston: Rowe and Hooper 1816), 205–6.
43. "Massacre at Dartmoor Prison," *Annals of Congress*, 14th Cong., 1st sess., 1535–36.
44. Ibid., 1523.
45. Andrews, *The Prisoners' Memoirs*, 176.
46. Melish, *A Description of Dartmoor Prison*, 10; Andrews, *The Prisoner's Memoirs*, 178; Reginald Horsman, *The War of 1812* (New York: Alfred A. Knopf, 1969), 264; Robin F. A. Fabel, "Self-Help In Dartmoor: Black and White Prisoners in the War of 1812," *Journal of the Early Republic* 9, no. 2 (Summer 1989): 186.
47. "Extract of a Minute of a Conversation Which Took Place at Lord Castlereagh's between His Lordship and Messrs. Clay and Gallatin," *Annals of Congress*, 14th Cong., 1st sess., 1507–8.
48. Henry Clay and Albert Gallatin to Reuben Beasley, April 18, 1815, in the *Annals of Congress*, 14th Cong., 1 sess., 1509. The London-based newspaper accounts, dated April 10, were later reprinted in a number of American newspapers including *New York Commercial Advertiser*, May 24, 1815; *Essex Register* (Salem, MA), May 24, 1815; *Boston Daily Advertiser*, May 25, 1815; *Dedham Gazette* (MA), May 26, 1815; *Daily National Intelligencer* (Washington, DC), May 27, 1815; *Republican Star* (MD), May 30, 1815.
49. "Report of Messrs. Larpent and King upon the Occurrence at Dartmoor Prison," *Annals of Congress* 14th Congress, 1st sess., 1512–18.
50. Ibid.
51. The official commission report can be found in the *Annals of Congress*, 14th Cong., 1st sess., 1511–17, and *American State Papers, 1, Foreign Relations*, 4:20–23. American officials declined the British offer to "make provisions for the widows and families of the sufferers" of the incident at Dartmoor, commenting, however, that they respected "the motives which dictated it." Congress itself eventually set aside a fund for the families of the deceased prisoners. See *Annals of Congress* 14th Congress, 1st sess., 1520.
52. *New York Commercial Advertiser* (NY) May 24, 1815; *Essex Register* (Salem, MA), May 24,

1815; *Boston Daily Advertiser,* May 25, 1815; *Dedham Gazette* (MA), May 26, 1815; *Daily National Intelligencer* (Washington, DC), May 27, 1815; *Republican Star* (MD), May 30, 1815.
53. *The Enquirer* (Richmond, VA), June 3, 1815; *Plattsburgh Republican* (NY), June 3, 1815; *Bennington Newsletter* (VT), June 5, 1815.
54. *Federal Republican* (Washington, DC), June 2, 1815.
55. *Northern Whig* (Hudson, NY), June 6, 1815.
56. *Daily National Intelligencer* (Washington, DC), June 1, 1815.
57. Ibid.
58. *New York Weekly Museum,* June 10, 1815.
59. *Independent Chronicle* (Boston), June 12, 1815; *Albany Argus* (NY), 13 June 1815; *Daily National Intelligencer* (Washington, DC), June 15, 1815.
60. John Hunter Waddell, *Horrid Massacre at Dartmoor Prison England* (Boston: Nathaniel Coverly, June 1815).
61. *New York Weekly Museum* (New York), June 10, 1815.
62. *Independent Chronicle* (Boston), June 12, 1815; *Albany Argus* (NY), 13 June 1815; *Daily National Intelligencer* (Washington, DC), June 15, 1815; *Niles' Weekly Register* (Baltimore), June 17, 1815; *Republican Star* (Easton, MD), June 20, 1815; *Western Monitor* (Lexington, KY) June 30, 1815; *Albany Argus* (NY), June 20, 1815; *The Patrol* (Utica, NY), June 22, 1815; *American Advocate* (Hallowell, ME), June 24, 1815; *Providence Patriot* (RI), June 24, 1815; *American Watchman* (Wilmington, DE), June 28, 1815; *True American* (Bedford, PA), June 29, 1815; *Republican Star* (Easton, MD), July 4, 1815.
63. Andrews, *The Prisoner's Memoirs;* Melish, *A Description of Dartmoor;* Waddell, *Horrid Massacre at Dartmoor Prison England.*
64. Waddell, *Horrid Massacre at Dartmoor Prison England.*
65. Melish, *A Description of Dartmoor Prison,* 15.
66. Andrews, *The Prisoners' Memoirs,* 175–80.
67. *National Advocate* (New York), June 16, 1815; *American Watchman* (Wilmington, DE), June 21, 1815; *Albany Argus* (NY), June 23, 1815; *Western American* (Williamsburg, OH), June 24, 1815; *Vermont Republican* (Windsor), June 26, 1815.
68. *Federal Republican* (Washington, DC), June 17, 1815.
69. *The Columbian* (New York), June 17, 1815; *Daily National Intelligencer* (Washington, DC), June 23, 1815.
70. *American Mercury* (Hartford), June 28, 1815; *The Ohio Register* (Clinton, OH), August 1, 1815.
71. *Niles' Weekly Register* (Baltimore, MD), June 17, 1815.
72. Ibid.
73. *Baltimore Patriot* (MD), August 3, 1815; *Rutland Herald* (VT), August 2, 1815; *The Columbian* (New York), July 5, 1815; *Baltimore Patriot* (MD), July 7, 1815; *Essex Register* (Salem, MA), July 8, 1815.
74. *Dedham Gazette* (MA), June 30, 1815; *Evening Post* (New York), June 30, 1815; *Alexandria Herald* (VA), July 5, 1815; *American Advocate and Kennebec Advertiser* (Hallowell, ME), July 8, 1815; *The Union* (Washington, KY), July 14, 1815; *Western American* (Williamsburg, OH), July 22, 1815.
75. *Baltimore Patriot* (MD), July 7, 1815; *Essex Register* (Salem, MA), July 8, 1815; *Rutland Herald* (VT), August 2, 1815; *Carlisle Gazette* (PA), July 5, 1815; *American Advocate* (Hallowell, ME), July 15, 1815; *The Columbian* (New York), July 20, 1815; *The Columbian* (New York), August 2, 1815.
76. *Essex Register* (Salem, MA), July 8, 1815.
77. *National Advocate* (New York, NY), July 25, 1815.
78. *Baltimore Patriot* (MD), July 24, 1815.
79. *New Hampshire Patriot* (Concord), August 1, 1815.

80. *American Watchman* (Wilmington, DE), July 22, 1815; *Northern Whig* (Hudson, NY), July 25, 1815.
81. This characterization of Beasley appears in Taylor, *The Civil War of 1812*, 366, and is far more kind than Eden Phillpotts's description in his 1904 novel, *Farm of the Dagger*, which characterizes Beasley as "either a knave or a fool, and never have unhappy sufferers in this sort endured more from a callous, cruel, or utterly inefficient and imbecile representative." Phillipotts quoted in Francis Abell, *Prisoners of War in Britain, 1756-1815: A Record of Their Lives, Their Loves, and Their Sufferings* (London: Oxford University Press, 1914), 249
82. *Newburyport Herald* (MA), July 21, 1815.
83. For a more complete discussion of the outfitting of the American squadrons, see Frederick Leiner, *The End of the Barbary Terror*, 53-85, and Frank Lambert, *The Barbary Wars: American Independence in the Atlantic World* (New York: Hill and Wang, 2005), 189-91.
84. *The Writings of James Monroe*, ed. Stanislaus Hamilton, 7 vols. (New York, 1969), 5: 377-379; Lambert, *The Barbary Wars*, 192-193.
85. Stephen Decatur and William Shaler to James Monroe, July 4, 1815. *American State Papers*, 1, Foreign Affairs, 4:6. For a more complete discussion of the last of the Barbary Wars, see Lambert, *The Barbary Wars*, 182-90, and Peskin, *Captives and Countrymen*, 192-203.
86. *Ulster Plebian* (New York), August 29, 1815.
87. *Daily National Intelligencer* (Washington, DC), September 9, 1815.
88. *Federal Republican* (Washington, DC), September 18, 1815; *Boston Daily Advertiser*, September 18, 1815; *The Columbian* (NY), September 19, 1815; *Poulson's American Daily Advertiser* (Philadelphia), September 21, 1815; *Alexandria Herald* (VA), September 25, 1815.
89. *Baltimore Patriot* (MD), October 17, 1815; *Vermont Republican* (Windsor), October 30, 1815; *American Advocate* (Hallowell, ME), November 11, 1815.
90. *New Jersey Journal* (Elizabethtown), November 21, 1815.
91. *American Watchman* (Wilmington, DE), December 30, 1815.
92. *Baltimore Patriot* (MD), December 19, 1815.
93. *American Beacon* (Norfolk, VA), January 2, 1816; *Daily National Intelligencer* (Washington, DC), January 15, 1816; *American Beacon* (Norfolk, VA), January 2, 1816; *National Advocate* (NY), January 19, 1816; *New Hampshire Patriot* (Concord), January 30, 1816; *American Watchman* (Wilmington, DE), January 20, 1816; *The Yankee* (Boston, MA), January 26, 1816; *Vermont Republican* (Windsor), February 5, 1816; *New Jersey Journal* (Elizabethtown), February 20, 1816.
94. *National Standard* (Middlebury, VT), October 18, 1815, reprinted in *Independent Chronicle* (Boston), October 23, 1815; *Albany Argus* (NY), October 24, 1815; *Centinel of Freedom* (Newark, NJ), October 31, 1815; *American Beacon* (Norfolk, VA), November 1, 1815.
95. *Northern Whig* (Hudson, NY), January 23, 1816.
96. *American Beacon* (Norfolk, VA), December 9, 1815, reprinted in *Green Mountain Farmer* (Bennington, VT), December 11, 1815; *Independent Chronicle* (Boston), December 11, 1815; *Washington Whig* (Bridgeton, NJ), December 11, 1815; *American Advocate and Kennebec Advertiser* (Hallowell, ME), December 16, 1815; *Weekly Recorder* (Chillicothe, OH), December 20, 1815.
97. *Daily National Intelligencer* (Washington, DC), September 9, 1815.
98. *Baltimore Federal Republican* (MD), June 8, 1816; *New York Commercial Advertiser* (NY), June 10, 1816; *Delaware Gazette* (Wilmington, June 10, 1816; *Alexandria Gazette* (VA), June 11, 1816; *American Daily Advertiser* (Philadelphia), June 12, 1816; *Rhode Island American* (Providence), June 14, 1816; *Portland Gazette* (ME), June 18, 1816; *Western Monitor* (Lexington, KY), July 5, 1816. For a more complete examination of the American focus on Palestine and the Middle East in this period, see Michael Oren, *Power, Faith, and Fantasy* (New York: W.W. Norton, 2007).
99. *American Mercury* (Hartford), June 28, 1815; *Ohio Register* (Clinton, OH), August 1, 1815.

Conclusion: "To Promote Each Other's Welfare, and Mutual Feelings of Peace and Good Will"

1. *Morning News* (New London, CT), June 16, 1847 and August 19, 1847; *Brooklyn Daily Eagle* (NY), July 2, 1846. For more on events in New York, see Edwin Burrows, *Forgotten Patriots: The Untold Story of American Prisoners during the Revolutionary War* (New York: Basic Books, 2008), 229–37. On David Kennison in Chicago, see Alfred Young, *The Shoemaker and the Tea Party: Memory and the American Revolution* (Boston: Beacon Press, 1999), 180–81.
2. Charles Herbert, *A Relic of the Revolution, Containing a Full and Particular Account of the Sufferings and Privations of All the American Prisoners Captured on the High Seas and Carried into Plymouth, England, during the Revolution of 1776* (Boston: Charles H. Peirce, 1847), 13.
3. Ibid., 30–34.
4. Ibid., 141–43.
5. Ibid., 242.
6. Ibid., 12–16.
7. Greg Sieminski, "The Puritan Captivity Narrative and the Politics of the American Revolution," *American Quarterly* 42, no. 1 (Spring 1990): 12–16.
8. Herbert, *Relic of the Revolution*, 10–11.
9. Ibid., 10.
10. Jay Sexton, *The Monroe Doctrine: Empire and Nation in Nineteenth-Century America* (New York: Hill and Wang, 2011), 60.
11. Ibid., 245.
12. Herbert, *Relic of the Revolution*, 10–11.
13. Campbell Craig and Fredrik Logevall, *America's Cold War: The Politics of Insecurity* (Cambridge, MA: Belknap Press of Harvard University, 2009), 6–9.
14. Ibid., 363.
15. Marie Anne Pagliarini, "The Pure American and the Wicked Catholic Priest: An Analysis of Anti-Catholic Literature in Antebellum America," *Religion and American Culture: A Journal of Interpretation* 9, no. 1 (Winter 1999): 97–128; Tyler Anbinder, *Nativism and Slavery: The Northern Know Nothings and the Politics of the 1850s* (Oxford, UK: Oxford University Press, 1992).
16. Craig and Logevall, *America's Cold War*, 369.

Index

Adams, Abigail: on British cruelty to American prisoners, 25
Adams, John, 116, 192; on British cruelty to American prisoners, 25; defeat in election of 1800, 87; naval success, 95 negotiation with Barbary States, 45–46, 51–53, 78, 216n48; on religious faith, 90; Tripolitan War and, 101
Adams, John Quincy, 89, 133
Adams administration: American navy, 93, 116–17; Federalist support, 87, 194; impressment and, 118–19; on sailors' rights, 115; tribute to North African states, 89
"Adventures of Col. Daniel Boone, The" (Filson), 34
Algeria: Algiers, prominent city, 44; American efforts at peace treaties, 51–52, 89; American victory in war, 184–85; Democratic-Republican position, 64–65; letter of demands by dey, 39, 206n1; right to seize non-believers, 51; threat to American vessels, 39; United States forced to carry tribute to Ottoman sultan, 89. *See also* Barbary captivity of Americans; *Maria* and *Dauphin* merchant ships; Mathurin order; Tripolitan War
Alien Enemies Act, 158

Allen, Ethan, 35–37, 192; account of captivity, 31–33
American Advocate, 161
American Captive—An Elegy, The, 69–70
American captives. *See* Barbary captivity of Americans; prisoners of war, American
American Citizen, 125–26
American Minerva, 72, 76
American Patriot, attack by Republican mobs, 141
American Revolution: Fiske's sermon, 16–17; veterans' treatment, 191–92. *See also* Patriot cause
Americans, colonial: split loyalties, 2–3
American Watchman, 186
Andrews, Charles, 166, 168, 170, 175–76, 179
anti-Catholicism, 196–97
Arbuthnot, Mariot, 29–30
Articles of Confederation: limits of, 9, 11, 41–42, 61; taxation, 58; weakness of, 45–46
Aurora General Advertiser, 106, 115
Awful Disclosures of the Hotel Dieu Nunnery (Monk), 196

Bainbridge, William, 89, 91, 104, 184
Baker, Anthony St. John, 166
Balance, 126
Baltimore Federal Republican, 189

229

Baltimore Patriot, 153, 157, 187
Bancroft, Henry, 131
Barbarossa, Tyrant of Algiers (Brown), 70–71
Barbary captivity of Americans: British ambassador's role, 49, 53–55; British citizenship claim, 50; captain's plea for help, 61; citizen proposals on solution, 66–68; Congress's efforts, 58; day of national thanksgiving, 80–82, 213n65, 213n67; *A Discourse . . . as Preparatory to the Collection*, 82; Monroe ransom attempt, 163–64; *Philadelphia* captives, 102–3, 106, 216n57; power of taxation problem, 49; ransom, private and public, 11–12, 57–59, 62, 72–73, 77–84, 208n34, 209n2; shaping American politics, 4, 6, 9, 73, 200n14; Smith's letter on American navy, 180–81; trust in elected representatives, 78; vulnerability of Americans to capture, 42. *See also* Tripolitan War
Barbary States: British admiration for American victory, 186; declaration of war by dey, 163; efforts at peace treaties, 89; final conflict, American victory, 162, 184–89; joint American and Dutch attack, 189–90; Madison declaration of war, 164–65, 184; settlement, 10; tribute, 39, 43–44, 56, 86, 90, 100, 102, 128–30
Barbary threat, 14, 42–43; American sailors false flag, 47; Mediterranean trade, 48–49, 87; military response, 12–14
Barclay, Thomas, 48, 63, 78
Barron, James, 121–22
Barron, Samuel, 105
Batterman, George, 27
Battle of New Orleans, 13–14, 160
Battle of Queenston Heights, 132; American soldiers captured, 142–43; Irish American prisoners, 143
Beasley, Reuben: blame in Dartmoor Massacre, 171–74; Dartmoor negotiations, 166–67; London accounts, 227n81; name cleared, 183; Shortland blamed, 175–76
Berkeley, George, 121
Blackstone, William, 146
Blake, Francis, 155–58
Bonaparte, Napoleon, 126, 133, 138, 146–47, 154
Boston Daily Advertiser, 147
Boston Gazette, 103, 116–17, 123, 148, 165

Boston Patriot, 134, 155–56
Boston Spectator, 149
Breen, Timothy H., 3
Britain: benevolent British Christians, 193; cruelty to American prisoners, 18–20; license for American vessels, 125; Orders in Council, 125, 140; role in Barbary crisis, 54–55; treaty with dey of Algeria, 45; United States becomes potential ally, 195; view of colonists, 2–3
British North American colonies, 199n7
British Prison Ship, The (Freneau), 36–37
Brown, John, 70
Brunsman, Denver, 7
Burnham, John, 68

captives. *See* Barbary captivity of Americans
captivity narratives, 7; American Revolution, 3–4, 31–37, 191–93, 195; Americans in Quebec, 150–51; anti-Catholic and slaves reports, 196; *Awful Disclosures of the Hotel Dieu Nunnery*, 196; British navy impressment, 135–37; prisoner ship treatment, 30
Carey, Mathew, 71
Carolina Gazette, 113
Castlereagh, Robert Stewart, 170
Cathcart, James, 91, 97–98, 100
Cheetham, James, 125–26
Chesapeake-Leopard affair, 13–14, 121–25, 129–30
Cincinnati and Revolutionary Societies, 73
City Gazette and Daily Advertiser, 78
Clark, Abraham, 75
Clay, Henry, 170–71
Cleves, Rachel Hope, 10
Clinton, De Witt, 122
Clinton, George, 25
Cobbett, William, 186
Coffin, Zachariah, 49
Cold War, parallels to Early American Republic, 10, 195
Colley, Linda, 3
Columbian Centinel, 68
Columbian Herald, 59
Commentaries on the Laws of England (Blackstone), 146
Congress: charges against Britain in War of 1812, 145; closed sessions in Algerian crisis debate, 74, 194, 211n14; limitation

on retaliation policy, 151–52; military solution to Algerian crisis, 74–75; public pressure in Barbary crisis, 73–74; sailors' certificates of citizenship, 111, 118
Connecticut Courant, 139, 141
Connecticut Journal, 47
Constitution: foreign affairs and ratification, 40; president's power to respond to Barbary threat, 92, 96; ratification debates, 200n14
Constitutional Convention, 5, 60; hope for captured seamen, 5, 11; restructured government, 60; structural issues of new nation, 193
Continental Congress, 27; Algerian crisis, 40, 49, 58–60; British cruelty investigations, 25, 27; Indians on western frontier, 58; treatment of prisoners rules, 19; weakness of, 54
Convention of Representatives (New York), 25
Craig, Campbell, 195

Daily Advertiser (New York), 67
Daily National Intelligencer, 164, 174–75, 177, 185–86, 189
Dale, Richard, 101
Dartmoor Massacre, 13–14, 162–63; Andrews account, 175–76; Anglophobia and, 224n11; commemoration of, 181–82; events of, 166–70; findings of the inquiry, 170–72, 182, 225n51; prison conditions 167–68; prisoners accounts and response, 176–77, 182; prisoners to serve in U.S. Navy, 173–74; reminder of British prison ships, 190; repatriation costs dispute, 167. Shortland blamed, 175, 180, 182. *See also* Shortland, Thomas
Davis, Joshua, 135–36, 220n10
day of Thanksgiving, 131. *See also* Barbary captivity of Americans
Dean, Silas, 192
Decatur, Stephen, 104–6, 163, 181, 184–89
De Jeane, Philip, 35
Democratic-Republican societies: on Algerian crisis, 74–75, 84; opposition to government's policies, 64–65. *See also* Republicans
Democrats, anti-communist position, 195
de Ternant, Jean Baptiste, 63

doctrine of indefeasible allegiance, 111–12
Dodge, John, 31–37, 192
Downer, Jeremiah, 29
Dunlap's American Daily Advertiser, 82

Eaton, William, 89, 91, 98, 100, 105, 216n46
Ebnallad, Al Koraschi, 39
Embargo Act of 1807, 125–26, 128–30; Madison's role, 133, repeal and replacement, 133
Entertaining Narrative of the Cruel and Barbarous Treatment and Extreme Suffering of Mr. John Dodge, An (Dodge), 33
era of free security, 13, 190, 202n32, 224n10; insecurity and, 196; replaces American vulnerability, 193. *See also* insecurity
Erskine, David, 121
Essex Register, 135, 144
Estes, Todd, 5, 84, 200n14
Evening Post (New York), 113, 148, 150; Madison, "Emperor of America," 146

Faris, Hyram, 56
Federalists: on Algerian crisis, 65–66, 74–75, 78, 83, 86, 194; on Dartmoor Massacre, 173–74, 177–78; efforts to regain federal control, 132; on Embargo Act of 1807, 125–27; nationalism of, 159–60; on policy of retaliation, 223n84; public opinion, 5–6, 88, 159; public will separate from policy, 63; Republican move toward tyranny, 132, 141–42, 145–46, 154, 160; Republicans and French, 138–39; on sailors' impressment, 110, 113–14; on sailors' impressment, Madison's role, 137, 158–59; Tripolitan War and, 88, 90–93, 96, 98, 103, 107–8; Washington support for, 63
Federal Republican (Georgetown), 148–49, 173, 177
Filson, John, 34
Fiske, Nathan, 16–17, 37
foreign affairs: American security and, 7–8, 40, 60, 76; Congressional action on Barbary threat, 194; public interest, 83–84; safe passage negotiation, 45; security abroad, 53, 55–56
foreign trade: Barbary threat, effect of, 49; importance of Mediterranean, 48; tribute demanded by Algeria, 39
France: demand for tribute, 87; impressment

France (*continued*)
  of sailors, 112; opposition to Britain's license for American vessels, 125
Franklin, Benjamin, 45, 78, 192; rumors about, 56
Freneau, Philip, 36–37
frontiersmen, Dodge's characterization, 34–35

Gage, Thomas, 2; treatment of British prisoners, 18–20
Gallatin, Albert, 170–71
Galusha, Jonas, 188
Gates, Horatio, 36
Gazette of the United States, 72, 76
George III, 50
Green-Mountain Farmer, 145
Groves, James, 169–70

Hamilton, Alexander, 5, 63–64, 83; "Lucius Crassus" on Tripolitan War, 96
Harford Convention, 159–60
Harrison, Richard, 47
Haynes, Sam, 10
Hendrickson, David, 8
Herbert, Charles, 1–3, 191–93, 195
Historical Discourse Concerning the Settlement of Brookfield, An (Fiske), 16, 37
Hixson, Walter, 8
Holmes, John, 180
Humphreys, David, 23, 78–82, 91, 93–94
Huntington, Samuel, 51

identity, American: foreign policy and, 8; prisoners of war, 4; sailors, 7, 9, 201n20
identity, British American, 2–3
impressment of sailors, 109–10, 129; British deserters on American vessels, 111–12, 121–22; British role, 6–7, 12–13, 111–12, 115–16, 119–20, 134–35; Congressional report, 115; Davis's account of treatment, 135–37, 220n10; France and Spain, 119; French role, 112; treaty effort, 120
Independent Chronicle, 26
Independent Gazetteer, The, 69
Ingersoll, Charles, 161
insecurity: Cold War parallels, 10, 195–96; demand for greater protection, 40, 56; early American identity, 4, 9–10; useful political tool, 62, 103, 114, 130, 133, 197
Irwin, Matthew, 61, 67

Jackson, Andrew, 13–14, 161–64, 172, 178, 190
Jay, John, 55, 118, 197; abuse of U.S. citizens by foreign powers, 40; Barbary threat, benefit of, 46–47; recommends well-armed vessels, 48
Jay Treaty, 5, 84, 118–20, 138, 158–59, 200n14, 213n3; Washington's support, 87
Jefferson, Polly, 56
Jefferson, Thomas: British impressment, 13; calls for war with Barbary States, 45–46; diplomatic efforts with Algeria, 51–52, 56–57, 92; effect of Embargo Act of 1807, 127–28, 131; Federalists on, 90, 93; impressment of sailors, 112; limited presidential powers, 90; loss of the *Franklin*, 98; Mathurins and, 58; Mediterranean trade, 48; military solution to Algerian crisis, 75; minister to France, 61; Monroe-Pinkney Treaty withheld from Congress, 138; on private intervention with Algeria, 62–63, 78; trade treaty rejected on impressment issue, 120–21; Tripolitan War and, 92, 94–96, 99–100, 105, 165, 214n9, 215n31
Jefferson administration: *Chesapeake-Leopard* affair, 121, 124; on Embargo Act of 1807, 125, 129; Federalist disparagement, 132; impressment of sailors, 113–19; loss of the *Franklin*, 99; Madison's role, 133; response to Barbary threat, 12–13, 130; response to Tripolitan threat, 87–88; on sailors' impressment, 110; settlement failure, 97; success in Tripoli, 108; trade treaty rejected on impressment issue, 120; Tripolitan War and, 91, 101–3, 106–7
Jones, John Paul, 63, 78
Jones, Philip, 26

Karamanli, Hamet, 105
Kennison, David, 191
King, Charles, 171, 182–83
King, Rufus, 49, 171
King Philip's War, 16
Know Nothing movement, 196

Index

Lamb, John, 55, 80; criticism and defense of, 53; negotiator with Algiers, 51–52
Larpent, Seymour, 171, 182–83
Lear, Tobias, 106, 128
Lewis, Philip, 141
Lewis and Clark's Corps of Discovery, 113
Lincoln, Levi, 92
Locke, John, 93
Logevall, Fredrik, 195
Logie, Charles, 49–50; treatment of Americans in Algiers, 52–55
London Courier, 146
lottery for sailor's ransom. *See* Barbary captivity of Americans
Louisiana, Spanish, access to Mississippi river, 42
Louisiana Purchase, 107–8, 113–14
Lovett, John, 151
Loyalists, 3; defense of prisoner treatment, 28–29

Mackenzie, Frederick, 20
Macon's Bill Number 2, 131, 133
Madison, James: abuse of power, 152–53; annual address includes North African war victory, 188; Barbary threat, 13–14, 128, 184; Barbary threat and tribute, 97; demands peace of the dey, 185; Embargo Act of 1807, 133; impressment issue, 119; policy of retaliation, 142–43, 146–49; Republicans and public opinion, 5–6; retaliation issue, 151; support for common vision of people, 64; trade treaty rejected on impressment issue, 120; on use of force in Barbary threat, 75, 91, 95
Madison administration, 142, 152; Alien Enemies Act, 158; Barbary threat, 13–14, 162–64; British in Worcester jail, 154, 156–57; Dartmoor Massacre blame, 173–74; declaration of war against Algeria, 165; on Embargo Act of 1807, 140; Federalist claim of anti-British sentiment, 178; relationship with French, 138–40; retaliation issue, 131–32, 159; sailors' impressment and, 137
Maria and *Dauphin* merchant ships, 11, 61–62, 65, 68, 74; Barbary threat, 42; captain's plea for help, 61; captured by Algerian corsairs, 39–40, 42, 45, 47–50, 52; public debate, 206n10; ransom for, 68; victims of independence, 45
maritime history, 7
Marks, Frederick, 8
Mason, George, 56
Massachusetts Gazette, 53
Massachusetts General Court, act regarding federal prisoners, 158
Massachusetts Spy, 153–54, 157
Mathurin order: Jefferson and, 57–58, 63; Jefferson pays for help, 63; Order of the Holy Trinity and Redemption of Captives, 50
Mazzei, Philip, 63
Merritt, Richard, 2
Monk, Maria, 196
Monroe, James, 162–64, 178, 184; Monroe Doctrine in annual address, 194; Monroe-Pinkney Treaty, 119–20; most-favored-nation status with Britain, 112
Monroe Doctrine, 194
Monroe-Pinkney Treaty, 138, 221n17
Morocco, 206n11; formal treaty, 44–45; seizes American ship *Betsey*, 44–45; threat to American vessels, 44–45
Morris, Andrew, 97–99
Morris, Charles, 131–32, 152
Morris, Richard, 101

Napoleonic War, 112
Narrative of Colonel Ethan Allen's Captivity, A (Allen), 32
Narrative of the Life of Frederick Douglass, 196
Nathans, Heather, 70
National Intelligencer, 100, 104, 177
nationalism: development of, 9–10, 14; early British attitude, 2; effect of Tripolitan War, 106, 108; effect of War of 1812, 162; fear of an 'other,' 6; Federalist-Republican effect on, 6–7, 178, 194; foreign policy and, 12; insecurity in Atlantic world, 40; partisan divide and, 62
Native Americans: British backing blamed for actions, 179–80; frontiersmen and, 34, 36; Ohio tribes response to American Revolution, 35; western frontier threats, 42, 58
New, Anthony, 74
Newark Centinel, 119, 145

Newburyport Herald, 102, 183
New Hampshire Patriot, 182–83
newspapers, letters with pseudonyms: Americanus, 139–40; Benevolence, 67; Benevolus, 57, 59; Centinel, 53, 55, 60; Coriolanus, 99–100; Franklin, 123, 218n40; Ghost of Montgomery, 163; Hampden, 157–58; Humanitas, 21, 23, 58–59; Militades, 151; Misercors, 24–25; Misercors on British cruelty, 24–25; Nautilus, 174–75; S on American captives, 135; Tit for Tat, 144; Volunteer on impressment, 134; Warren, 70, 76–77
newspapers and pamphlets: on American victory in North Africa, 186–88; battle between *Enterprise* and *Tripoli*, 94–95; British treatment of prisoners, 25–27, 29–30; Dartmoor Massacre findings, 172–74, 182; on Embargo Act of 1807, 125–27; "Era of Good Feelings," 162; Federalists on Dartmoor Massacre, 183–84; Federalists on retaliation policy, 146–50, 153–54; Federalists on Tripoli War, 86, 96–98, 102; Humphrey's lottery plan to ransom sailors, 79–81; impressment of sailors, 113–14, 116–17, 123; Madison, "Emperour of America," 142; military solution to Algerian crisis, 76–77; North African reports, 47–50, 52–53; O'Brien letter on Algerian crisis, 65; poems on Barbary captives, 69; private funding for captives' release, 59, 67, 164–65; Republicans on Dartmoor Massacre, 182–83; Republicans on fishermen's impressment, 109; Republicans on retaliation policy, 154–58; Republicans on Tripolitan War, 99–100, 102, 104; role in Early Republic, 8, 63–64; rumors and fear of travel abroad, 56–57; Smith's letter on American navy, 180–81; trust in elected representatives, 76–77; violence by Republicans denounced, 141–42; Washington-Gage debates, 19–20. *See also* Batterman, George
New York Gazette, 98
New York Weekly Museum, 175
Niles' Weekly Register, 14, 165, 179
Noah, Mordecai M., 163–64
Norfolk Ledger, 123
Norristown *Herald*, attack by Republican mobs, 141

North Africa: dealings with European nations, 50; more American vessels seized, 62, 64–65. *See also* Algeria; Barbary captivity of Americans; Morocco
North Africa, crises of: Algerian crisis challenge, 45–46, 52–65; American identity and foreign policy, 67, 69–71; American nationality and nationalism, 40; failure of Humphreys to meet with dey, 78–79. *See also* Barbary captivity of Americans
Northern Whig, 173
North's Act, 22, 199n4

O'Brien, Richard, 47–49, 52–53, 61, 65, 72, 97–98, 100, 216n46
Onuf, Peter, 8
Otto, Louis Guillaume, 56

Page, John, 75
Patriot, 94
Patriot cause, 6, 11, 27, 37; public support, 2–4; redefinition of relationship with England, 17–19
Patterson, William, 68
Pennsylvania Evening Post, 25
Pennsylvania Packet, 26
Penrose, William, 81
Philadelphia Gazette, 76
Pickering, Timothy, 89
Pinkney, William, 119–20, 134
Pintard, John, 78
Plumer, William, 133
Political Calendar (Newburyport), 102–3
Portland Gazette, 138
Portsmouth Oracle, 164
Preble, Edward, 101–2, 104–5
Prince, James, 152, 155–58
Prisoners' Memoirs, or, Dartmoor Prison, The (Andrews), 175
prisoners of war: Federalist-Republican opinions, 132; international practices, 2, 146; naturalization of citizens, 147; typical British treatment, 20
prisoners of war, American: in Britain, 4, 9, 11, 13, 22, 204n11; in Canadian prisons, 6, 21; defense of prisoner treatment, 27–29; escapes or enlistment in British armed forces, 30–31; failure of American government, 14–15; French treatment

of, 138–39; in occupied American cities, 21, 24–25; policy of retaliation, 142–44; prison ships, 6, 21–24, 26, 37, 128; private initiatives, 5, 11–12; public support, 5, 8–10; treatment of, 20–23, 26, 31–33, 35–36, 132–33. *See also* Barbary captivity of Americans; captivity narratives; Dartmoor Massacre
prisoners of war, British: treatment of, 18–19, 21, 27, 135; War of 1812, 132; Worcester prisoners, 152–58
prisons, Britain: Forton Prison, 22; Mill Prison, Plymouth, 1, 22, 31
privateers or piracy: Declaration of Paris abolishment, 43; North African, 43–44; U.S., 43
Provoost, David, 54–57, 60
public opinion, plight of American captives, 6, 20–21, 23, 26–27. *See also* Federalists

Quasi War, 87
Queen Anne's War, 16

Ramsay, Robert, 179
Randolph, Edmund, 67, 79
Redeemed Captive, The (Williams), 17
Reign of Terror in America, The (Cleves), 10
religion, Tripoli, infidel, 90
Repertory, The, 146–47
Republicans: anti-British sentiment, 110, 127, 177–80; attack on Tripoli treaty, 90; British relationship, 132–34; call for war with Britain, 116–17, 137, 139–40; on Dartmoor Massacre, 173, 177–79; Democrats soft on communism, 195; on Embargo Act of 1807, 127–28; nationalism of, 116, 118; policy of retaliation, 144–45; public information on Algerian crisis, 65–66; public opinion, use of, 5–6; on sailors' impressment, 110, 114–18; Tripolitan War and, 103–4, 106–8; view of nationalism, 159
Rhode Island American, 146
Rhode Island Gazette, 147
Robertson, Peter, 29
Rouleau, Brian, 7
Rowlandson, Mary, 17–18, 31–33, 37
Rowson, Susanna, 69–71, 165
Rumsfeld, Donald, 197

Salem Gazette, 79, 149
Salem Register, 109, 118
Scott, Winfield, 142–43
Seabury, Samuel, 82
Seaver, Mary, 131
security. *See* foreign affairs
Sedition Act of 1798, 87, 158
Shays' Rebellion, 60
Sheehan, Colleen, 5
Short Account of Algiers, A (Carey), 71
Shortland, Thomas, 166–68, 170, 172, 174–76, 178, 180, 182
slaves. *See* Barbary captivity of Americans
Slaves in Algiers (Rowson), 69, 71
Slotkin, Richard, 34
Smith, George, 68, 180–81
Smith, Robert, 102
Sovereignty and Goodness of God, The (Rowlandson), 17
Spectator, 126
Sproat, David, 27–29
Stephens, Hannah, 57
Stephens, Isaac, 47–49, 57
Sterrett, Andrew, 94–95
Stewart, Charles, 187
Story, Isaac, 82
Strong, Caleb, 131

Taylor, James, 170
theaters: Algerian crisis portrayal, 70; Barbary captivity portrayal, 12, 69–72; Tripolitan War, 106–7
Thomas, Isaiah, 131, 152, 155
Tories, American: defense of prisoner treatment, 27–28
Tripolitan War, 87–88, 92; American position in the Atlantic world, 91; American ships seek protection, 91; battle between *Enterprise* and *Tripoli*, 94; battle defeats, 97; declaration of war, 12; demand for tribute, 90; expanded assault, 105; Federalist or Republican credit, 95; *Franklin*'s capture, 97–99; limited American response, 92; offer to overthrow dey, 105; peace treaty, 100–101, 106; *Philadelphia* destruction, 104, 106; U.S. blockade, 97–99, 101. *See also* Jefferson, Thomas
True American, 117–18
Tyler, John, 134

Unbecoming British (Yokota), 10
Uncle Tom's Cabin (Stowe), 196
Unfinished Revolution, The (Haynes), 10
U.S. Navy, 49, 54, 74–76, 78; complaints by Federalists, 112; establishment by Congress, 194; increased for North African combat, 103, 186; in Mediterranean to protect ships, 88, 92–95; military solution to Algerian crisis, 75; Republican opposition, 116–17; understanding of limits, 124

Van Rensselaer, Stephen, 142–43
vessels, American: *Adams*, frigate, 117; *Aurora*, merchant ship, 36–37; *Betsey*, 44–45; *Constitution*, 101; *Dalton*, privateer, 1; *Eagle*, 128; *Edwin*, merchant ship, 163–64, 180; *Enterprise*, 94–96, 98–99; flying Union Jack to avoid capture, 52; *Franklin*, merchant ship, 97–99; *George Washington*, 89; *Intrepid*, 106; *Mary Ann*, 128; Mediterranean crisis, 49; *Philadelphia*, 102–4; *President*, 81; USS *Chesapeake*, 13, 121; *Violet*, 128; *Yankee*, privateer, 21, 23. See also *Chesapeake-Leopard* affair; *Maria* and *Dauphin* merchant ships
vessels, British: *Africa*, 134; *Halifax*, 121; *Hunter*, hospital ship, 37; *Jersey*, prison ship, 27–30, 128, 152, 179; *Melampus*, 121; *Raisonnable*, man-of-war, 1; *Strombolo*, prison ship, 29; *Ville de Milan*, 109–10, 116. See also *Chesapeake-Leopard* affair
vessels, North African: *Estedio*, Algerian brig, 184–85; *The Gift of Allah*, 102; *Mashouda*, Algerian flagship, 184–85; *Tripoli*, corsair, 94
vessels, Swedish: *Maria Christiana*, 175

Waldstreicher, David, 73
War of 1812: American victory, 194; Baltimore riots, 141–42, 221n38; Battle of New Orleans, 161, 178; charges against Britain, 145; declaration of war, 141; Federalist opposition, 13, 131; Federalist-Republican divide, 219n3; freedom of the seas, 13; nation's self-confidence, 10, 13, 162–63, 165, 189–90; policy of retaliation, 142–50, 223n78; Republican move toward tyranny, 141–42; Second War of Independence, 162; security at home, 10; Treaty of Ghent, 162, 188. See also Battle of Queenston Heights
Washington, George: Algerian crisis, 11, 61, 81; Dartmoor Massacre and, 180; day of national thanksgiving, 80; impressment of sailors, 118–19; on private intervention with Algeria, 62, 84, 213n68; respect for office, 63; retaliation in American Revolution, 144–45; secret foreign negotiations, 63–67, 83, 194; support used for Jay Treaty, 87; treatment of American prisoners, 2, 18–19
Washington administration: on public opinion, 5; secret foreign negotiations, 63
Washington *Federal Republican*, 148, 173; office destroyed, 141
Weekly Aurora, 161
Wellesely, Richard, 134
White, Charles, 131
White, Samuel, 169–70
Whitman, Walt, 191
Williams, John, 17, 31–33, 37
Wochentliche Philadelphische Staatsbote, 26
Woodward, C. Vann, 4
Worcester (Mass.) Gazette. See *Massachusetts Spy*

Yokota, Kariann Akemi, 10

www.ingramcontent.com/pod-product-compliance
Lightning Source LLC
Chambersburg PA
CBHW032213230426
43672CB00011B/2540